The
History
of
Fantasy
Sports

AND THE STORIES OF THE PEOPLE
WHO MADE IT HAPPEN

LARRY SCHECHTER

ISBN (Paperback): 979-8-218-42470-1
ISBN (E-Book): 979-8-218-42471-8

CONTENTS

PREFACE

My first book, *Winning Fantasy Baseball*, was published in 2014. Since then, I've sometimes asked myself if I have any other ideas worthy of writing another book. This is the only idea I've ever had that I thought was worthy. In December of 2018, I decided I would write it. Almost immediately, unexpected life circumstances made me put it on hold.

It remained on hold for more than three years. On April 30, 2022, I had a heart attack. I ended up on a ventilator for five days. I spent my 64th birthday on a ventilator. There was a period of time where I was consciously aware that my life was in grave danger. I thought, "This can't be real—I'm too young to die..." I had time to think of all the things I wanted to live for and be able to do—including my kids, marrying my current girlfriend, traveling, etc.—and I thought about a few regrets I would have. One was "I should have written that book."

I got off the ventilator and within a few days it became clear that my heart was okay, and I would survive. I was very, very lucky and happy to be alive. Unfortunately, my kidneys had shut down due to the heart attack and I needed to start dialysis. I was in the hospital for three and a half weeks and then spent another 11 days at rehab. During these five weeks, I became 100% resolved that as soon as I was well enough, I would write this book and I would not let anything deter me.

I wrote this because I felt it was needed. Nobody has ever written this story. I wanted to make this contribution to the fantasy sports community.

During those five weeks, I received many messages of support. Mike Carter, a fantasy writer from Chicago, tweeted, "This community needs you." That was very meaningful to me and gave me even more motivation.

During those five weeks I became excited about the prospect of writing this book. I wanted to learn the history myself, and then share it with everyone else. I even started writing some of this preface and Chapter 1 in my head. I memorized it as I was incapable of writing anything.

After leaving rehab, I was on dialysis for another month as an out-patient. My kidneys recovered and within a few months I was back to normal. My cardiologist called my recovery a miracle.

Before all this, I had a family history of heart disease, as well as two prior incidents of Afib. Due to Covid shutdowns and my losing track of time, I had been overdue for a follow up with my cardiologist. Had I seen him earlier, perhaps he would have spotted my problem and done a pre-emptive procedure that would have prevented the heart attack. I will never know. But I encourage you...if you are due for any medical appointments, colonoscopy, etc. do not procrastinate. Do it.

And donate blood. Donate organs. I will never know who they are, but someone—or several people—helped save my life by donating blood. They will never know they helped save my life, but they did.

I thought this book was something I could knock out in a few months. Oh my God, was I ever wrong. I had absolutely no idea what I was getting myself into. It was a humongous project that required massive research, dozens of zoom interviews—as many as three hours total for a couple of people—follow-up e-mails, more follow-up e-mails; tracking people down on LinkedIn, Facebook, Twitter, through contacts, contacts of contacts, even grandkids; learning something new, which then required going down four more rabbit holes; being maddened by getting conflicting information, ...and information that turned out to be inaccurate; wanting to throw up my hands in frustration many times and say, "Forget it!" But here I am, on January 27, 2024 and after 18 months, it is done. I did it. And it feels damn good. And I know this book is needed.

I realized early on that I could write this as a research paper with just the facts and figures, but that would be incredibly boring. So, instead, I share the facts and figures while focusing on the stories of the people involved and how they did it. There are many stories that are interesting, some inspiring, some humorous, and a few will even put tears in your eyes.

And, by the way, my health continues to be great.

I would like to thank:

My cardiologists Dr. Eli Levine and Dr. Michael Schechter (no relation).

The doctors, nurses, and staff at Delray Medical Center, in Delray Beach, Florida.

The doctors, nurses, and staff at the Cleveland Clinic, in Weston, Florida.

The doctors, nurses, therapists, and staff at the Sunrise Rehabilitation Center, in Sunrise, Florida.

The technicians and staff at Fresenius Kidney Care, in Boca Raton, Florida.

And especially to my brother Barry, whose help and support during that time was immense.

CHAPTER 1

In the Beginning

We started as cavemen. But now we can put a man on the moon, a person in Nebraska can pick up something called a "telephone" and talk to someone in Thailand, a tiny computer chip can process millions of bits of information in a second—and you can go to something called Starbucks and get a pistachio latte.

I often marvel at this, wondering how it all occurred. If it were up to me, we'd still be rubbing two sticks together to make fire. But this is the story of how our modern civilization evolved, and it includes names like Albert Einstein, Thomas Edison, Marie Curie, and the Wright brothers.

The fantasy sports industry is obviously insignificant compared to our entire civilization, yet I also often marvel at how some people came up with ideas for games based on professional sports, started playing them with friends, and it has evolved to where an estimated 50 million people participate in the United States alone, plus millions more all over the world. There are versions of these games for baseball, football, basketball, hockey, golf, NASCAR, cricket, Formula 1, alpine skiing, Iditarod, ski jumping, bull riding, biathlon, bass fishing, wakeboarding and more. It is one of the most popular forms of entertainment today.

And it has created a worldwide industry worth an estimated $25 billion. There are hundreds of companies offering fantasy games..., plus fantasy sports writers, news and information websites, podcasts, magazines, and companies that keep track of statistics. Newspapers and broadcasts cover fantasy sports, and there's a SiriusXM radio station solely dedicated to them. How we went from those initial ideas to the present is the story of the evolution of fantasy sports, and includes names such as Andy Mousalimas, Peter Pezaris, Carol Matthews, and the Ford brothers.

I have played fantasy sports since 1992. I have played in two fantasy baseball "experts" leagues, LABR and Tout Wars. So, I have seen a lot of this growth myself, and from my involvement in LABR and Tout Wars, I know some of the people responsible for certain aspects of the growth. And yet, prior to writing this book, I knew very little about how we got from the initial ideas for games to where we are now.

This book tells the story of the evolution of fantasy sports. I could have written 1,000 pages, but for the sake of practicality needed to keep it much shorter. It's like choosing an All-Star team where there's never enough room to include every worthy player. I apologize to anyone or anything I didn't have room to include.

To write the history of fantasy sports, it would be wise to first define the term. According to *Merriam-Webster*, the applicable definition is: *of, relating to, or being a game in which participants create and manage imaginary teams consisting of players from a particular sport and scoring is based on the statistical performances of the actual players.*

If you look at other dictionaries and encyclopedias, you will find similar definitions. One aspect they don't usually mention is whether the statistical performances of the players are based on past or future events.

The fantasy sports industry that has an estimated 50 million players just in the US and has grown into a $25 billion worldwide industry is based on sporting events that haven't yet occurred. For example, a fantasy football league will draft players before the NFL season starts, and participants accumulate statistics for their players as the actual NFL games are played. Another example would be a daily fantasy baseball contest where participants choose players and are awarded statistics for their players' performances that same evening.

Before the advent of this industry, there were board games based on actual professional players' statistics for *prior* seasons. Some people say these games were a pre-cursor to modern fantasy sports. And several of these games have remained popular to this day. Some even say that the first fantasy baseball game dates to an 1866 tabletop game called Sebring Parlor Base-Ball, which simulated baseball games by sliding a penny from pitcher to batter, whereupon a spring-activated bat propelled the coin into one of the cavities in the field. It was advertised in popular periodicals.

A similar game, William Buckley's Game Board, was patented in 1867. In Buckley's game, a marble-sized ball was rolled by the mechanical "pitcher" toward a spring-activated bat that would drive the ball into the field of play. But Sebring's game went into commercial production while Buckley's did not. In 1869, Milton Bradley started producing its own table game that used cards, called Base Ball: The New Parlor Game.

The first game to ever replicate performance of actual players based on a prior year was developed by Cliff Van Beek. National Pastime was a board game with dice and cards. Its first (and only) commercial release was in 1931, based on the 1930 Major League Baseball (MLB) season. Perhaps the game wouldn't have been successful anyway, but the Great Depression was a difficult time to launch a business.

In 1936, Cadaco-Ellis, a toy and game company, came out with Elmer Layden's Scientific Football, a board game that sold successfully until the 1950s. Cadaco-Ellis introduced All-Star Baseball in 1941, after former MLB player Ethan Allen approached them about an idea for a baseball game. They agreed to manufacture it, and it went on to become one of the most popular sports games of all time. The board game has player disks for hitters that are divided into sections such that when you place the disk on a spinner the probability is that the player will achieve his real-life statistics. Since there are no disks for pitching, a hitter's probable outcome is always the same for every at-bat. It was intended to be easy to play, since their initial target audience was ages 9-12. The first edition came with disks for 40 star players. Participants could create their own teams from these disks. In 1946, they started a "special edition" option that included 20 Hall of Famers such as Babe Ruth, Ty Cobb, and Lou Gehrig.

Cadaco-Ellis later also offered board games for basketball, hockey, and horse racing. The last edition of baseball player disks was released in 1993. Since their first year, Ethan Allen had personally obtained written permission from the included players to use their name and statistics. But Allen died in 1993 and the Major League Baseball Players Association (MLBPA) had become stricter in wanting compensation for using players name and statistics. Cadaco-Ellis couldn't afford the licensing fees being requested and stopped production.

In 2003 and 2004, the company came out with a commemorative Hall of Fame version, by working out a better licensing deal through the Hall of Fame. Past versions of All-Star Baseball can still be purchased on websites such as eBay.

APBA

When National Pastime came out in 1931, Dick Seitz, a 16-year-old from Lancaster, Pennsylvania, bought the game and played with friends. When it was clear National Pastime was never going to release a second edition, Seitz invented his own game, somewhat based on National Pastime. The boys continued to play and called themselves the American Professional Baseball Association, or APBA for short.

Seitz took his game to war in the 1940s and played with three comrades in the barracks at Fort Eustis, Virginia. He printed player cards on his own printing press. After the war, he went back to Lancaster, kept refining his game, and kept playing with friends.

In 1951, he launched APBA baseball commercially and sold it by mail-order. The board game, which could be played alone or against another person, used dice and had cards for various Major League players. The original game had 20 player cards for each of the 16 major league teams. Seitz sold 150 games at $10 each. Continuing to work part-time from 1952-56, he produced new versions annually and, in 1957, went full-time with it. The company later produced similar games for football, golf, hockey, soccer and—subsequently discontinued—basketball, bowling, boxing, and horse racing.

Some similar games have come and gone, but APBA's main competitor has been Strat-O-Matic, which first launched their baseball board game in 1961. These baseball games certainly qualify as "fantasy," as they allow people to manage their own team of professional players, set batting orders, choose starting pitchers, decide when to steal bases, bunt, put in a relief pitcher, etc. For football games, participants can call plays on offense, decide when to go for it on fourth down, decide when to have their defense blitz, etc. And for golf, they must decide which club to use based on the conditions.

Strat-O-Matic

In 1948, 11-year-old Hal Richman played All-Star Baseball but was not pleased that the game didn't account for the pitcher's ability. He also felt its spinner was an imprecise method of determining outcomes and was susceptible to wearing down. In his bedroom in Great Neck, New York, he began working on creating his own game. His first decision was that using dice would eliminate the deficiencies of the spinner. He started playing his own invented game and continued to work on improving it throughout his childhood and then as a student at Bucknell University. He shared the game with a few friends throughout those years, but mostly played himself.

After he graduated from Bucknell, his mother arranged for him to pitch a man in the toy business. The man said Richman's game had promise, but that it just wasn't commercial. After this meeting, Richman sat at the table in his kitchen, grabbed a few multi-colored dice and overcome with frustration, just kept rolling and rolling. That's when he had an epiphany. He would add a third die to the roll, so that half the time the result of the at-bat would be dictated by the hitter's card (if the third die was a 1, 2 or 3) and half the time by the pitcher's card (for a 4, 5 or 6).

"That step is what made the baseball game," Richman says. "This would not have happened if I hadn't been stimulated by this man's criticism."

In 1961, he used his Bar Mitzvah savings to launch Strat-O-Matic by buying ad space in *Sports Illustrated* and working from home. During 1961 and 1962, he sold several hundred games but lost the few thousand dollars he had invested. In 1963, he borrowed $5,000 from his father with the understanding that, if he didn't pay it back, he'd follow his dad into the insurance business. That was the year Strat-O-Matic sales took off.

Strat-O-Matic football launched in 1968, followed by basketball in 1973 and hockey in 1978. When the MLBPA started demanding licensing fees—the same demand that caused Cadaco-Ellis to stop producing All-Star Baseball—Richman complied. "We made a deal we could live with," he said.

Richman has been secretive about sales and revenue, but in 2006 he did say the total number of Strat-O-Matic games sold over the years was in the low millions. In 2016, he stated that the previous year had been their most profitable one ever.

Ball Park Baseball

A similar, though lesser-known, tabletop game was created in 1957 by Charles Sidman, a Kansas University student and later history professor. He organized a league to play the game with friends. Players could use any team that had won a pennant from 1920 to 1970. There were cards for hitters and pitchers, as well as park charts. And they included unusual possible outcomes, such as a fielder getting ejected for arguing.

In 1971 the friends pooled resources to open a restaurant they called The Ball Park in a local Lawrence, Kansas shopping center. The idea was you'd have a sandwich and a beer and play a game or two of Ball Park Baseball. The restaurant was successful for about five years—some customers played the game while they ate, others came just to eat or get a drink—but the game has lasted until at least 2024 and can be found at BPBaseballGame.com. Lawrence resident and famous baseball writer

Bill James played the game at the restaurant and, as of 2024, still played in that same league.

Computer Games

Computer versions of APBA and Strat-O-Matic games started in the mid-1980s. But the first computer-based simulation game was created in 1961, in Akron, Ohio, by John Burgeson, an IBM engineer. Users would pick a lineup of nine players from a roster of 50 retired players, the computer would pick its lineup from the remaining list, and the simulation game was then played based on the statistical probabilities for each batter and pitcher. At about three characters per second, the computer would print out a play-by-play baseball game.

Burgeson wrote the program on his own time for enjoyment, and then shared it with the company. IBM included it as part of the software that shipped with the IBM 1620 computer. At a cost of about $120,000 per computer, the game was never going to catch on with the masses like APBA or Strat-O-Matic. IBM salespeople used it to help convince corporate clients to shell out their $120,000: "With this machine, you'll get free programs for linear regressions, curve fitting, and managing your own baseball team!"

Although only 50 to 200 copies of Burgeson's game were ever distributed, his invention was officially recognized by the National Baseball Hall of Fame.

Rege Cordic, a Pittsburgh radio personality, featured the game on his KDKA radio show. For three evenings in the fall of 1961, drive-time listeners heard Cordic calling out the play-by-play of a baseball game with the likes of Willie Mays in center field and Stan Musial at first base. Cordic read the computer printout with enthusiasm, as though it was a real game happening right then.

APBA and Strat-O-Matic Leagues

Many APBA and Strat-O-Matic players compete against each other in a variety of leagues. Some leagues play games in person and others compete online. There are also in-person tournaments.

Some leagues, such as Phil Zangari's South APBA Baseball League, in Lancaster, Pennsylvania, have lasted for decades. Since 1978, their team owners draft players from all major league teams' previous season. They have a 138-game schedule. Some games are played at their houses, while others are played at a social club that they all belong to. Each game can be played in as little as 30 minutes. Their World Series and then next year's draft occur every March.

There are similar leagues for both APBA and Strat-O-Matic baseball, football, and other sports that have been around for years, as well as Facebook groups for APBA and Strat-O-Matic baseball. The APBA Suncoast Football League, based in Tampa, started in 1979 and was still going as of 2024. It was co-founded by Ray Dunlap, who became the head statistician for the Tampa Bay Buccaneers for six years during the 1980s. The National Card Football League, also for APBA, started in 1981 as a face-to-face league in Columbus, Ohio. In 2013, they expanded to online play via Skype, which has allowed them to have teams from across the USA. The National Strat-O-Matic Hockey League began in 1996 and is still going. Some 24 teams compete and play 82 games over the course of a 22-week season. Games are played head-to-head over the internet or by the home team following the road team's Computer Manager.

Jim Drucker was commissioner of the Continental Basketball Association from 1978–86, the Arena Football League from 1994–96, and the East Meadow Strat-O-Matic Baseball League (EMSBL) from 1972-78. In 1972, at age 20, Drucker founded the EMSBL, based in East Meadow, New York. The 2023 season was their 52nd consecutive year of play. After starting with just three friends, they expanded and typically have seven to nine teams competing in a 60-game season and World Series. The other three original members dropped out over the years, but Drucker has played 48 of the 51 years (he took a sabbatical for three years) and Jeffrey Weintraub, who joined the league in 1975, has played for 48 consecutive seasons.

Playing Strat-O-Matic based on the prior year's season, Drucker said he's always a year behind. Someone will ask him, "Wow, have you noticed what a great year Bryce Harper is having?" and Drucker will reply, "No, but I can tell you what he did last year."

Larry Burkholder, of Ephrata, Pennsylvania, started playing APBA Baseball as a senior in high school. Along with five classmates, he started the SEATO APBA baseball league in 1970. A man named Randy Walker joined the league in 1979. In 2014, Walker was diagnosed with ALS. He was going to quit, but his wife Lisa told him, "If you want to play, I'll do whatever I have to so you can play." She started playing APBA with him. She would roll the dice and he would tell her what players to put in the game. By 2018, he could no longer speak and communicated through an eye reader and computer, body gestures, and Lisa could read his lips. In 2018, Walker's team came from two runs behind in extra innings to win his first World Series after 39 years in the league. He burst into tears.

As of 2024, the league was still going—although Randy no longer plays, he keeps up with the latest scores, standings, and trades on the SEATO website. He sometimes sends an e-mail when he sees a lopsided trade, just to poke fun at it. And when he felt well enough, Lisa brought him to the yearly drafts. (If you google "SEATO APBA" you can see an *Ephrata Review* story and picture about Walker.)

If you're wondering what SEATO stands for, so are they. None of them—not even Larry Burkholder—can remember.

The Illowa APBA League is named after its geographical area, which includes parts of Illinois and Iowa. It started in 1975 and still has two original members—three others have played since 1980. Marcus and Dan Bunch, the sons of one of the original owners, Mike Bunch, have been in the league since 1998 and 2012, respectively. They play a 162-game season, plus an All-Star game and playoffs. During the year, they have three get togethers at locations such as a hotel conference room, where they will play 30 games in a weekend. The rest of the games are played at members' homes and in some cases, such as with one owner who moved to Montana, with a video call.

One of their members since 1980, Thomas Nelshoppen, an IT consultant for the University of Illinois, started APBABlog.com in 2008. According to his blog, celebrities who have played APBA include former MLB star Joe Torre, former Cincinnati Reds general manager Walt Jocketty, and former Texas Rangers managing general partner, President George H.W. Bush. Nelshoppen wrote he has "talked to several members of the Bush family over the years about APBA. They all share a love for this game."

Many other players, sports executives and celebrities have played APBA or Strat-O-Matic. In Alan Schwarz's 2002 book *The Numbers Game: Baseball's Lifelong Fascination with Statistics*, he surveyed 50 decision-making baseball executives and found that half of them had played Strat-O-Matic when they were younger. The games are so realistic that famed baseball writer Bill James noted in his 1986 *Baseball Abstract* that Strat-O-Matic and APBA should be employed as teaching tools for new managers the way major airlines put pilots through flight simulators before taking to the skies.

Keith Hernandez played Strat-O-Matic baseball as a teenager, and after his 17-year MLB career resumed playing on his computer. He recreated the 1964 NL season three different times. He became an analyst for Mets games on SportsNet New York and admits to using Strat-O-Matic to prepare. "I don't see the American League that much," Hernandez said, "so I look at player's cards to see the running rating to see if they are good bunters, good hit-and-run guys, what kind of arm they have, what kind of range they have—it's absolutely helpful."

Famed sportscaster Bob Costas started playing Strat-O-Matic baseball at age 12, when he would play hundreds of games each summer. He continued to play sometimes as an adult. He also played Strat-O-Matic football briefly. Costas says he will always fondly remember a game he played in 1967 at age 15. He put up light-hitting Gary Geiger as his last resort pinch hitter in the bottom of the 12th of a game he was losing 6-3 with 2 outs and the bases loaded. Boom...walk-off grand slam!

Another famous broadcaster, Jon Miller, played Strat-O-Matic baseball as a teenager. In fact, you could say it prepared him for his career. Miller said, "When playing Strat solo, I would broadcast the games—to myself, as I was the only one listening—to seem more like the Giants games I listened to on the radio. I added my own sound effects such as crowd noise, ballpark organists, and vendors."

During the baseball strike of 1981, when Miller was broadcasting Red Sox games with Ken Coleman, they decided to broadcast Strat-O-Matic games as if the strike had ended. They started with a Red Sox/Yankees series that was scheduled for those dates in real life. Local celebrities, politicians and Bruins players came to the station and were the managers for either the Red Sox or their opponent. "Ken and I would take the score sheets from the games and do old-time re-creations of the games," Miller said. "We had crowd noise, ballpark organists, and I did impressions of the public-address announcers in all the different parks where the games were played."

Miller went on, "The first night's broadcast sounded so authentic—even though we stated clearly at the beginning of the broadcast that it was a re-creation of a Strat-O-Matic game played at our studios—that the station was flooded with calls from people thinking the strike was over." One irate man said, "I'm a season ticket holder at Fenway and I'm outraged the Sox didn't notify me the strike was over."

Meanwhile, newspapers in some MLB cities resorted to playing every canceled game with Strat-O-Matic and writing up summaries.

The strike continued and canceled the 1981 All-Star Game in Cleveland. Media members created a replacement game, using Strat-O-Matic cards, on a card table over home plate at Cleveland's Municipal Stadium. Opera singer Rocco Scotti sang the national anthem. Bob Feller rolled the first dice. The stadium scoreboard was in operation. That set is now in Cooperstown as part of the Hall of Fame's collection.

This massive publicity in 1981 gave a boost to Strat-O-Matic sales.

In 1984, Jon Miller was broadcasting Orioles games. Player Ken Singleton asked Miller to bring Strat-O-Matic on the team flight from Baltimore to California. Singleton managed a team with Mike Flanagan as his pitching coach. Lenn Sakata also managed a team. Cal Ripken, Jr. came walking by, asked what was going on and wanted to play, too.

"Cal took the Orioles, and I took the Tigers," Miller said. "In the fifth inning, with the Orioles leading, I changed pitchers and Cal proceeded to pinch hit for his platoon players. By the seventh inning, the Tigers had gone ahead, and I changed pitchers again, trying to nullify his platoon changes. When the Tigers won the game, I used a Howard Cosell impression: "Manager Cal Ripken, Jr. was thoroughly out managed by the wily Tiger skipper, Sparky Anderson. In the late innings, he had no one left on his bench, having fallen into Sparky's cleverly set trap in the middle innings."

Cal took the score sheet, went to the back of the plane to sit with his dad—a coach for the Orioles—and they reviewed his game strategy. Several minutes later, he came back and said, "All right, I know where I screwed up. Let's play another one."

CHAPTER 2

Origins of Fantasy Baseball

Daniel Okrent is the man generally credited with having invented fantasy baseball. Legend has it that the idea came to him in the fall of 1979 on a flight from Hartford, Connecticut, to Austin, Texas. But there is a lot more to this story and the legend isn't true.

The story begins with Bill Gamson, an eminent sociologist who taught at the University of Michigan and later Boston College. Gamson, a past president of the American Sociological Association, published the influential books *Power and Discontent* and *The Strategy of Social Protest*. He also liked games and incorporated them into his teaching. *He* drew praise for his development and use of simulation games to teach aspects of sociology and political science.

While a young research associate at Harvard in 1960, Gamson was looking for a diversion from his studies and created a game he called the National Baseball Seminar. Gamson said, "In my apartment for five hours, two buddies and I hashed out the rules for an auction of all MLB players using four statistics: batting average, RBIs, ERA, and wins. We felt these statistics reflected productivity, but in truth there wasn't a tremendous availability of statistics back then. We knew these four would be published in all the papers."

When Gamson moved to the University of Michigan in 1962 as an associate professor, he recruited about 25 people to his game, including Robert Sklar, a history professor. In 1966, Sklar mentioned it to a student he was advising: Daniel Okrent. Years later, this led to the creation of modern fantasy baseball.

Besides Gamson, there are several others known to have played a version of the game prior to 1979.

Bill Winkenbach created the Superior Tile Summer Invitational Home Run Tourney around 1959 or 1960. (Winkenbach is discussed extensively in Chapter 3, as just a few years later he created what became modern fantasy football.)

Joe Blandino, a teacher at Bridgeton High School in southern New Jersey, was concerned that his friends, who had recently graduated from college, might drift apart and tried to think of a way for them to stay in touch. He knew the seven friends all liked baseball and got the idea of creating a league where they would each draft major league players and have their own team. They would assign a point value to the players' statistics and whichever team earned the most points would win the competition. They used the categories of batting average, runs scored, home runs and RBIs, as well as wins and ERA for pitchers.

His friends loved the idea. They began their league in 1976 and called it the Baseball Owners Club. They started with a $50-per-year entry fee and their first pick was Joe Morgan. They each draft 18 players, using both AL and NL players; and they add one extra player on the first Sunday in June and one more at the All-Star break. To determine the winner at the end of the season, they take the stats of their best eight hitters (one must be a catcher) and their three best pitchers (there must be two starters and one reliever).

One of the members, Art Frank, became the president and CEO of Niagara Fallsview Casino. Because of this connection, they've held their annual draft in Niagara Falls a few times and once in the Bahamas. Their year-end banquet has often been an overnight stay at an Atlantic City casino. Most importantly, Blandino achieved his goal of keeping the group together. Blandino told me they were all "retired, gray and balding" as they prepared for the 2024 season, their 47th year. One dropped out in the early 90s, but the other seven have been in the league all these years.

Dennis DiOrio, owner of DiOrio's Bar and Grill in Somers Point, New Jersey, and a few of the other league members had seasons tickets for the Phillies. Mike Dunleavy, an accountant who sat in front of them, was very confused as he listened to some of them rooting for Phillies players, then opponents' players, with no rhyme nor reason. After several games, he asked them who they were rooting for, and they explained their game. A few games later, they brought a copy of the rules for him, and, in 1979, Dunleavy started his own league at his firm.

Brian Matthews, one of the co-founders of fantasy company CDM, played a game in college with two friends in the late '70s. They each drafted eight MLB teams and acquired stats in certain categories for the entire team. It never occurred to them to take individual players.

When well-known fantasy radio host Lenny Melnick was 7 years old, he was good friends with another seven year old, and Melnick played a game with that friend's father. They each chose three players for the entire season and got a penny for each win, home run or stolen base.

Lary Bump and some friends started a league in 1979 wherein you were given points for eight categories: wins and strikeouts for pitchers, and batting average, runs scored, hits, HR, RBI, SB for hitters. They took turns drafting one player per category. For example, someone might take Reggie Jackson for the home runs category, and Jackson could also be selected for the RBIs (or another) category. Their first year, one participant took slugger Larry Hisle for both HRs and RBIs. Hisle was injured in May and was out for the rest of the year. Nothing in the rules allowed for a replacement. They changed the rules for the second year to draft a backup player for each category. Other than that, the rules have changed very little. As of 2023, they had 19 guys playing in three leagues with several playing in all three leagues.

Dan Okrent said he learned of a Chicago book publisher, Ivan Dee, who played a game like Okrent's that started a few years earlier. Ron Shandler, of BaseballHQ, said one of his subscribers, Ed Klein, had played a game prior to 1979. And well-known fantasy analyst John Benson reportedly played a game around 1977.

I just happened to stumble upon these examples of people playing prior to 1979, so undoubtedly there were many others. But these leagues were all isolated. When Dan Okrent created his version of the game, not only did he create a league, but it caught on with the public and led to what we have today. Therefore, Okrent is the person primarily credited with having invented fantasy baseball (he called it Rotisserie Baseball).

Okrent is a very accomplished man. He has been the editor at magazines such as *Esquire, Life* and *Time,* and was the first public editor of *The New York Times.* He has written books about baseball, immigration, and prohibition. His 2003 book *Great Fortune: The Epic of Rockefeller Center* was a finalist for the Pulitzer Prize for history. His 2010 book *Last Call: The Rise and Fall of Prohibition* won the Albert J. Beveridge award by the American Historical Association as the year's best book on American history. And it was a major source of information for the 2011 Ken Burns/Lynn Novick miniseries *Prohibition.*

Okrent also invented the baseball statistic WHIP, which became a commonly used measure of a pitcher's performance by calculating how many walks and hits are allowed per innings pitched.

And Okrent helped discover the famed baseball stats guru Bill James.

When Robert Sklar told Okrent about the National Baseball Seminar in 1966, Okrent was not interested in playing. But Okrent was a student in several of Sklar's classes and they became friends. After college, Okrent moved to Manhattan and Sklar arrived three years later, taking a job as a professor at New York University. Their friendship continued—among other things, they often attended baseball games together.

From 1978-1982, Okrent flew often from Hartford, Connecticut, to Austin, Texas, as a publishing consultant for the *Texas Monthly.* The legend is that his idea for a fantasy baseball game came to him on one of these flights in the fall of 1979. There has been conflicting reporting about this. Some accounts imply that the idea just magically came to him on this flight, even that he jotted the rules down on a cocktail napkin; others claim that the germ of the idea was from the National Baseball Seminar and basically sat in his unconscious for 13 years until this plane ride; some have even said he had been consciously trying to improve upon the National Baseball Seminar game.

I asked Okrent about this and he told me, "I fiddled around with the idea of doing something more elaborate and more representative of how baseball worked. The kernel was there, and I planted the kernel, and I nurtured it. Before the plane ride to Texas, I spent many long, wintery evenings in the Berkshires, in Western Mass., developing it, and then wrote up the rules and took them to Texas."

He decided arbitrarily that pitching and hitting would each count for half the total points. He chose to use only National League players to make teams more like real teams. In a 2010 *ESPN The Magazine* article, by Morty Ain, Okrent said, "I prototyped various statistical combinations against the actual performance of the NL East division over the preceding five years. I found that if you had taken those six teams and ranked them by eight categories—batting average, home runs, RBIs, steals, wins, saves, ERA, and WHIP—it tracked close to the actual standings." Okrent confirmed with me that this prototyping was done during those long, winter nights prior to the flight to Texas. "I was a barely working freelance writer," he told me. "I had a lot of time on my hands."

He did test other categories, but these eight were the combination that tracked the best to the actual standings. He even tested fielding percentage, but that had no correlation at all to the actual standings. Per a 1999 *USA Today* article, by Chris Colston, Okrent said, "In reality I don't think stolen bases are all that important ... but for some reason adding them improved the statistical correlation between rotisserie and real baseball."

Okrent has said in other interviews that he knew On Base Percentage (OBP) was a better stat than batting average, but walks—which are necessary to compute OBP—weren't yet shown in the newspaper box scores.

Other details of his game were that players would be selected in an auction format, just like the Seminar, but every position on the field had to be filled, including historically light-hitting ones like catcher and second base. In the Seminar, teams could load up on as many sluggers as they wanted.

In the Morty Ain article, Okrent said, "Not to disparage Gamson's game, but the difference between his game and mine was the difference between a covered wagon and a rocket ship."

Sklar said that in the Gamson game "there were no trades, you just sat back and watched your numbers. Dan's intent was to make you a virtual GM."

Another piece to this story is that in 1970, when Okrent was 22 years old, he started playing Strat-O-Matic with a literary agent friend, David Obst. They played so obsessively that they were included in a 1976 *Newsweek* article about the popularity of dice baseball games. They were photographed playing the game in an office, wearing baseball caps. "I remember just getting an enormous amount of ridicule about that," Okrent said. He also said, "If there hadn't been Strat-O-Matic, I still think I would have come up with rotisserie, but unquestionably it helped."

Okrent admits that his inspiration for creating WHIP was a fatigue rating in Strat-O-Matic; namely, that after a certain number of innings, a pitcher's performance worsened if he gave up a combination of three hits and walks in one inning or four hits or walks over two innings. "That was absolutely in the back of my mind when I was putting together the first categories for rotisserie," Okrent said, "which is to say that walks are as important as hits in demonstrating a pitcher's weakness."

Okrent was 31 years old when he took that trip to Texas. The next day, at lunch with four of the *Texas Monthly* guys who he knew liked baseball, he handed them each the rules he had typed up for his proposed game.

He received blank stares in response…indicating somewhere between simply not being interested to thinking he was totally nuts.

Okrent had moved to western Massachusetts in 1978 but went to Manhattan frequently for work and would regularly have lunch with friends there to talk baseball. A month after his trip to Austin, he had lunch with five of these friends at La Rotisserie Francaise in Manhattan on East 52nd Street. Okrent pitched the idea to them: *we will acquire players for our own team by an auction, we will be required to have them at certain positions, we will follow their statistics and whoever scores the highest in various categories gets the most points. The team with the most overall points wins the pennant.*

Two of the five friends— Lee Eisenberg, an editor for *Esquire Magazine*, and Cork Smith, an editor at Viking Press—wanted to play. They needed to recruit more players to have enough for a league, so they contacted friends who loved baseball. While some said it sounded boring, stupid, or crazy, others thought it was great. They ended up with a total of 10 teams—Okrent wanted to limit it to that so there would be enough good talent available.

Okrent recruited Sklar. Sklar asked Glen Waggoner, who at the time was an administrator at Columbia University. Waggoner couldn't afford the planned $250 buy-in fee, so he partnered with Peter Gethers, an editor at Random House and a sitcom writer. Okrent also got his lawyer, Michael Pollet, and another friend, Bruce McCall, who was a very talented artist and writer for the *New Yorker* magazine. Eisenberg recruited Rob Fleder, who worked with him at *Esquire*. Cork Smith enlisted Tom Guinzberg, a colleague at Viking Press.

The original league had one female owner. Valerie Salembier, then the advertising director for *Ms.* magazine, was asked to meet Okrent and Eisenberg for a drink to talk about Rotisserie League baseball. She knew Dan because her boyfriend had worked with him at *Texas Monthly*. She said they quizzed her about her baseball knowledge as though she were on a job interview. They called two days later to tell her she had been accepted into the league.

In all, they had a total of 11 owners and 10 teams. Most were in their 20s and 30s. A few of them were editors, a few writers, a lawyer, a college professor, a university administrator, and two from the advertising industry.

In March 1980, after that initial discussion at La Rotisserie Francaise, seven of the original members met at PJ Moriarity's, on Third Avenue in Manhattan. Over burgers and Bloody Marys, they officially hammered out the rules. "That was really the birth of Rotisserie," Okrent said.

Among other things, they decided at this session that they would bid $250 for 22 players. (Okrent said he wanted the league to be an auction because it was a way of forcing people to allocate resources like a real MLB team owner.) They would each have 14 hitters and eight pitchers. The $250 per team would go to a prize pool. Additional fees for trading and calling up players would also go to the prize pool. The winner would get 50%, second place 25%, third 15%, and fourth 10%. The next year, they added a pitcher and raised the budget to $260. This has remained the standard for fantasy baseball auctions until today.

They decided to call the game Rotisserie League Baseball, in honor of the restaurant where Okrent first mentioned the idea, because it sounded better than Moriarity League Baseball, and it was a nice pun on the popular term Hot Stove League, which refers to people talking about baseball during the offseason.

The Rotisserie Baseball League held their first draft on the Sunday after opening day, which was April 13, 1980, at Cork Smith's Manhattan apartment. They've said they didn't really know what they were doing.

"It's like having sex for the first time," said Rob Fleder. "You don't know what you're doing, but you know something's about to happen, and then it happens—and it wasn't exactly what I expected, but I'm coming back for more."

They were all very intense about their teams. Gethers said, "Rotisserie took over my life completely." But they also had fun. Bruce McCall made team logos, and he wrote a newsletter, which mostly just made fun of everyone.

The internet didn't exist, so Okrent had to get the MLB game results from the newspaper—or a week later in *The Sporting News*—in order to compute the standings by hand and then fax them to everyone in the league.

Waggoner and his partner Gethers won the first year. They wore tuxedos and white tennis shoes to the awards banquet at Cork's apartment. Their girlfriends wore cheerleader outfits. They celebrated by pouring a bottle of the chocolate drink Yoo-Hoo over the winners, as MLB teams do with champagne. It would become an annual tradition. Okrent finished 7th that first year.

The winner was awarded the Wigge Cup. "It was named after Larry Wigge, the statistics editor of *The Sporting News*, who was providing us with the precise statistics," Okrent explained. "We didn't know him, never spoke to him, we just thought it was a funny name."

Gethers said he called Michael Pollet one day during that first season and Pollet told him, "I can't talk trade because I'm in Washington arguing in front of the Supreme Court in an hour." Gethers said, "But we are talking about Omar Moreno! Sixty steals!" There was a pause, then Pollet responded, "Hold on, maybe I have a few minutes."

Rotisserie Baseball Spreads

The 11 original owners would tell their friends about Rotisserie at work and at dinner parties, and it was fascinating to many people. Some wanted to play. Some would mention it to their friends.

Eight of the 11 owners were in the media, and many of the people they told were as well. Fred Ferretti, a *New York Times* writer, wrote an article about the league that was published in the *Times* on July 8, 1980. He had heard about it from a friend who knew one of the players. The article was titled "For Major-League Addicts, A Way to Win a Pennant," and it began: "What George Steinbrenner is to the American League, Lee Eisenberg is to the Rotisserie League."

More articles followed, and the league was featured on *CBS Morning News*, *The Today Show* and National Public Radio. Okrent did a five-minute segment with Bryant Gumbel on the *Today Show*. (Gumbel later requested the rules and formed a league.)

These articles and media appearances only showed the league as unusual, interesting, and even humorous. None of them ever explained the rules or how the winner was determined, only that they picked players and used their stats for their imaginary teams. After *The New York Times* article, people would contact them asking how to get the rules. Okrent said they generally didn't share the rules with anyone except friends, because they thought they might have something of value. They also trademarked the name.

In 1981, they created a second league, using only American League players. Gethers and a few others played in both leagues, and they gave the remaining spots to other friends.

Okrent wrote an article for the March 31, 1981 issue of *Inside Sports* magazine, "The Year George Foster Wasn't Worth $36." Okrent said,

"The article was not supposed to include the rules—and I didn't want the rules published—but midway through the process an editor asked can we have the rules just for fact-checking...but then they published the rules."

This was a watershed event, as it was the first time the rules had been published, and it was now easy for people who read the article to start their own leagues. Many, many did just that. Before the issue even went to press, some of the magazine staff had formed their own league, including John Walsh, the editor-in-chief.

By 1981, their second season, there were Rotisserie leagues in nearly every major league press box, Okrent said. MLB players went on strike during the summer of 1981. Chapter One mentioned how without games to write about, some media used Strat-O-Matic games as a substitute. Many other baseball writers wrote about their Rotisserie leagues as a source of content. Okrent said, "I always thought the thing that spread the word in the pre-internet world was the strike."

While many writers were playing Rotisserie, according to Okrent there were other baseball writers who were incredibly dismissive of Rotisserie and said it was ruining the game, played by "numbers' nerds who don't appreciate baseball."

In this pre-internet era, it was hard to get information. Gethers said they started doing things like calling the Phillies' front office, pretending to be from *The New York Times*, to ask about Mike Schmidt's hamstring. Within two years, teams' publicity offices were inundated with calls asking about players' injuries, who was going to make the roster, etc.

During the winter of 1980, Okrent met Steve Wulf, a writer for *Sports Illustrated*, and invited him to join the league. Wulf did so, and won the 1981 title. He later wrote a May 1984 article for *Sports Illustrated* and their three million readers, about his experience in the league.

Bantam Books approached the founders about writing a book. They agreed, and *Rotisserie League Baseball: The Greatest Game for Baseball Fans Since Baseball* was published in March 1984, before the MLB season started. The book went into detail about the rules, had tips on strategy, and made the game sound like fun. It was primarily written and edited by Waggoner and Sklar, but each owner wrote a chapter about their own team. Many people who bought the book recruited friends and started leagues. One was well-known fantasy analyst Matthew Berry, who bought the book at age 14, and said, "They were such talented writers they made the game sound appealing."

Once again, they garnered publicity when Robert Thomas Jr wrote an April, 1984 book review for *The New York Times*. They knew they had something good when Bantam asked them to write another book the very next year. The second edition was published in April of 1987 and, starting with a 1989 edition, it was published annually for several years. Fairly early on, the books started including players statistics.

Sometime in the early 1980s, real MLB players started to become aware of Rotisserie. Former Atlanta Braves outfielder Dale Murphy, for example, said he was in New York to play the Mets on a Sunday in the early '80s and took a cab to church before the game. As he paid, the cabbie said, "Have a good game today. I just traded for you." Steve Wulf relates he was at the batting cage before that same game at Shea Stadium when Dale Murphy asked him, "How is your Rotisserie team doing?" According to Wulf, "That was the first official acknowledgement that real players knew about Rotisserie."

As time went on, more and more fans would tell major league players, "Hey, have a great year—because you're on my Roto team." Players would hear this when signing autographs, in the on-deck circle, at bars, everywhere.

Rotisserie League Baseball Tries to Monetize

As Rotisserie became popular, entrepreneurs and companies started their own games, stat services, advice services, and more. All of this is covered later in this book. For now, we'll stay with what happened with Okrent and his league mates through the years.

Very early on, they had trademarked the name "The Rotisserie League." When the first book came out in 1984, they started the only "official" Rotisserie League Baseball Association (RLBA). Membership cost $50 per league and members received a position eligibility list; opening day rosters, mailed after opening day; four annual updates about rules changes, new variations of the game, news from other leagues; and a certificate signed by Okrent for the league winner. In addition, the RLBA would adjudicate disputes and rules interpretations.

For a few years, they held Rotisserie conventions in Clearwater, Florida, during spring training. And they sold RLBA-logo caps and T-shirts. They advertised the conventions in their own book, as well as in *Baseball America* and *The Sporting News*. Each year, approximately 70-90 people from around the US would pay money to come and meet the founders. "People actually paid money to meet us," Gethers said. "How sick is that?"

They started to offer their own stat service. The advent of computers made this possible, but it was still pre-internet and thus they had to rely on USA *Today* for the statistics. They would mail or fax weekly league stats, transactions, and standings the same day they would appear in *USA Today*. An attorney named Lew Fidler had volunteered to run the stat service because he had an early computer, a fax machine, and free time. Fidler wrote his own computer program to do the stats.

Despite these efforts, they never made much money. Although they had trademarked their name, and sometimes issued cease-and-desist orders, individuals and companies would simply change the name to "Fantasy." The rules were so simple that there was nothing to protect, and nobody had to buy anything to play the game. Thus, by the late 1980s many people were playing "fantasy baseball" rather than "rotisserie baseball," even though it was the same game, albeit sometimes with minor tweaks to the rules used by the original Rotisserie league.

In 1989, the RLBA had more than 1,000 leagues. It created and sold a video, hosted by Reggie Jackson, that was like a VHS version of the Bantam book. It hired a full-time marketing director, John Hassan, and rented a Manhattan office—but Hassan's employment ended after only two years, when the RLBA basically gave up on the idea of making money.

Okrent estimated none of them ever made more than $10,000-$15,000 from the game. He has said that for a while it bothered him that he didn't make any money from his idea, but in the pre-internet age it was hard to do. Waggoner has said he is not bitter that the game took off and they didn't make money. He said their original goal was to have fun, not make money, and they succeeded in that.

Hassan said perhaps he could have been more effective if they'd brought him in during 1984, when the first book came out, but by 1990 the "horse had left the barn." Hassan couldn't bring in more revenue. He would pitch deals with many people, but ultimately, they would all realize they could do it themselves and didn't need the RLBA. He remembers that they met with one man several times before he disappeared—a year later, they saw the idea in USA Today.

Hassan said part of his job was taking calls from RLBA members from all over the country, to adjudicate trade and transaction disputes. "I'd be on the phone with three guys, and whoever I ruled against would throw a shit fit," he said.

They also published a Bantam Rotisserie Basketball book in 1990 and 1991, overseen by Greg Kelly, an editor for Sports Illustrated, and a football book written by Sklar for 1991-92.

Okrent never won the league he created. He finished second three times, once losing the title on the last day of the year by half a point. Hassan said, "It's amazing that Dan Okrent never won a league, it's like finding out that Hugh Hefner never got laid." Okrent quit the league in 1995. The original league continued without him through the 2008 season. After a hiatus, Okrent started playing again in 2001 with some of the original guys, but this time it was a simpler format of rotisserie baseball.

Wulf hosted the 2008 draft in the main conference room at ESPN The Magazine. It included Okrent, Waggoner, Fleder, Wulf, longtime commissioner Cary Schneider and John Hassan. At one point, Wulf looked at the rosters and saw Ken Griffey Jr., Tony Gwynn Jr., Prince Fielder, Chris Duncan, Aaron Boone, Jose Cruz Jr., Scott Hairston, Jason Kendall, Justin Speier, Daryle Ward, and Jayson Werth, and realized he had, at various points, bid on all their fathers.

Okrent said that by the mid-1980s everyone would ask him how much to pay for a player, or about a trade they wanted to make, or tell him about their teams. "It got exhausting," he said. "There is nothing more interesting than your own Rotisserie team, and there is nothing more boring than someone else's."

One time he was followed into a men's room by someone asking him questions. The guy continued doing so even after Okrent went into a stall and locked the door.

In the late 1980s, having founded *New England Monthly* magazine, Okrent gave a speech about New England's economic outlook. While he was taking questions afterwards, a pinstriped banker rose and asked, "How much should I pay for Ryne Sandberg?"

Okrent, who was featured in Ken Burn's 1994 baseball documentary, has often said, "If I bring peace to Israel and find a cure for cancer, my obituary will still say, 'He invented Rotisserie Baseball.'"

Lew Fidler became a New York City councilman and, in September 2008, gave a ceremonial presentation to give the original team owners credit as the founders of Rotisserie Baseball. Only Waggoner and a couple of others attended.

Over the years, Okrent received a few letters from wives accusing him of breaking up their marriages.

While Okrent invented the game, Glen Waggoner helped make it popular, and edited their series of books. "Glen was the closest thing we had to an official spokesman," Okrent said. "He never lost his enthusiasm for his connection to the original league."

In 2000, Okrent and Waggoner were inducted into the inaugural Hall of Fame class of the Fantasy Sports Trade Association (FSTA). Waggoner attended the induction, but Okrent had no interest in going. "You couldn't pay me to go," he has said in the past. I asked him why and he explained, "It wasn't important to me. I had stopped playing five years earlier. I did get tired of being known for this part of my life—this was a hobby, we tried to make it a business, we didn't succeed. Big deal. I got books to write, I got magazines to edit, I'm moving on with my life. I'm grateful that they did it, and for the acknowledgment, but it just wasn't an important part of my life then."

In 2005, members of the original league were invited to the Baseball

Hall of Fame in Cooperstown to honor the 25th anniversary of their league. Okrent and most of the others did attend. Their winner's trophy, the Wigge Cup, is now at the Hall of Fame.

Okrent has said his proudest Rotisserie moment came when he moved to New York City. His 10-year-old son had started at a new school and the kids were mean to him—nobody wanted to talk to him, and he was very unhappy. One day, a kid who he had become friendly with took him home and introduced him to his parents. His father asked, "Are you related to Dan Okrent?" Okrent's son responded, "Yeah, that's my dad!" The friend's father said, "He invented Rotisserie baseball, he changed my life." The next day, Okrent's son was the most popular kid at school.

CHAPTER 3

Origins of Fantasy Football

Bill "Wink" Winkenbach was a successful Oakland businessman. He owned a company called Superior Tile, a 10% limited partnership of the Oakland Raiders, and the building that was home to the Raiders offices. In the mid-to-late 1950s, he created a fantasy game based on the PGA Tour. Each week, participants would select a team of pro golfers and whoever had the lowest combined total strokes would win.

Around 1959, Winkenbach created a baseball game, the Superior Tile Summer Invitational Home Run Tourney. Team owners drafted a fixed number of pitchers, catchers, infielders, and outfielders and earned points based on their players' actual performance. The league continued for more than 40 years.

Fantasy football was born in October of 1962, when the Raiders went to New York for a game against the Titans (now the New York Jets). Information about the details is slightly conflicting. The most reported story is that one night at their Manhattan hotel—what is now the Row NYC —Winkenbach created the game with the help of Bill Tunnell, the Raiders PR director, and Scotty Stirling, who covered the Raiders for the *Oakland Tribune*.

Stirling said the men got together for drinks, and Winkenbach told them about his golf and baseball games. Someone suggested, "Why don't we do a football game?" They stayed up all night talking about the game and creating the rules, according to Stirling. "Winkenbach deserves the lion's share of the credit for developing the game," he said. "We chipped in with rules, but the germ of inspiration was these earlier games he played with golf and baseball." When they were back in Oakland, they added George Ross, the *Oakland Tribune*'s sports editor, to the group.

The slightly different version of events states that on the flight to New York, Wink was sitting with George Ross, told him about his baseball game, and Ross suggested they do one for football. This conversation then led to Winkenbach discussing the idea with Tunnell and Stirling at the hotel. One further discrepancy: In a 2010 article, Stirling said that Ross was also at the hotel with them on the night they created the game.

Since the 1962 season had already started, they waited until August 1963 to hold their first draft. They called the league the Greater Oakland Professional Pigskin Prediction League (GOPPPL). (The acronym rhymes with "topple" and is often referred to with the word "Prognosticators" in place of "Prediction," but that is not correct.)

Their rules dictated that owners must (1) be affiliated with an AFL team in some capacity, (2) be a journalist for pro football, or (3) have bought or sold 10 season tickets for the Raiders' 1963 season.

They recruited four more owners: Raiders radio voice Bob Blum, ticket manager George Glace, and season-ticket sellers Phil Carmona and Ralph Casebolt. In 1963, there was only one preview guide, *Street & Smith's*, and it was difficult to get injury news. An owner had to really follow the AFL and NFL religiously and dig to get information. Because of this difficulty, each owner selected a second person to help as team "coach." Essentially, they were co-owners.

Stirling asked a friend, local entrepreneur Andy Mousalimas, to be his coach. George Glace asked Ron Wolf, a Raiders scout, to be his coach. (Wolf went on to become a Hall of Fame general manager for the Packers in the mid-1990s. Stirling later became GM of the Raiders, then of the NBA's New York Knicks; he also served as the NBA's VP of operations and spent 24 years as the Sacramento Kings' scouting director.)

The roster requirement was 20 players: four receivers, four halfbacks, two fullbacks, two quarterbacks, two kick returners, two kickers, two defensive backs or linebackers, and two defensive linemen. The owners submitted a weekly starting lineup consisting of about half of their 20 players. If a player was known to be hurt, owners could apply to the commissioner for permission to select a temporary replacement from the undrafted players.

Their scoring system was 50 points for a rushing touchdown, 25 points for a thrown or caught touchdown, 25 points for a field goal, 10 points for an extra point and 200 points for a kick or interception returned for a touchdown.

The first draft was held, in August 1963, in the basement recreation room of Winkenbach's house. Stirling and Mousalimas had the first pick and took Houston Oilers quarterback George Blanda (he was also the Oilers placekicker and could be drafted again separately as a kicker). The second pick was Cleveland running back Jim Brown. Others taken in that draft included YA Tittle, Mike Ditka, and Frank Gifford.

Winkenbach was the league commissioner because his office had phone lines, typewriters, and a mimeograph machine—especially rare in 1963. He distributed weekly reports to everyone on Tuesdays.

Stirling has said, "Winkenbach would sit with other limited partners at home Raider games, and their big concern wasn't how the Raiders were doing, but how their GOPPPL team was playing."

"We'd go and root for the opposition," Mousalimas recalled, "and fans would look at us and say, 'Why the hell are you rooting against the Raiders?'"

With no internet and no ESPN, they did much of their research by reading out-of-town newspapers at their local newsstand. Mousalimas would call newspapers for information— sometimes he got it and sometimes they hung up thinking he was a bookie.

GOPPPL held a banquet in January for the club owners, coaches, and wives. Winkenbach personally made a trophy for the last-place team with a wooden football face and a dunce cap on top. Stirling and Mousalimas, with the first pick, finished last. Every year, the person who placed last was required to display the trophy at his home until handing it off to the following year's loser.

Although GOPPPL was mentioned in a 1965 *San Francisco Examiner* article, through 1968, very few people heard about the game. The original members only shared it with a small number of friends and some co-workers at the Raiders and at the *Tribune*. Per their own rules, they only allowed football journalists, Raiders season-ticket sellers or buyers, or those affiliated with an AFL team. Only a few other leagues sprouted from the small number of friends and co-workers who were told about it. Ross said he noticed many *Tribune* staffers putting in extra hours in the sports department, studying information to help their personal GOPPPL teams. He said GOPPPL made his sportswriters better at their jobs, as they all became NFL and AFL experts.

At some point, *Tribune* staff also started GOPPPL baseball and basketball leagues.

Tribune columnist Dave Newhouse said the leagues were great for morale, giving people something to talk about and needle each other over.

In 1969, John Madden was hired as the Raiders' coach, and Wink had lunch with him often. According to Winkenbach's daughter, her dad used this friendship with Madden to "pick his mind about who to draft." Wink was also a good friend of owner Al Davis. On game day, Wink would set up radios around the family TV so he could watch one game and listen to others.

The phrase "fantasy football" didn't yet exist. Instead, people referred to this game as GOPPPL, both for Wink's original league and for anyone else who created a league. It would be many years before "fantasy football" became the common name.

Andy Mousalimas and the Kings X

Bill Winkenbach is the man credited with inventing fantasy football, but Andy "Sam" Mousalimas was the guy who spread the word. Yet this was far from Mousalimas' biggest accomplishment in life. Born to Greek immigrants, he was a 17-year-old high school senior when the Japanese attacked Pearl Harbor. One year later, he volunteered for the Army and soon became a member of the Office of Strategic Services

(OSS), which was the forerunner of the CIA. Mousalimas later recalled, "The recruiting officer said 97% of you will probably not return."

Fluent in Greek, he was assigned to a group that secretly parachuted behind enemy lines in Nazi-occupied Greece. They blended in with the Greek resistance and raised havoc among the German forces, destroying infrastructure and incredibly pinning down 31 German divisions that otherwise would have been sent to France to stop the Allied invasion on D-Day. He always had a cyanide pill in case he was captured.

The activities of the OSS were not declassified until 45 years after their last mission. Mousalimas never spoke of it until that happened, even to his own family. He was awarded a Purple Heart and the Congressional Gold Medal.

After the war, he came home, got married, and was the manager of a bar on Telegraph Avenue, in Oakland, called the Lamp Post. He was known as one of the few bartenders who would serve African Americans. He became friends with Scotty Stirling, a regular customer, leading to Stirling asking Mousalimas to be "coach" of his GOPPPL team.

In 1968, Mousalimas left the Lamp Post and bought the Kings X bar on Piedmont Avenue, in North Oakland, turning it into what was probably the Bay Area's first sports bar. To attract customers, he offered competitions such as gin rummy, backgammon, and trivia contests. One day, in 1969, he decided it would be fun, and good for business, to offer fantasy football to the public. He started his own 10-team Kings League and invited his regulars to join. He had no problem filling it.

Demand required Mousalimas start a second league for the 1970 season. He called it the X League. He altered the scoring system to include points for yardage gained and an escalating reward scale for length of TDs. "The rules were terrible," he said. "They were great to begin with, but when you got 25 points for a rushing touchdown—whether for a yard or up to 74 yards—then it was double after 74 yards. How many times you score from 75 out? And then you got 200 points for a defensive player score or a return player. So, we changed a lot of that. In those days, OJ Simpson was running wild, while Pete Banaszak was scoring one-yard touchdowns. You got points for the one-yard touchdowns, but no points for the guy rushing for 100 yards."

The scoring unit was called "points," but really meant "cents." The leagues would have different amounts of money at stake. For example, a "20 cent" league meant that for every point you score, the other nine owners give you 20 cents, so you win $1.80 per point. They called them "points" rather than "cents" because they were worried about trouble from the vice squad. Some of the divisions typically had $25,000 to $35,000 of side bets at stake.

After the 1970 season, Mousalimas said, "Winkenbach sends me a letter that he didn't appreciate that I changed the rules, and I'm persona non grata. He didn't invite me back for the 1971 GOPPPL."

By 1978, there were six leagues of 10 teams each, including an all-female Queens League. (According to long-time league member Pasquale Franzese, the men back then didn't want to allow women into their leagues.) Mousalimas also created a "mid-season draft" where, halfway through the season, each league would hold a four-round draft to replace injured or underperforming players. The last-place team would get the first pick and proceed in order, with the first-place team getting the last pick.

And yes, this was all great for his business. For draft night, he served prime rib and hired extra staff. It was a rollicking event with more than 200 participants, as most teams had multiple managers, sometimes as many as seven managers for just one team.

The Kings X was packed on Friday nights, since players were required to go and write their starting lineups on a chalkboard so everyone could see them by 10 p.m. Everyone had a great time eating, drinking, talking about their teams, and trash talking. Sundays were packed, with the games on NBC and CBS. Mousalimas would often call newspapers and TV networks during the games to try and get details on who scored. They mostly ignored him, assuming he was a bookie.

On Sunday nights, Mousalimas would leave his bar around 3 a.m., drive to a local newsstand, and get the first edition of the *Tribune*. He then went home and worked until dawn so that he could have the leaderboards posted on the wall for the standing-room-only Monday lunch crowd, who were anxious to see the results. After *Monday Night Football*, he would need to do it again in time for Tuesday lunch.

Rarely mentioned in articles about Mousalimas is that he purchased Kings X along with his wife, Mary, and his brother-in-law John Kumarelas. There is never any mention of Kumarelas being involved with the creation of fantasy football, although he helped operate the bar for 23 years. One of Mousalimas' grandchildren, Harry Ahlas, said that Mousalimas was the biggest decision maker, but both Kumarelas and Mary were a vital part of Kings X.

Fantasy Football Spreads

The Kings X was well known for its trivia contests and other competitions. Trivia teams would come from across the bay in San Francisco to challenge Kings X teams. Men would fly in from Los Angeles overnight just to play in the gin tournament. And everyone who came would see the football leaderboards in the main dining room and inquire what this was. Starting with the first league in 1969 and increasing as time went on, word spread about this new game. People started their own leagues, both in the Oakland area as well as those visiting from around the country who happened to go to the Kings X. PGA Golfer Tom Purtzer reportedly started a Phoenix-based league after seeing a GOPPPL member prepare for a draft in the early 1970s.

"Guys in offices and in bars would talk about it," Ross said, "and pretty soon it was all over town, and then it spread to San Francisco and the rest of the Bay Area."

"I think the thing first spread in the Bay Area," Stirling said. "Once it got to Montgomery Street, which is to San Francisco what Wall Street is to New York, it spread like wildfire."

Kings X players also started their own leagues throughout Northern California.

Bars from all over the country, including Hawaii, started calling and asking for the rules. Mousalimas always obliged. Helped by bars and offices and other word of mouth, it eventually spread throughout the entire United States.

Norman Brooks, from southern Florida, saw the game while visiting San Francisco in 1975 and launched a league in his home state. He subscribed to 28 newspapers to keep up with every NFL team.

A September 1980 article in *Inside Sports* outlined the basic rules of fantasy football. (This was six months before the same magazine published Dan Okrent's rotisserie baseball article.)

The article was written by Glenn Ferry, a San Francisco bartender who played in two leagues. He mentioned that trading and selling players was allowed, and that when one owner had several injured running backs late in the year, Ferry sold his sixth-best running back to him for a bottle of Brolio Chianti.

The rules published in the article were presumably the same, or close to, what the Kings X leagues had been using, after the modifications made by Mousalimas: The leagues had 10 owners, who used a snake draft, meaning that whoever goes first has the last pick in the second round, then first pick in round three, last in round four, etc. Participants were required to draft 25 players: six running backs, six wide receivers, three quarterbacks, two kickers, two kick returners, four defensive backs and two linebackers. Each week, they started two running backs, three wide receivers, one quarterback, one kicker, one kick returner, two defensive backs and one linebacker. A mid-season draft allowed them to add five additional players.

The scoring system gave 10 points for a rushing touchdown of less than 50 yards by a quarterback, running back, or wide receiver, or 20 points if more than 50 yards; 5 points for a quarterback making a touchdown pass of less than 50 yards, plus 5 points for the running back or receiver who caught it, or 10 points each if the pass was more than 50 yards; 20 points for a touchdown scored by a defensive back or kick returner, or 40 for one scored by a linebacker; and 5 points for a field goal of less than 45 yards, or 10 if 45 or longer.

Many people read the article and formed leagues. Two students at Case Western Reserve University in Cleveland, Tom Spear and Jeff Kornreich, recruited four classmates to begin the Indoor Football League (IFL). The following year, one of the six quit and was replaced by a new owner. As of January 2024, they had just completed their 44th consecutive year, with all six of these owners still playing, plus two more who were added in 1985 when they expanded to eight teams. While college friends tend to drift apart and lose contact, the league has made it possible for them to remain friends even while most of them now live in different parts of the country, with one member even splitting his time between San Francisco and Singapore.

Spear had the unusual opportunity to roster his own son, Carey, who was a placekicker at Vanderbilt. Carey signed with the Eagles but was released before the season started. The next year, he signed with the Browns, but again was released before the season. Nonetheless, Spear kept his son on his IFL roster both seasons.

Spear says the reason the league has lasted all these years is the trash talking. They still bring up years ago when someone drafted Frank Pollard as a kick returner. Kick returners ideally run one back for a touchdown occasionally. It turned out Pollard was only returning kicks because he never dropped the ball, but he wore a neck brace and never returned a kick more than about five yards.

In 1980, a group of New England beat writers heard about the game while in Seattle for a Patriots-Seahawks game; one of those writers, Jim Donaldson, of *The Providence Journal*, later wrote *The Official Fantasy Football League Manual* in 1984. By the end of the decade, fantasy football games were being offered by several companies and fantasy football magazines were being published.

GOPPPL and Kings X Leagues Continue

While the game spread throughout the country, and many people started using different rules and formats, the two original leagues remained strong.

Mousalimas sold the Kings X in 1991 and retired to spend more time helping the Greek Orthodox Cathedral of the Ascension in the Oakland Hills, which he had helped build. The new owner, Nicholas Haney, kept the football leagues going until he sold the bar in 2005, and it became a tiki bar named the Kona Club. Fantasy football didn't fit their theme, so the Kings X league moved to the Grand Oaks sports bar. As of 2023, they were still holding their drafts there. They were down to three 10-team leagues, including the Queens league. Ann Cooke, a 40-year league veteran, was the commissioner, and her 35-year-old daughter Danielle Sullivan, a 15-year league veteran, was the official scorekeeper.

In 2012, 87-year-old Mousalimas did his 50th draft, teaming with his son-in-law and grandson. (Google an ESPN article "50 years of fantasy football," by Tim Keown, and you can watch a three-minute video of Mousalimas at this draft.) At the time he planned this to be his last season, but ended up playing until he was 90.

In 2018, the OSS Operations Groups were given the rarely awarded Congressional Gold Medal. At age 92, Mousalimas flew to Washington, DC to receive the medal. He was the only survivor of his group well enough to attend, so he accepted the decoration in honor of his brothers in arms, living and dead.

Meanwhile, GOPPPL was also still thriving. Their 2015 draft, held at Francesco's Italian restaurant, included, among others, the current commissioner, Stan Heeb, who had been in the league since 1974, and defending champion 91-year-old Fred Thomsen, who won $300 for his 2014 victory. There were 10 teams for this draft, and they still used the original scoring rules. Several members have been joined by their sons in the league. Thomsen marveled that his grandson could draft fantasy teams on a computer. Thomsen said that while on the phone with him, his grandson drafted three Yahoo teams in an hour.

Winkenbach and the other original owners never tried to make money from their creation. In the very early days, Mousalimas suggested to Wink, "I think this will spread, what do you think about copyrighting it?" Wink was not interested in that. Mousalimas then asked, "How about me? I'd like to copyright it." To which Wink replied, "Over my dead body."

We will never know what might have happened if they'd copyrighted it, but, looking at the example of Dan Okrent and Rotisserie League Baseball, they may not have fared much better financially, since the rules are simple and people can just change the name.

Wink played GOPPPL right up until his death in 1993 at the age of 81. In 2011, he was inducted into the FSTA Hall of Fame posthumously. The San Francisco 49ers stadium created a fantasy football section that included gold busts of Winkenbach and Mousalimas.

Emil Kadlec, co-founder of the World Championship of Fantasy Football (WCOFF), invited Mousalimas to the WCOFF in Las Vegas and, just before a draft with 2,000 participants, brought Mousalimas on stage. To Mousalimas' surprise, he was treated like a rock star.

Shortly before his death, Mousalimas was asked if he had any regrets. "Only one," said this true American hero. "I should have drafted Jim Brown."

CHAPTER 4

First Commercial Games

It's unclear who started the first commercial for-profit fantasy game, but one possibility is Larry Burris. The former Bainbridge Island, Washington, parks and recreation director started a company called Fantasy League Baseball in 1983. Advertising in *The Sporting News* and possibly elsewhere, he grew to have 1,000 players—from almost every state, plus several foreign countries—for the 1990 MLB season, grossing $150,000. During the season, he managed everything over the course of 8-to-12-hour days, seven days a week.

Participants mailed in draft sheets listing the players they wanted, ordered by position. Burris ran the drafts where someone randomly was given the first pick for the first position to be chosen, then they had the last pick for the next position, second pick for the third position, next to last for fourth, etc. until they all had 15 hitters (two from each infield position and five outfielders) and 10 pitchers. He then mailed everyone the results of the draft and weekly reports with their team's stats, league standings and the national standings. It was roto scoring, with five hitting categories (batting average, runs, home runs, RBIs, stolen bases) and four pitching categories (wins, ERA, WHIP, saves.)

It was free to replace a player on the disabled list, but it cost $10 for what Burris called "replacing failures." Burris offered cash prizes for league winners as well as for the top teams nationally. He also ran private leagues that did live drafts in the Seattle area, and had a partner who ran a similar football game. Fantasy League Baseball shut down after the 1991 season, most likely because the way Burris awarded cash prizes based on the number of entries—and the amount of transaction fees received—violated gambling laws.

Burris estimated that by 1990 there were about 50 companies offering various fantasy games. The number increased significantly in the 1990s. Some of these companies had unique formats; others had unique drafts, such as by a live conference call; some grew very large and made their owners millions; others remained small, but are still in business even today; and many never lasted long. This chapter will highlight some of them.

Ultimate Fantasy Sports

John Zaleski was one of the many who bought the Bantam *Rotisserie League Baseball* book in 1984. He immediately organized a league with SAE frat brothers from Long Beach State and a second league with sales associates he worked with selling Canon copiers in Costa Mesa, California. Although he ran these leagues for free, from the beginning he intended to turn them into a business one day.

His friends all thought the roto rules were too complex, so he switched immediately to a point-style version, awarding points for various accomplishments, e.g. 1 for a single, 2 for a double, 4 for a homer, etc. and other points for pitchers. He also had "head-to-head" (H2H) games, meaning contestants played a game against one individual opponent at a time. Everyone loved that format. They initially used only MLB games played Friday through Sunday, so Zaleski would have time to process lineups, calculate results, and mail reports.

In 1986, he launched his business, Ultimate Fantasy Sports (UFS), advertising in magazines, offering MLB, NFL, NBA, and NHL fantasy games. Baseball had a 162-game season, and there were 14 for football, 82 for basketball and 80 for hockey.

In 1990, he started Lifetime Leagues, where participants kept all their players from year to year. (The terms "keeper" and "dynasty" weren't yet used in fantasy and only became popular in later years. They refer to leagues where participants keep their team every year, though often they are only allowed to keep a limited number of players rather than the entire roster.)

Many people told Zaleski the lifetime concept wouldn't work, but they were wrong. It was quite popular—at his high point, Zaleski had 52 baseball Lifetime Leagues, as well as 42 for football, 23 for basketball, and five for hockey. He also continued to run many one-year-only leagues. He charged $200 per team, maxing out at $500,000 gross revenue.

Zaleski says one key to his success was offering a $20 Team of the Week prize. It kept most owners engaged the entire season. But the biggest key was that he never started a new Lifetime League until all open teams from the prior year had been sold. All leagues started the season full.

Over the years, many competitors emerged in the lifetime market, but Zaleski believes they all failed because they would start new leagues before making sure all open teams had been sold.

The first several years, Zaleski ran UFS alone, working 80-hour weeks processing entries and lineup changes, mailing results, handling customer service—everything. In 1992, he hired one part-time worker, which later changed to one full-time employee. When the internet allowed people to enter their own lineups, changes, and get the results online, Zaleski said, "I got my life back, only needing to work 40-to-50-hour weeks."

The downfall of UFS was the economic recession that hit around 2010. Zaleski was not collecting payment in full for teams prior to seasons beginning and had a large percentage of customers who didn't pay for several years. He sank about $400,000 of his own money into the business, until he realized he was never going to dig out of the hole. He tried unsuccessfully to find a partner or a buyer and shut down in 2016.

Scoresheet Baseball

David Barton was teaching computer science and working on his PhD in math at Cal Berkeley when he joined his first rotisserie league in

1986. He was shocked when Vince Coleman was the first pick in the draft. It shouldn't have been surprising, as Coleman had stolen 110 bases in 1985, but Barton thought, "This can't be right! Coleman is not the best player in baseball!"

Barton had played Strat-O-Matic and thought it was more realistic, giving credit for walks, defense, and other skills. He called his brother Jeff, a bartender, and said, "There's this new rotisserie baseball thing, it's a simple game, just add up some stats. I'm a computer programmer, I can devise a simulation game—like Strat-O-Matic but with current year's stats—but I need someone to run it because I need to keep my job."

Jeff agreed to run it. David spent his spare time in 1986 creating the game, and they launched Scoresheet Fantasy Baseball in 1987. They ran tiny ads in *The Sporting News* and *USA Today*, and 300 players signed up. Jeff worked part-time bartending until going full-time with Scoresheet in 1988. When they had 1,200 players in 1989, David quit his job. He never got his PhD.

The game was $75 to enter, plus fees for making weekly lineup changes, typically costing about $50 more for the season. Each week, players set their lineups and strategy choices for things such as lefty/righty matchups, steals, and bunts. Each Monday morning, the prior week's MLB stats were used to run six or seven simulated games for every team, playing a 162-game season against the other teams in their league. Most leagues had 10-12 teams, using players from only the AL or NL. A good 90% were "keeper leagues," meaning participants would continue with the same teams in the same leagues every year. Each spring they would select 13 players on their 35-man roster to keep for the next season, and the other 22 would go back in the pool for that season's draft. There was no overall contest against all other entries—just a league competition—and there were no cash prizes. The league winners were given small $15 trophies.

The Bartons hired typists to process entries and weekly lineup changes, and mailed reports every Monday showing the league standings and a scoresheet of each simulated game. "Some of our customers the first year or two didn't even care about our game rules," Jeff said. "They just didn't want to have to enter everything by hand from the *USA Today*."

Their third year, someone called and asked, "Can I use a fax?" Jeff replied, "What's a fax?"

They did start offering a fax option, and eventually everything transitioned online. That eliminated the transaction fees, and the Bartons no longer needed typists.

Scoresheet was still operating as of 2024. After peaking at seven staff members in an office, since about 2018 it's been back to just Jeff and David running the business from their homes. For the 2023 season, they had 3,000 players and—with many owning more than one team—a total of 5,000 teams. Ten leagues from their first two years were still going, with about half of the original owners.

By 1993, the Bartons had added games for the NFL, NBA, and NHL, partly just to give their typists something to do when it wasn't baseball season. But baseball was always 80 to 90% of their business. David couldn't come up with a good way of developing simulation games for the other sports, so they were more traditional fantasy games. When the NBA demanded licensing fees, the Bartons shut down their game, since there wasn't enough business to justify the expense. The NHL was never very big, and they stopped when they no longer needed typists. They stopped football when Covid hit.

In 1989, Pittsburgh mailman Don Klosinski and his brother Ron started a very similar company called Robot Baseball. It peaked at 750 teams by 1993, but later went out of business and Scoresheet bought its client list, netting a few dozen new players.

Jeff said, "The biggest mistake we made was having no idea how successful it was going to be, so we started on a shoestring—had we known rotisserie was going to have millions of people playing, we would have borrowed money from family and friends and gotten more customers."

Jeff also said occasionally wives would call asking him to kick their husband out of the league, since it consumed so much of their time. One of those calls came from the girlfriend of the Bartons' father, who complained, "All your dad does is study stats for Scoresheet." Their dad started playing Scoresheet the very first year in 1987 and kept playing until he passed away in 2014.

Terry Bradshaw Football and Miller Lite Football

Patrick Hughes started playing fantasy football in 1983. After five years of seeing the league's commissioner spend many hours a week calculating the stats and standings, Hughes asked his brother Michael—a computer programmer—if he could create a software program to run a fantasy league.

Hughes, a 33-year-old who had a sales and marketing background and owned an equipment leasing company, invested $150,000 to launch Franchise Football League (FFL). He got a 1-800 number and placed ads in fantasy football magazines. He also placed the software into the primary software retail stores at the time, Egghead Software, Electronic Boutique and CompUSA. That first year, in 1988, he sold 200 copies at $49.95 each.

The IBM-compatible software allowed people to run their drafts, make trades, and calculate the weekly scores and standings. It was customizable to allow for various scoring rules. And for $10 a week, FFL would send a 3.5" floppy disk by Priority Mail on Tuesdays, so that you could download the weekly stats rather than having to enter everything manually from newspaper box scores.

The next year, Hughes enlisted the help of distribution company Ingram Micro to produce retail packages and get them into the big bookstore chains. And FFL was the subject of perhaps the first nationally televised fantasy football feature story on *Inside the NFL*, which included an interview with Hughes.

When NFL Properties, the marketing arm of the NFL, told Hughes he needed to be licensed, he paid the fee and became one of the first fantasy sports companies to be licensed. Two months later, NFL Properties called and said, "Miller Brewing asked if we have a different twist on coverage of the NFL and we told them to contact you." Hughes went to Milwaukee for a meeting, and they created Miller Franchise Football.

It was a simple game, where teams would draft 25 players and start 11 each week, awarding points only for touchdowns. A 1-to-9-yard touchdown by a quarterback, running back or receiver would get points, with more awarded for 10-39 yards, and even more for 40 yards or longer.

Miller had John Madden make a video pitching the game to their 350 distributors. The distributors sold the idea to approximately 6,500 bars and taverns across the United States. The game was free to play, with each location hosting drafts and offering prizes. Hughes worked a deal with FedEx, so that as soon as the *Monday Night Football* game ended, Hughes would e-mail the week's stats to FedEx, whereupon they would make 350 copies and deliver them the next day to the distributors, who would then drop off a copy to each participating bar. This made it easier for someone at the bar to calculate the team scores and standings rather than having to look at all the newspaper box scores. Hughes and his brother would make a list of all Sunday touchdowns from the newspaper, watch the Monday night game, and record the touchdowns so that they could e-mail FedEx immediately after the game.

Miller Franchise Football ran three years, from 1989-1991, with about 6,500 locations annually. Hughes was told that the average bar had 10 leagues of typically 10 teams each. This means 650,000 players per year, not to mention that many teams undoubtedly had co-owners. This makes Miller Franchise Football one of the biggest keys to spreading fantasy football in the late '80s and early '90s. Surveys found that men and women from age 14 to 80 played.

Hughes said, "I think Miller Franchise Football was instrumental in the expansion of fantasy football, with all those bars and taverns showing people how to play, how to get your buddies and set up a league."

Miller also produced the *Miller Lite Football Handbook* for the NFL and inserted 12 million copies in 12-packs of Miller Lite during August and September. The handbook included the rules of the game as well as an ad for Hughes software. Miller paid Hughes $150,000 per year to run the game and gave him this advertising for free.

FFL had an office in McLean, Virginia. Before long, Michael, who worked for FFL on the side, created league management software for baseball, basketball, and hockey. Hughes's wife, Cheryl, also worked part-time after her day job. In 1994, Hughes sold his leasing company.

In 1995, Hughes created a game for Fox Sports. Fox Fantasy Football only lasted a year, but during that time he was invited to attend an *NFL on Fox* Sunday show hosted by Terry Bradshaw and Howie Long. During a break, he asked Bradshaw if he'd be the spokesman for FFL football and Bradshaw replied, "Absolutely!" The game was then called FFL Terry Bradshaw Fantasy Football and featured Bradshaw's picture on the cover. The agreement lasted three years and sales went from $500,000 in 1995 to $2 million in 1997.

One day in the summer of 1996, someone called their office with an FFL software problem. Their tech rep spoke to the man, solved his problem, and then the man identified himself as Bobby Bonilla (then currently a member of the Baltimore Orioles). He said, "Thanks a lot, you've been great. I'm the commissioner of the Orioles' fantasy football league. If you're ever coming to a game let me know and I'll introduce you to the players."

The tech rep asked Bonilla to hold, told Hughes about this, and Hughes couldn't grab the phone fast enough to say, "Hi Bobby, would love to!"

Hughes, an Orioles season-ticket holder, attended a game with two employees—before the game, Bonilla took them into the clubhouse to meet the players. Cal Ripken's brother, Billy, who also played for the Orioles, told Hughes that he and Cal, along with Cal's agent, all co-managed a team in the league. Billy said, "Why don't you have Cal endorse your fantasy baseball game?"

Billy introduced Hughes to Cal and his agent, and they had a deal done before the following baseball season to rebrand as FFL Cal Ripken Jr. Fantasy Baseball.

Hughes paid Bradshaw $100,000 a year and Ripken $33,000. Hughes subsequently recruited Grant Hill to endorse his NBA game and Mike Richter for his NHL game. He sold 20% of his company stock to raise $1,700,000 to pay for the endorsements and increased needs for inventory and staff.

FFL sales peaked in 1997 at about 10,000 users a year—the vast majority were football players—and then declined as competition grew with Yahoo, ESPN and CBS SportsLine entering the arena. By 2009, sales nosedived as the internet made their software mostly obsolete and, after 21 years, Hughes shut down the company. He took a job with IBM and left the fantasy industry.

An FFL Terry Bradshaw Fantasy Football box is displayed in the Pro Football Hall of Fame. And a Cal Ripken Jr. Fantasy Baseball box is shown at the Baseball Hall of Fame.

BoxScore Baseball

Dan Polisano, a bartender and substitute teacher in the metro Detroit area, played Larry Burris's game for several years and enjoyed it. But he felt Burris was overcharging and that he could create a game that would offer more and charge less.

Polisano created a game very similar to Burris's. He bought his first ever computer, without a hard drive, because it struck him as an unnecessary frill. In 1990, the 32-year-old founded BoxScore Baseball, running two free test leagues with friends to work out the kinks. And in 1991—investing $10,000 in advertising in magazines like *The Sporting News*, *Fantasy Index*, *Fantasy Baseball* and *Baseball Weekly*—he received 200 entries at $75 each. He provided a 1-800 number where players could make in-season transaction moves for a cost.

After Burris went out of business after the 1991 MLB season, Polisano's entries jumped to 400 for 1992. He had occasional help from family but primarily did all the work himself, working BoxScore during the day and bartending at night. He added a couple of live drafts in the Detroit area, as well as conference-call drafts.

The 1994 MLB strike hurt business, followed by increased competition in the industry. One competitor that angered him was when

The Sporting News started advertising their own game. He was paying the magazine good money to advertise and now they were competing against him.

BoxScore Baseball never grew beyond a little over 400 teams per year, but was still getting about 200 teams per year as of 2023. Polisano tried an NBA game in 1996 and 1997, but it didn't catch on. In 2000, he started dynasty baseball leagues (meaning you keep most of your players every year and the league is continuous from one year to the next) and these accounted for 50% of his business before long. In 2003, he started an NFL game that is still going as of 2023. And, of course, he added a website and online drafts.

The first BoxScore national competition, in 1991, was won by Charlie Wiegert, who later co-founded CDM (Chapter 6). Since he couldn't play his own game, Polisano played CDM, winning their 1993 mid-season overall competition.

One loyal BoxScore player has played every year since the mid-90s until 2023, including the one year he was in jail. Incarcerated just before the draft, he gave his girlfriend instructions and she drafted for him. During her weekly visits to see him in jail, he would give her the transactions to call in. He won the league, and later married the girlfriend.

"I've got a core group of 100 people," Polisano said. "We've got a Vegas league where we go out every February and have a live draft and that's a blast. I didn't get rich from this, but these guys are my buddies now. I've been talking to them for 20 years."

First Online Baseball Game

Rick Wolf graduated from the State University of New York at Binghamton with a BS in computer science and a BS in mathematics. In 1987, 23-year-old Wolf started working as a programmer for IBM's Prodigy, a pre-internet online service that offered news, weather, sports, bulletin boards and e-mail.

Of their 120 developers, only Wolf and a few others liked sports. Thus, Wolf was placed on the team that worked on sports projects and they developed the first ever online fantasy baseball game. Launched in 1991, Baseball Manager was based on an idea by John Butterfield, who also designed it.

It wasn't like the Dan Okrent Rotisserie game, it was a simulation game. Participants played head-to-head games against other people from around the continental United States. The cost was $119.95 for a 162-game season or $59.95 for a shorter, 54-game season. There were 10 people in a league, each major-league player was assigned a salary, and entrants had an $18 million budget to spend on players.

Participants could let the computer manage their team, or they could manage it themselves, setting the hitters lineup, pitching rotation, pinch-hitters, and relief pitchers—even adding free agents or making trades. Each night, the computer would run a simulation game against your opponent. The next morning, players would receive a mock newspaper with a headline such as "Cecil Fielder's 2-run homer leads Black Sox 6-4 over Mustangs," accompanied by the game's full box score and updated league standings. The headlines were generated automatically by programmers having inputted dozens and dozens of possible scenarios.

The season didn't start until the middle of May, so that six weeks of actual game stats were collected. When the computer ran simulations, it would use each player's stats from one of the games—randomly chosen—previously played during the season and not already used. And it differentiated their stats against left- or right-handed pitchers.

In 1992, they had more than 200 leagues. The rock star Meat Loaf managed seven teams in 1991 by long-distance phone while on tour in Australia and for 1992 had eight teams. (Meat Loaf went on to play fantasy sports the rest of his life, including baseball, football, basketball, and NASCAR.)

Wolf and his team developed tools for all sports. In 1992, they put ESPN on Prodigy, in the sports section, called ESPN.com. They developed online applications to help themselves do better at their own fantasy sports and they put those on ESPN.com. Baseball Manager was acquired by GameLine LLC in 1998 and then by Blue Goat Systems in 2022, and can still be found at www.BaseballManager.com._

Head2Head Sports

Bill Reinking, a federal bank examiner, got an idea for a company that would offer points-style salary cap fantasy games, and wrote a business plan on a cocktail napkin. He founded Head2Head Sports in 1994. Salary cap means all MLB players (or NFL, NBA, etc.) are assigned a salary—participants must choose a roster filling certain position requirements for hitters and pitchers, and stay under the assigned cap for total salary.

It started slowly but grew into a major player in the fantasy industry, with millions of dollars in sales. Reinking drove sales for the Scottsdale, Arizona-based company by personally securing partnerships with NASCAR.com, PGATOUR.com, Knight Ridder Digital, Tribune Newspapers, FOX TV, Clear Channel Communications, and other leading media. In 2005, they partnered with Major League Lacrosse to offer what may have been the first-ever fantasy lacrosse game.

Reinking sold the company in 2007 to an East Coast-based private equity fund, stayed on for three years managing the business and then left the industry. It remained very successful for a number of years, but closed in 2024.

Wall Street Sports

Larry Cotter and Bill Carey grew up together in Mahopac, New York, a small town about 40 minutes north of New York City. They became friends at age 12 when they played together on a travel baseball team. They both went to James Madison University, graduated in 1992 as CPAs, and took jobs at accounting firms in Washington, DC.

In 1995, Cotter got the idea to start a stock simulation company where people could buy and sell the stocks of professional sports players. He asked Carey to help him, and in early 1996 they launched Wall Street Sports. They each invested $50,000, and both worked 20 hours a day, seven days a week, which included 12-to-14-hour days at their accounting jobs.

The game set "analyst expectations" for every player, such as Mark McGuire will hit 45 home runs and have 100 RBIs. His stock price would go up and down during the season as he would fall behind—or get ahead—of those numbers. Participants could buy and sell their stocks in real time. If many people were buying Mark McGuire, his price would go up, and vice versa. Their website featured a scrolling stock ticker—each athlete had a symbol, such as FAVR for Brett Favre, and the ticker would scroll their real-time stock price.

Wall Street Sports was free to play, and offered prizes such as T-shirts, mugs, signed baseballs and footballs, other sports memorabilia, and large prizes such as a trip to the NCAA men's college basketball Final Four tournament. It was a monthly competition, so in the summer everyone would have all baseball players—in the fall, they would add players from the NFL, NBA and NHL as those seasons began.

An early player was a writer for *The Wall Street Journal* and in late 1996 published an article about the game on the front page. Membership went from 5,000 to 36,000 in just two weeks. Cotter and Carey quit their day jobs.

At the time, Cotter was 25 and had been married for just a year—his father-in-law got in his face and called him "the most irresponsible husband ever, leaving a real job at a real company to chase this game." But Cotter's wife was okay with the decision, knowing that if it didn't work out, he could always go back to a CPA firm. Meanwhile, Carey's supervisor at work thought he was crazy. One concern was that some people thought the internet might just be a fad.

They added golf in 1998, and when Fred Couples was leading the Masters on Sunday, he hit a ball in the water on 13 and his stock price crashed. That's when Cotter and Carey knew they had something special. By 1999, they had 185,000 members trading a daily average of 150 million shares of 800 professional athletes.

In 1997, they created an NCAA March Madness bracket game called It's Madness. There had been similar games offered in newspapers, but they were perhaps the first to offer a $1 million prize for anyone who could pick the perfect bracket. It only cost them $14,000 to insure it, as the odds of winning were more than one in a billion.

This game was free to enter and garnered a lot of press. All the local newspapers, radio and TV mentioned it. Some out-of-town newspapers picked up the story as well. In two weeks, 130,000 people registered. They used this game to promote their other games. Although nobody predicted the bracket correctly, they gave away prizes to people based on how well they did.

The next year, after Bobby Knight had been fired from his coaching job at Indiana University, they hired him as spokesman and upped to a $10 million prize. Knight helped get national attention and they had 300,000 entries. That month, their website had 1.15 million unique visitors, more than NFL.com and FoxSports.com.

Sandbox

In 1998, Wall Street Sports merged with Phoenix-based Sandbox.net, which had done a stock market simulation game for CNN and a fantasy game for Yahoo, but hadn't been able to monetize well.

The company name was changed from Wall Street Sports to Sandbox. com. The Wall Street owners had 70% of the new company while the Sandbox.net owners had 30%. This put Cotter and Carey into the fantasy sports arena, leading to games for MLB, NFL, NBA, NHL, NASCAR, PGA—and later a partnership with the Olympic committee to run a portfolio of games for the Olympics.

At their height, there was a staff of about 100 employees in the Reston, Virginia, office, with sales offices in New York and Los Angeles to sell advertising. They also kept the Phoenix office and staff of about

35 employees from the original Sandbox.net company. John Fullmer, the Sandbox.net chairman, became the Sandbox.com chairman of the board. Because they wanted sports nuts working for them, they would interview job applicants with 100 questions, such as, "What was Rod Carew's batting average in 1973?"

Cotter and Carey say that they invented "incentive-based direct marketing." For example, participants would start with $1 million Wall Street Sports dollars to acquire their portfolio. They would be offered things such as five extra Wall Street Sports dollars if they clicked on a sponsor's banner, or 50 dollars to download and try a piece of software. This incentivized members to support advertisers— including National Geographic, IBM, Microsoft, AOL, Dell Computer, and Intel— and created a profitable business model. With their free games, Sandbox. com grew to 8 million members—the third largest membership behind ESPN and Yahoo.

When ad revenue declined, they transitioned from free games to a paid format. For about $7 per month, contestants could have two teams in all their games, plus access to news and their forums. A little under 10% signed up to pay, which gave them a much smaller base, but it was also much more profitable.

In April 2000, Sandbox.com entered a $15 million, two-year exclusive agreement with Time Warner to develop more than 30 co-branded fantasy sports and arcade games for CNNSI.com, Time Warner's sports website. In return, Sandbox received cross-promotional advertising across Time Warner media outlets, including *Sports Illustrated*, CNN, CNN Headline News and CNN/SI.

In 2000 they launched Sand Lotto, which was perhaps America's first national lottery, and offered a $100 million daily jackpot. It was free to enter, and they allowed phone entries on an automated line, as back then only 65 million people had access to the internet but 275 million had access to a phone.

CHAPTER 5

Newspaper Games

Bill Gibson and Geoff Ford became friends at age 13, played sports together, and when they both attended the University of Calgary as business majors, they carpooled every day for four years. By 1985, at age 31, they were still great friends and had season tickets to the Calgary Flames. Gibson worked in marketing for TransAlta Utilities and Ford had just started an IBM programming and consulting firm called Spectrum InfoSystems.

They both played in their office hockey pools, which were contests where typically four to 10 people would each draft 10 or less NHL players. They earned one point per goal and one point per assist and whoever had the most points at the end of the NHL season was the winner. These pools were very popular throughout Canada and dated as far back as 1975 or earlier.

Gibson thought it would be great if this game could be played by more than just 10 people at a time, perhaps even by all the other season-ticket holders. Since it wouldn't be possible to have dozens or hundreds of people playing a game where each NHL player could only be on one person's team, Gibson came up with the "box" format. He would create an entry form with many boxes that each contained four or five players of equal caliber, and the participants would choose one player from each box. Gibson knew it would have to be computerized, so he explained the idea to his buddy Ford and asked if he thought this was something he could program. Ford said he could, and they became partners on the project.

Gibson put together a pitch with the help of a graphic designer at TransAlta, and they landed a meeting with Calgary Flames management. After the meeting, management reviewed the proposal and ultimately answered, "Liked it, but not right now."

Gibson said, "We now had two options, call it a day or give one more team a try." Gibson and Ford decided to try the Edmonton Oilers, since they were close to Calgary. In early 1986, they had a meeting with Oilers marketing director Mark Hall. He loved the idea but saw no reason to limit it to just their season ticket holders. Hall recruited the *Edmonton Journal* as a partner, which wanted to offer the game to their entire readership of 300,000. Gibson and Ford only had a concept—they had no employees, no computers, no office space, no code had been written—but they told the Oilers and *Journal*, "Sure, we can do it."

They created a game with 21 boxes of four players each. The results would be published weekly in the *Journal* showing the leaders for the season, and there were also prizes for the best teams each week.

They formed a company, SportsMark, Inc. Ford's consulting firm bought a used IBM S/34 mini mainframe (about the size of a washer and dryer side by side) and Ford designed software to handle all the entries and calculate the stats and standings.

The contest, Hockey Draft Sweepstakes, was for the NHL season beginning fall of 1986. The *Journal* published several full-page ads with an entry form to be mailed in. The Oilers promoted the contest during their pre-season games, and a local Dodge dealer offered a new car for the grand prize. Another company offered ski trips for whoever had the most points during each month. Each week, a contestant would be drawn randomly to win an autographed Oilers hockey stick or tickets to an Oilers game. And one lucky random winner would get tickets, airfare, and accommodations to an out-of-town Stanley Cup final game.

"We were thrilled," said Gibson. "The grand prize was more than we could have imagined. And when the first ad came out, we were so excited we went to Billy's News in downtown Calgary to buy up all the *Edmonton Journals* they had." Ford added, "We were very proud to see our SportsMark logo next to the Oilers and *Journal* logos on that first entry form."

Entries were limited to one per person, and they received 27,500. With little time to process everything, they hired a temporary team of 20 people to open and batch entries, and a local keypunch firm to digitally key and verify the information. It took two weeks of long days and nights. Each week, the Oilers sent them the official NHL stats. Employees entered them into the IBM system, which would run overnight and, by morning, create the list of the top 500 contest leaders and the weekly winners. The *Journal* published the results and paid SportsMark $1 per entry, which resulted in a small profit.

The success of the contest led them to signing up several other Canadian newspapers for the following 1987-88 NHL season. With the *Edmonton Journal* renewing, they had seven newspapers total. Gibson and Ford were still working full-time at their day jobs. They worked for SportsMark at night and needed temporary help to handle the entries. Ford's receptionist at Spectrum recruited 10 friends from her church. During the pre-season, they brought entries home at night, opened the envelopes, batched them, and put them into a filing system so they could be retrieved easily if needed. They hired a local Calgary keypunch firm to enter them.

In 1988, they hired their first full-time employee, Rob Moser. And they took a booth at the International Newspaper Marketing Association (INMA) Conference in Colorado Springs, attended by newspaper people from across the globe. By 1989, they ran the hockey contest for 25 Canadian newspapers, as well as a few non-profits, and they did a MLB game for the *Toronto Sun*. They also signed their first US-based newspapers. *The Salt Lake Tribune* and the *Deseret News*, also in Salt Lake City, ran an NBA game jointly. Their baseball and basketball games were the same format of picking one player from several boxes of four or five players per box. In baseball they awarded points for hits, runs, RBIs, pitchers wins and strikeouts, etc. and in basketball for points scored, rebounds, assists, blocks, etc.

Once the Salt Lake game was underway, they received a cease-and-desist letter from the   National Basketball Association Players Association (NBAPA), threatening to sue them for $1 million if they didn't stop. Panicked by this, Gibson and Ford were soon on a flight to the NBAPA's office on Park Avenue, in New York, where they worked out a deal to become licensed by the players association.

Ford continued to run his computer consulting firm (which also handled the SportsMark programming) and work part-time for SportsMark. But in 1989, Gibson and Ford decided that SportsMark could support Gibson working on a full-time salary and he handed in his resignation at TransAlta Utilities. When Gibson told his boss why he was leaving, his boss was blown away. He had been playing the *Calgary Sun* Hockey Draft for two years and was amazed Gibson was involved with it.

Gibson's wife was supportive of the move, but his mom didn't like his leaving the stability of a major utility company. She asked his brother to talk him out of leaving TransAlta, but the brother never made the call.

More U.S. newspapers followed, including the *Buffalo News*, *Indianapolis Star*, *Minneapolis Star Tribune*, *Denver Post*, *New York Daily News*, *Chicago Sun-Times*, *Houston Chronicle*, and *New Orleans Times-Picayune*, and others. Some ran games for more than just one sport. The sponsors got great advertising, as the newspapers would typically run six to seven full-page pre-season ads with entry forms, and then about 25 weeks of full-page results with ads during the seasons. The newspapers saw increased circulation on results days.

SportsMark hired retired NHL legend Gordie Howe as their spokesperson. He signed pucks and hockey sticks for the newspapers to give as prizes. Each year, a handful of winners would get to attend a dinner and an NHL game with Howe.

Starting in 1989, they ran a Stock Market Challenge for several newspapers. Stocks were placed in boxes by category such as oils, textiles, etc., and, as with the other games, contestants selected one stock per box. Whoever's portfolio increased the most during the contest was the winner. The biggest contest was for the *Toronto Star*, which invited teachers to get their classrooms to play the game. The contest drew about 100,000 entries, including 30,000 students from approximately 1,000 classrooms. The $5,000 grand prize winner was a 12-year-old. The newspaper interviewed her and asked, "How did you beat all of these experts, stockbrokers and everyone else?" The girl explained she picked stocks because she liked the names, such as Hummingbird and Gandalf.

During those years, they increased revenue by offering optional services such as mailing reports and offering player trades by a 1-900 number. This allowed contestants to change a few of their chosen players for someone else in a box. SportsMark used an IBM IVR (Interactive Voice Response) system to make the changes without the need for someone to answer the phone call. They started with a 24-line system. When a contestant called, they were greeted by a recording of Gordie Howe welcoming them to the contest. Ford said, "It was exciting when the IVR lit up with 20 lines going at once...we knew we had something good."

They later added another 24-line system, and more than 100,000 contestants regularly used this phone service for several years. Live operators were also available for customer support issues. The increased profits allowed them to start revenue-sharing programs with newspapers.

In the early '90s, newspaper clientele on both sides of the border continued to increase. SportsMark was much more exciting and fulfilling for Ford than his other business, so he sold his consulting company and went full-time. Rob Moser was made VP of operations and a SportsMark partner. Ford's brother, Peter Ford, joined as a partner and VP of sales.

Hockey Draft Sweepstakes had become a staple promotion in virtually every major newspaper in Canada. SportsMark peaked at 53 newspapers in one year. The *Edmonton Journal* had surpassed 50,000 entries per year and many others were in the 30,000 to 45,000 range. This is more impressive considering all contests were limited to one entry per person. The check-box format—sometimes also called "pick em"—remained the same, although some years Wayne Gretzky and Mario Lemieux were so superior to every other NHL player, they had a box for just the two of them. And one year, they split Gretzky into two choices, "Gretzky goals" and "Gretzky assists."

In 1993, they wanted to pitch their skills to the marketing directors of major corporations, and with the help of their ad agency came up with an idea that would let this audience experience their product firsthand. They ran a golf contest based on the major tournaments. The Marketing Masters ran for five consecutive years and resulted in great corporate connections, which led to SportsMark running national box format sports contests for Coors Light, Owens Corning, John Deere, Boston Pizza, Sony Corporation and more, including a national hockey contest for Gillette Canada. The contest was promoted, and entry forms provided in participating retail stores. This contest sparked a cease-and-desist letter from the National Hockey League Players Association (NHLPA), which resulted in SportsMark becoming the first fantasy company licensed by the NHLPA. In addition to hockey, NBA, MLB, and the stock market, they had games for the Canadian Football League, the NFL, and the PGA.

SportsMark decided to enter the pay-to-play arena and bought ads in all the sports annuals such as *Lindy's*, *Athlon*, and *Street and Smith*. The game, Ultimate Draft, kicked off in 1992. Whereas the newspaper games were free to enter, and prizes paid by the newspapers and their sponsors, these "check box" games cost $25 to $30 to enter, plus fees for making player changes. SportsMark paid cash prizes to the winners.

In 1995, they aligned with *Inside Sports* magazine as a partner and the game was rebranded as *Inside Sports Ultimate Draft*. They had a game for all four major league sports and attracted over 30,000 contestants. That year, their 10-person staff processed more than one million unique entries from their various contests. Their staff and computer equipment were all located in their Calgary office, and they had contract companies doing keypunching and processing entries. Geoff Ford said, "A million entry forms sure took up a lot of office space." They grew organically, never needing investment or taking on debt.

By the late '90s, newspapers were in decline due to the advent of the internet, and there was more competition for fantasy games. In 1999, online company Internet Sports Network (ISN) made an offer to buy SportsMark and the partners felt it was a good time to sell. Gibson described it as "a great opportunity for us to capitalize on our years in the industry." Geoff Ford became the COO of ISN, with Gibson, Moser, and Peter Ford also being given prominent roles.

Within two years, in December 2000, the dot-com bubble burst and ISN folded, taking down SportsMark with them. The four partners bought back their intellectual property from ISN and partnered with a large Dallas-based company, SCA Promotions, in 2001, later changing the name to SCAinteractive. The company was still operating successfully as of 2024 and has run hundreds of promotions for major corporations over the past 20 years. The biggest was the 2006 *Pirates of the Caribbean* contest they ran for McDonald's, which drew 13 million entries as McDonald's gave away thousands of food prizes and one car per day for 28 days.

While having mostly transitioned away from fantasy sports into consumer promotions, they still run fantasy contests for Hockey Night in Canada, SportsNet, TSN and the Score. The operations side of the business is still based in Calgary and is run by Moser. Dallas handles the marketing, led by Peter Ford and Geoff's son Adam. Gibson and Geoff Ford are retired.

In 2023, Gibson said, "I know I am biased, but I believe that no other company can profess to be involved in fantasy sports for over 37 years. The crux of our success was our flawless execution of our contests. This is a testament to Geoff and all the programmers involved in the design and coding of so many different iterations of a fantasy contest."

After all these accomplishments, and given the millions who've been exposed to fantasy sports via SportsMark, it sure is a good thing that Mark Hall of the Oilers liked the idea, or else it all may have never happened.

Dugout Derby

In 1989, Bill Junkin, who owned a Los Angeles-based ad agency Wakeman & deForrest (W+D), teamed up with a company called Phoneworks to launch a baseball check box game. Called Dugout Derby, it was first offered in the *Los Angeles Times*. Some 6,250 people entered, which was 5% of the paper's circulation. The participants who weren't already subscribers converted to being subscribers at a rate four times higher than normal.

The next year, the game spread to papers such as the *Arizona Republic*, *Los Angeles Times*, *Chicago Sun-Times*, *Miami Herald*, *New York Post*, *Philadelphia Inquirer*, and *Newsday*. As with SportsMark games, the papers would run many full-page ads and trade ad space to companies for sponsoring weekly prizes. The *Newsday* contest was sponsored by sports radio station WFAN, with more than $100,000 in prizes. The grand prize was a two-week cruise to Alaska plus $7,500 cash.

Unlike SportsMark, rather than mailing in a free entry, participants called a 1-900 number and had to pay by the minute to enter their team of nine hitters (one per position plus a DH) and four pitchers. They were also allowed to trade two players per week via the 1-900 number. They earned points for singles, doubles, triples, home runs, runs, RBIs, stolen bases and lost a point for an error. Pitchers were given points for wins and strikeouts, and lost points for earned runs and a loss. During that 1990 season, they received several million dollars of 1-900 calls. Wakeman & deForrest administered the games.

During fall of 1990, they introduced an NFL game called Pigskin Playoff. This ran in 12 newspapers and drew 135,000 players. For the *Los Angeles Times* game, each weekly winner of the 17-week NFL season won a seven-day trip for two to Hawaii. There were 50 other prizes per week, such as a SONY Watchman, CD player, sweatshirts, and mugs. The season-long champion won a weeks' cruise for two.

A fantasy golf game for Spaulding helped promote their introduction of three new golf balls.

It appears that Junkin and Phoneworks created these games without knowing that SportsMark was already running newspaper games. W+D patented their game, and around 1990 sent a cease-and-desist letter to SportsMark. SportsMark replied by showing their games had already started in 1986 and never heard from W+D attorneys again.

In August 1992, W+D filed for bankruptcy. It is unclear how much money they had made—or possibly lost—from their fantasy games. It is also unclear what percentage of the 1-900 number revenue they received.

In their bankruptcy filing, a handful of newspapers were shown as being owed money by W+D, which makes it appear they may have been paying the newspapers to do the games and/or promising revenue sharing with the papers. What is clear is that their core ad agency business had lost some of their biggest clients in the prior 16 months and their income was significantly reduced. And W+D had spent a lot of money on patents for their games.

30 Years Later

In a 2011 interview, Dan Okrent described the worst moment in his career as being "when this guy came to us in the '80s. Bill Junkin was a newspaper promotion guy, and he was interested in buying rotisserie baseball, and was going to use it to build circulation games. But we were so naïve— and our lawyer never composed a non-disclosure agreement—and he spent weeks interviewing us, and then he disappeared. Suddenly, these circulation games are popping up all over newspapers that were connected to the chain he was working for. He just stole it. And there was nothing we could do about it."

After I learned that Junkin's company had gone bankrupt, I e-mailed Okrent: "Maybe it will make you feel a little better after all these years to know his company went bankrupt?"

Okrent replied, "How gratifying!"

Replica

Replica Corporation, based just outside of Boston, started running stock market contests for college and high school students in 1987. One was sponsored by AT&T and another by CNBC/USA Today.

In 1990, they entered the fantasy sports arena, offering very simple football games, called BlitzPicks, through newspapers in cities such as Reno, Spokane, Tulsa, and Allentown. Participants simply had to pick one NFL quarterback, one running back, any two receivers and one kicker. It cost $6.95 to enter by a 1-800 number.

In 1991, they introduced a national salary cap game, sponsored by AT&T, called the Sports Challenge Football. With ads in the USA Today, 6,240 people entered, vying for a $10,000 grand prize. The following year, they added a salary cap baseball game, and both baseball and football were now sponsored by USA Today and athletic apparel company Champion USA.

The baseball game required people to choose one hitter per position, but, in an unusual twist, they chose one team's entire pitching staff rather than taking individual pitchers. And they had to choose to play either with only American League or only National League players for each entry.

By 1993, the salary cap baseball and football games were garnering up to 15,000 entries each. A call center manned by 80 operators allowed people to enter teams and make changes for these contests, plus for the BlitzPicks and student stock market contests.

In October 1995, without any warning, Replica suddenly went out of business. The season abruptly ended, with no refunds, for everyone playing their football games. Many stock market game players also didn't get refunds. Replica's 15 full-time workers and even more part-timers lost their jobs without warning.

Their spokesman told the press they had poured a lot of money into an internet project expecting to get 6,000 signups for the NFL, but got less than 1,000. All total, they only had 12,000 entries for football, and they had promised a $1 million grand prize having expected at least 25,000 entries. Plus, their 1995 baseball game was down by about 50% from the prior year due to fan resentment caused by the 1994 strike.

The spokesman said their investors got tired of losing money. "I don't think the sports fans who play our games even know what the internet is," he added. "Maybe four or five years from now it'll be a viable internet business, but right now it isn't."

Sports Buff

Jeff Thomas was a software developer from Kenosha, Wisconsin, who had played the Replica games in *USA Today* and was aware of the SportsMark games, and thought he could improve on them. In 1993, he ran a small test market for his own game, Buff Ball. It went well, so, in 1994, 32-year-old Thomas took a leap of faith, borrowing $30,000 from friends and family, quitting his job, and opening an office. He signed deals with 10 newspapers, including local papers in Racine, Sheboygan, and Chicago. Thomas cold-called newspapers, often competing with SportsMark to sign them. He also attended newspaper trade shows and often closed deals at night over a couple of beers.

Like SportsMark, people would see an ad in their local newspaper, complete the entry form—choosing two quarterbacks, three running backs, three wide-receivers, a kicker, and a team defense—and mail in the entry. Thomas developed an IVR system so people could make weekly changes without the need for a call center.

You could enter the contest for free, keeping the players you chose for the entire season. But if you wanted to change any player selections during the season, you paid a small fee and called the IVR. Thomas gave the papers a portion of his revenue. Participants were required to choose players from certain positions and earned points for touchdowns, yardage gained, receptions, etc.

Thomas picked up entry forms every day at his post office box and did the data entry himself until his volume required hiring a data entry company. Through these games, Thomas built a large customer database. He made $3-$4,000 profit from the small newspapers and $20-$30,000 from large papers. The most successful included the *Charlotte Observer*, *Chicago Tribune*, *Miami Herald*, *Schenectady Gazette*, and the *Minneapolis Star-Tribune*, which had 40,000 entries one year for the football contest. They had run 12 full-page ads as well as advertising at the state fair. The *Sheboygan Press* said their ad revenues increased significantly and their single-copy sales increased 6% over the prior year during the football contest.

After starting with football, Thomas ran a MLB game the second year and added the NBA and NHL a few years later. In 1995, while still increasing the newspaper game business, Thomas upgraded his software to offer his own national salary cap game. He somewhat copied the Replica game, but by using IVR rather than a call center felt he would be more successful. He changed the name to Sports Buff, and using direct mail to his newspaper customers, he converted more than 5% to his own higher revenue game.

He gave cash prizes for the weekly, league and overall winners. To do something different and fun, he brought the top four winners (along with a significant other) on a three-day Carnival Cruise, and he invited two "experts" from *Pro Football Weekly* magazine, where he had advertised. While soaking up the sun in the Bahamas, they held a playoff competition draft on the cruise.

Next was a trip to Cancun, after which he settled into always bringing the top winners to Las Vegas for a few days, including a playoff draft. At the Vegas drafts, each participant was paired with a retired MLB, NFL, NBA, or NHL legend—such as Fergie Jenkins, Jim Plunkett, Sidney Moncrief, and Steve Shutt—to be a draft partner. They also had a golf game which didn't have a playoff competition, but he gave the top winners a trip to the Tour Championship one year and to Vegas in other years.

Sports Buff ran games for almost 500 newspapers during the '90s and 2000s, typically with about 100 newspapers running a game at any time. Its database accumulated almost one million customers over the years. A website was launched in 1996, and by 1998 many people made their moves online rather than calling. Thomas worked out of an office from day one, even when it was just him. As he grew over the years, he hired a salesperson and support staff as needed.

Soon after buying SportsMark, ISN also bought Sports Buff, controlling the entire North America newspaper fantasy games market. ISN also purchased an online company and a content/magazine company, and thus was one of the first ever fantasy sports roll-ups. The friends and family members of Thomas who had invested made six times their money back.

After the sale, Thomas worked as an employee for ISN, but, as mentioned earlier, things didn't go well and ISN was soon out of business. Thomas gave ISN $5,000 to buy their current customer base for the salary cap game and went back into business himself. But it was never nearly as successful as it had been, primarily because now there was so much more competition, with the likes of ESPN and Yahoo offering fantasy games. Newspaper games fell by the wayside due to the advent of the internet.

Thomas had an idea for a game people could play alone and immediately when, for instance, it was 2 a.m. and they couldn't sleep. He called it RapidDraft. He interviewed 11 fantasy football experts about their draft strategy and built Artificial Intelligence "bots" to represent each strategy. Adding these experts' personal player rankings with their individual strategy created a draft that was extremely realistic. The experts from places like Footballguys.com and *USA Today* were happy to do it, since they were given free publicity. Each player had an avatar that would come to the podium and announce their pick.

Using the experts' weekly rankings each week to make lineup changes, the participants would play out the season against the 11 bots. Then a playoff competition was held for only the real people who qualified for the playoffs. In 2008, about 7,000 people paid to play the game.

After Thomas sold RapidDraft to a billionaire who later reneged on the deal, he had to shut down the company in 2012. He went on to other pursuits in the fantasy industry and later started a company growing hemp in Colorado. Thomas was also on the FSTA board for 12 years, serving as president from 2006 to 2008. In 2009, he played in a national fantasy football contest where the top 12 winners won a trip to Vegas— and, ironically, the man who was probably the first to ever bring fantasy winners to Vegas won a trip to Vegas for himself.

According to Thomas, "The regional newspaper games played a huge part in growing the industry in the 1990s. They introduced the concept to a lot of players and made it simple to play with the check box game. You didn't have to devote hours and hours to it."

CHAPTER 6

CDM Sports and the Landmark Legal Case

Very few fantasy players have heard of Brian and Carol Matthews, but they were instrumental in the success of the fantasy industry. Brian and Carol met while both working for aerospace manufacturer McDonnell Douglas in St. Louis. Brian was an engineer and Carol a software developer. They were married in 1989.

Brian played in a fantasy baseball league with co-workers as well as others in the aerospace industry who worked for Northrop Grumman in California. Their draft was held at a secure building at McDonnell Douglas, hooked up by satellite with the Northrup building in California. The league bid real money on players with no limit. Participants typically spent $3,000-$5,000 for their team. One year, somebody spent $2,000 for Ricky Henderson. The prize money was split 50% for first place, 25% for second, 15% and 10% for third and fourth. The teams finishing second, third or fourth sometimes won more money than the first-place team because they had spent less.

A friend of Brian's knew a man, Charlie Wiegert, who loved fantasy baseball. Brian invited him to join their league. Charlie had worked for the *St. Louis Suburban Journal* newspapers for almost 20 years, doing a little bit of sports writing but primarily selling advertising. He started playing fantasy baseball in 1984 when a group of sportswriters at the newspaper formed a league after reading the Bantam Rotisserie Baseball book. Wiegert won this league the first three years and was hooked on the game. By 1990 he was in eight leagues, including the aerospace league. He had also won a national competition against 700 participants. His prize was a trip to the 1989 All-Star game, where he saw Bo Jackson crush a 448-foot home run (this can be seen on YouTube). He also won a national contest with BoxScore Baseball against approximately 500 entrants.

Brian, who always had a bit of entrepreneurial spirit, thought of starting a national fantasy baseball game. He asked Wiegert if he'd be interested in working with him. One weekend, at the Matthews' kitchen table, the idea for CDM Fantasy Sports was born. The Matthews asked Wiegert to design his ideal game by combining what he liked about other games with his personal wish list.

More kitchen table meetings followed. In 1991, 41-year-old Wiegert, 33-year-old Brian, and 27-year-old Carol launched CBC Distribution & Marketing, d/b/a CDM Fantasy Sports. (CBC was for "Carol, Brian, Charlie" and CDM was for "Carol Diane Matthews.") They all thought this would just be a part-time side gig.

Their office was in the basement and a spare bedroom in the Matthews house. They invested $5,000 for two Macintosh computers, a printer, a copy machine, and a toll-free phone line.

Wiegert created a salary-cap game where he assigned all players a salary. Participants had to fill a roster with players at specific positions and stay under the cap. There were prizes for leagues of 25 teams as well as prizes for an overall competition against all entries, with a grand prize of $5,000. Brian and Carol developed software to run the league. The game was called Carol's Fantasy Baseball Challenge, and their only marketing consisted of tiny ads in the back of the *Sporting News'* annual baseball magazine, the *USA Today Baseball Weekly*, and *Fantasy Baseball* magazine.

The first year they got 275 entries. They charged $99 to enter, plus weekly transaction fees for lineup changes. By the end of the year, the average team had spent a total of $250. They named it after Carol because players could pay an extra $10 for a chance to go up against Carol and win $25. As Wiegert explained, "We wanted to appeal to a guy's male ego of 'I can beat a woman!'" What they didn't know was that it was Wiegert who ran that team.

They downloaded the baseball stats from a Vegas gambling website. Computers were so slow that it took eight to 10 hours to calculate the weekly stats for just 275 teams, something that today would take less than one second. On Mondays, Brian and Carol would start running the program before leaving for work and take turns coming home at their lunch break to make sure it was working properly. After work, they printed the results and stuffed envelopes to mail to their customers.

For the second year, they decided to add a basketball game. They added John Brison, also from McDonnel Douglas, as a 20% partner and gave him the task of creating a basketball software program. The owners then realized that having a major sports brand put their name on the game could take it to a new level. *The Sporting News* was an obvious choice, since it was in St. Louis. During the summer of 1992, Wiegert tried several times unsuccessfully to get a meeting with Bill Topaz, the general manager of *The Sporting News*.

One day that fall, Wiegert stopped by the *Sporting News* offices to check on an ad they placed in the basketball preview magazine. The ad was not in the magazine—and Wiegert was irate. This ad was their only marketing for their new NBA game. (They did subsequently offer the game to their existing baseball clients and 75 people entered.) At the *Sporting News* office, the irate Wiegert ran into Gary Levy, a guy he knew from his softball league who worked there. Wiegert told Levy he wanted to meet with Bill Topaz. Levy was able to arrange a meeting, and 10 days later, at 6 a.m. on a Tuesday, the Matthews and Wiegert met with Topaz.

Brian Matthews said they "put together a kick-ass presentation" because both he and Carol had experience pitching for government contracts. But Topaz gave them a cold shoulder. He was only taking this meeting because he felt he had to after the screw-up with their NBA ad. Topaz was listening half-heartedly until the last page, which showed projected revenue for *The Sporting News* would be $125,000 for the first year and $1 million for the first three years (based only on the baseball game). That got his attention and he said, "I've been a terrible host. Does anyone need a cup of coffee? I want to go through this again."

By noon, Topaz called Wiegert and said, "Okay, let's do this—but if we're gonna do it, I want to do it for all four sports we have annual magazines for: baseball, football, basketball, and hockey."

Although they had no current plans for a football or hockey game, the co-owners immediately agreed. Carol's Fantasy Baseball Challenge was renamed the Sporting News Fantasy Baseball Challenge.

Weekly space in *The Sporting News* was extremely expensive, so instead Topaz offered to give them free space in their yearly special editions for each of the four sports. When the fantasy baseball edition came out, there was a burst on the cover of the magazine: "Win $10,000 playing our fantasy baseball game...details inside." Inside was a six-page spread that included an entry form and an explanation of the rules, prizes, and the players' salaries.

The entries came with $99 checks—first at a trickle, then a flow. "By the middle of February, we saw we were going to have to do something other than meet in the basement," Wiegert said. In March, they moved into a 3,000-square-foot rented office space and hired a receptionist. They invested $150,000 to buy more Macintoshes, printers, copiers, and a phone system.

They took turns periodically stopping at their post office box to pick up entries. When Wiegert made a stop around the first week of March, the box was empty, except for a note with a yellow card directing him to the counter. He was a little nervous as he approached the counter—back then, they weren't sure whether fantasy sports would be considered gambling in some states, and he was afraid he was going to be arrested or something. But when he gave the man the card, the man handed him a bucket with about 400 entries. Wiegert said, "I had the biggest smile on my face." He knew then they were on to something big.

To keep up with all the entries that had to be keyed into the computer system, they enlisted help from family members and then from co-workers at McDonnell Douglas. That first year, there were 4,200 baseball entries. After that bucket came in, Carol soon quit her job to work full-time managing CDM. The other three owners would come in after their day jobs and work all night. But by late April, Brian

Matthews, Wiegert and Brison had all quit their day jobs. When Wiegert quit his job to work full-time in fantasy, his dad thought he had gone completely crazy.

Topaz had also agreed to run a small strip in the weekly magazine showing the current Baseball Challenge leaderboard, and they added free agents—a weekly list of players who could be added to teams without the normal transaction cost—which meant participants needed to buy the weekly magazine to see who the free agents were. CDM's exposure was increased by being in the weekly magazine and *Sporting News* sales increased due to CDM players wanting to see the free agents. Topaz allowed CDM to offer subscriptions to their customers at a discounted rate and CDM became the largest source of new subscriptions to *The Sporting News*.

The first year of football brought about 2,000 entries. Basketball and hockey each had about 1,000. And they added baseball games for mid-season and the playoffs. Their first year with *The Sporting News* earned CDM $4.8 million in gross revenue and a profit of $1 million. They gave the hockey contest winner a trophy that looked like the Stanley Cup, but they named it the "Topaz Cup."

By 1997, football grew to 15,000 entries and baseball peaked at almost 17,000. They had players from all 50 states and at least 25 foreign countries. Wiegert remembers getting a call from a man in Italy—it took 90 minutes to sign him up because he spoke very little English. The man had seen the ad in *The Sporting News* when visiting Miami.

In these pre-internet days, participants would call their toll-free number to make lineup changes. The weekly baseball deadline was Sunday at 11 p.m. CST. CDM had 100 employees answering phones and more than $150,000 in monthly long-distance charges, making them Sprint's largest customer in St. Louis. Since they couldn't handle the Sunday volume, they offered participants a 50-cent-per-transaction discount if they called in by Saturday.

They hired friends and relatives, including Wiegerts' two daughters, who recruited many of their high school friends. The employees each had a cubicle with a computer and a headset, and the phones would stay busy all weekend. Sometimes callers had to wait 30 minutes to get through. Staff members were paid an hourly wage plus a 10% commission on all transaction fees and typically made $400-$500 per day on the weekends. During weekdays, there were only about a dozen of them in the office to answer phones, print and mail reports, etc. Weekly reports were printed on Mondays, and two Phillipsburg mailing machines were used to stuff envelopes. Wiegert would pack his car with envelopes and get to the post office by 11:30 at night.

In 1995, CDM began offering their games online. Rather than paying an Internet Service Provider (ISP) to host their games, the entrepreneurial Matthews chose to start their own. All four partners co-founded the ISP and had financial interests in it, but only Brian actively worked for the company. Three years later, the ISP, which also hosted sites for other companies, eclipsed $11 million in revenue, equaling CDM. Brian Matthews then raised $53 million from investors and bought several ISPs in five states. In June 2000, they sold the company, then known as Primary Network, for $140 million.

CDM had a five-year contract with The Sporting News. By the end, Bill Topaz was no longer with them. Increased competition in the industry meant CDM had to up their prize money, which hurt profits. They tried explaining this to the new management, asking to lower the percentage they paid. Their new management didn't understand—in fact, they thought they should be getting a bigger share—so negotiations to renew didn't go well.

The Sporting News had made about $10 million over the five years, but there was no renewal. Instead, they used a new company to provide their fantasy games. That company screwed up, and three years later The Sporting News was out of the fantasy business.

Meanwhile, CDM, in need of a new partner, approached USA Today, who agreed to a deal. This went well, with CDM revenue peaking in 1999 at $18 million. Around 2003, they bought TQ Stats and Roto Times. In 2004, Gannett (owner of USA Today) offered to buy CDM. The four co-owners were happy to sell, as it would be an opportunity to further grow the business, and would allow them to cash out. And, as Wiegert explained, "Back then a lot of people thought fantasy sports was gambling, so we always had in the back of our minds a fear that it could be outlawed."

But just when they were on the verge of selling to Gannett, there was a cruel twist of fate.

CBC vs. MLBAM

By 2005, fantasy sports were estimated to be a $1.5 billion-a-year industry, with 15 million participants and at least 200 fantasy providers.

In January 2005, Major League Baseball Advanced Media (MLBAM), operator of MLB.com, made a deal to pay the Major League Baseball Players Association (MLBPA) $50 million over five years—in return, MLBPA transferred selected rights to player names and images to MLBAM, which would use them in cutting deals with companies seeking to put out fantasy games.

Like many other fantasy baseball companies, CDM had a licensing agreement with the MLBPA. (They also had agreements with the NFL, NBA, and NHL players associations.) From 1995 through the 2004 season, they paid royalties to the MLBPA, just as Harold Richman had been paying a fee for every Strat-O-Matic game sold. CDM had paid them more than seven figures for those 10 years. At the time, Yahoo, the largest fantasy sports site, was paying a licensing fee of about $3 million per year. But after acquiring the rights, MLBAM decided to dramatically restrict licenses to potentially just the three biggest providers: ESPN, CBS SportsLine, and Yahoo. They were also offering their own games on MLB.com.

One of the requirements to complete the sale of CDM to Gannett was that CDM needed to get their licensing agreement signed over from the MLBPA. Attempts to do this were surprisingly met with delays by the MLBPA, until finally the MLBPA told CDM they had sold the rights to MLBAM. Wiegert and their company attorney, Mike Torrence, flew to New York to meet with MLBAM.

Nothing was resolved at this meeting. A week later, during a conference call, MLBAM told them, "We aren't giving you a license, and our intent is to put you out of business...you can turn all of your business over to us and we'll give you a 10% royalty for the first year on what they spend—and then you're done." (This 10% commission was also offered to other companies who had their license requests denied.)

For CDM, it was essentially a life-or-death situation. They either had to fight this or go out of business. In February 2005, CBC, the parent company of CDM, sued MLBAM, hiring attorney Rudy Telscher. The suit was filed in Missouri's Eastern District as CBC *Distribution and Marketing Inc. v. Major League Baseball Advanced Media*. The lawsuit claimed they could do business without a license, arguing that players' names and statistics are readily available in newspapers and online, and therefore are not the intellectual property of MLB.

MLBAM countersued CBC, alleging its fantasy products were in violation of the players' rights of publicity, which is the ability to profit from the commercial use of a person's name. The MLBPA joined the case on MLBAM's side.

Not only did this cause the deal to sell to Gannett to fall apart, but Gannett also pulled out of the current partnership, not wanting to risk being associated with CDM while it operated without a license during the legal battle. "USA Today" was dropped from the name and the game became the CDM Diamond Challenge. CDM continued running ads in USA *Today*. Losing the sponsorship didn't hurt sales much, since their players liked the game and didn't care if there was a sponsor.

It took until November for both sides to meet for court-ordered mediation. MLBAM and MLBPA flew 13 lawyers to St. Louis. CDM had just one attorney, Rudy Telscher, and the four co-owners attended. Telscher described what he told the opposing attorneys, "If we win, this has implications not only for fantasy sports, but also for your baseball licensing revenue, and your EA Sports licensing revenue. Why would you take a chance? We're probably the only company who can afford to fight you, so why don't you let us into the party—we'll pay you money—even though we don't think we should—we're willing to do it just so we can be under the tent."

The main lawyer for MLBAM stood up and said, "Rudy, we're here just to deliver one message: We are going to sue your client for everything they've got unless you stop right now."

This quickly ended the mediation attempt. Telscher later said, "That was the most expensive 'flip me the bird' in my entire legal career. It had to cost them at least 25 grand to fly in 13 lawyers and put them up at the Ritz Carlton."

The conflict was going to be resolved by summary judgement, meaning both sides would submit their arguments and the judge would make a ruling without a trial. CDM felt they provided an accounting and news service by compiling and delivering the data, and that they should receive the same immunity as newspapers that print box scores. MLB countered that CDM was using player names for a purely commercial venture and that, like video games and baseball cards, fantasy providers must pay a licensing fee.

MLBAM spokesman Jim Gallagher said, "What people have to understand is, this is a baseball game with a single purpose. How do they make money? They do it on people building a team using named baseball players. Not fictitious."

Telscher countered, "If this applies to baseball players like MLBAM says, then in a Trivial Pursuit game, I can't use Sylvester Stallone, Arnold Schwarzenegger, presidents? They have a right of publicity? If you're using player identities, singling them out, promoting products individually, of course players should get something for that. If you're using raw, mass data, that is owned by the public. It's historical facts."

There was another question: Even if this did violate player rights of publicity, does the First Amendment trump any such rights of publicity?

"We wanted a license because we didn't want to get into litigation," Brian Matthews said at the time. "It's better to be partners in this than to fight. But if they don't want to settle, we will fight it to the end. Do they want to make this the landmark case? If they do, they picked a tiger to fight with." The CDM partners said they were willing to spend an anticipated $500,000 for legal fees.

The case was going to have massive ramifications for the entire industry. Whatever was ruled would set the precedent not just for fantasy baseball, but for all other sports. A ruling against CBC would put them—and many other companies—out of business, and would hinder growth for the industry. A ruling for CBC would mean nobody would have to pay licensing fees to run fantasy games, and anyone could enter the business without this concern. Fantasy companies large and small, as well as leagues and players associations, were all watching the case. Even companies not directly involved with licensing were affected, such as magazines and stat services that needed a healthy growing fantasy player base.

"They really don't have a legal precedent to rely on," Wiegert said. "That's why they're all nervous about the MLBAM case. It will become the defining moment in the fantasy sports industry. A judge will decide, once and for all, 'Do you have to pay these guys licensing fees to operate or do you not?'"

Another very important factor in this case isn't often mentioned. The licensing agreement CDM had had for several years with MLBPA included a provision that prohibited the company from using players' names and records after it expired, as well as a clause stating that CDM acknowledged MLBPA's right to publicity and could not challenge their rights. Telscher argued that the clause wasn't enforceable. But if the court upheld the clause, CDM wouldn't be able to contest the case on First Amendment rights or in any other fashion.

In August 2006, US District Court Judge Mary Ann Medler granted summary judgment to CDM. She ruled that CDM did not violate player rights of publicity under Missouri law and that the First Amendment would trump any state law to the contrary. She further ruled that "the strong federal policy favoring the full and free use of ideas in the public domain rendered unenforceable the licensing agreement's no-use and no-challenge provisions."

But MLBAM and the Players Association appealed the decision. They received support from the NFL, NBA, USGA, NHL and NASCAR, in the form of amicus briefs. The FSTA funded attorney Glenn Colton's firm to file amicus briefs for the initial ruling and the appeal. This showed the court that CBC wasn't alone—there were many companies affected by this.

Wiegert said, "MLBAM couldn't understand how they possibly could have lost, so they hired a highfaluting law firm from Washington that wins appeals all the time." They came to St. Louis for the oral arguments at the 8th Circuit Court of Appeals and according to Wiegert the three justices "just tore those guys up."

Telscher's view of this was that the judges appeared to all be on CDM's side regarding First Amendment rights. He said, "The panel was hostile to MLB's view that something they didn't invent, didn't build, didn't complain about for 25 years, is something they should now get to own—and this was more protected free speech than something like selling tennis shoes with MLB's logo on them, which is a more classic type of rights to publicity."

On October 16, 2007, the 8th Circuit upheld the ruling in a 2-1 decision. They concluded that CBC's use of the names and statistics was for a commercial purpose and thus infringed on the players' rights of publicity. However, they agreed with the lower court that "CBC's first amendment rights supersede the players' rights of publicity." In balancing this First Amendment interest against the right of publicity, the court started with the caution that "it would be strange law that a person would not have a First Amendment right to use information that is available to everyone."

The three judges agreed unanimously on the above points, but as for the prior contract's provisions, they ruled 2-1 for CBC. The contract stated that MLBPA possessed the exclusive right to use baseball statistics. Since the First Amendment trumped such an exclusive right, the court found that MLBPA "breached a material obligation that it undertook in the contract," which rendered the contract unenforceable. One judge dissented, arguing that section of the contract used the word "agreed," which, in his view, meant that this was a bargain between the parties. Therefore, the contract would be enforceable, and he would have denied summary judgment.

MLBAM and the MLBPA then appealed to the US Supreme Court. Wiegert said, "We were still nervous about the outcome. It was like David vs Goliath—and we knew Supreme Court justices sometimes attended Nationals games. And MLB had deep pockets and big political connections."

In June 2008, the Supreme Court declined to hear the case, issuing no comment. This gave a final decision that fantasy baseball leagues and providers could use the names and statistics of major league players without having to pay for a licensing agreement.

"This definitely feels great," Telscher told the *Sports Business Journal*. "Baseball had a fairly arrogant tone through this thing and was an aggressive opponent. You've got a bunch of smaller guys who built this industry into what it's become, and for baseball to come in like they did, 25 years after the fact, and try to push everybody out, that just wasn't right."

Jeff Thomas, then the president of the FSTA said the decision "marks potentially the single biggest day in the history of the fantasy sports industry. The FSTA, its members, and all others in the fantasy sports business owe a debt of gratitude to the management team at CDM, and its lead counsel Rudy Telscher."

15 Years Later

Paul Charchian, an FSTA board member at the time (and later president) said, "Most of us across the industry thought we would lose the case, because it was just us tiny companies against MLB and the NFL and players associations. We all thought we were going to get our asses kicked. That's one of the big reasons my partner and I sold Fanball in 2005."

In January 2023, I interviewed Telscher. I asked how confident, or not, he was when the case started. He told me, "When I first got the case, it looked bad. This was a case about using player names, without permission, to make money—which makes it a right-to-publicity violation. But it occurred to me that newspapers sports pages use player names, without permission, to make money. And there are games like Trivial Pursuit. So, it occurred to us there would be a First Amendment protection that would be involved here. I hired a guy from Washington University named Neil Richards, who clerked for the US Supreme Court and was a First Amendment expert. The more he read the better we felt we had a good case, but it was far from certain."

Telscher also said, "If you want to win, you've got to be right on the law, but you've also got to tell a story that causes whoever's deciding the case to believe that it would be unfair to rule against you."

Although there was no actual trial, "witnesses" signed declarations, to submit to the court, that told the story Telscher wanted to tell: MLB played no part in creating or developing fantasy baseball, and fantasy baseball had made MLB more money because fantasy players watched more games than non-players, they bought more merchandise, television packages, etc. *The fantasy industry had helped MLB and its players*, not damaging them in the least.

One declaration was from Dan Okrent, who explained how he created a game, it grew by a grassroots following, and nobody ever complained or said players rights were being violated. Several other fantasy players from around the country filed declarations explaining things such as "We know who the second baseman is for the Angels when nobody else would...we buy TV packages...we attend spring training games...not only is fantasy not hurting baseball...it's helping baseball."

But was this "story" even relevant if the court had to decide whether players rights to publicity were violated, and if so, did the First Amendment trump those rights? When I asked Telscher, he explained there's a balancing act between the right of publicity and First Amendment rights, so telling the story can influence the decision.

Looking back 15 years later, Telscher said, "I've handled many big cases, but they are usually one big company suing another big company, and very few people care about the outcome. This was the only case in my career that had such a big public attachment. I had law professors... fantasy players...emailing me in the middle of the night, saying, 'You gotta win,' 'This is not right,' 'Everybody's counting on you.' All these 200 companies that MLBAM was trying to put out of business were relying on our team to win."

According to Wiegert, one important fact that rarely gets mentioned is that, before the appeal, they had a meeting and tried to negotiate a settlement. CDM offered a deal where MLBAM would allow CDM to operate their games, MLBAM would pay their legal expenses, and CDM would have the judge vacate the order. This would have ensured MLBAM could continue collecting millions of dollars of fees from the big companies such as ESPN.

Wiegert said that Judy Heeter, the Director of Business Affairs and Licensing of the MLBPA, told them, "You guys are crazy, we are going to get the ruling overturned, and put you out of business."

Wiegert said Clay Walker, who oversaw licensing issues for the National Football League Players Association (NFLPA), was upset they didn't accept this offer, because he knew it would affect them as well. Wiegert explained, "Judy Heeter is the one who needs to be lambasted in history, because she had the opportunity to enable the players association to continue to collect millions of dollars in royalties but, in her arrogance, chose not to do that."

NBA vs. Motorola and STATS, Inc.

In the mid-1990s, STATS, Inc. was doing a pager product for Motorola that would report the scores and limited statistics of NBA games as the games were in progress. They were in discussions with the NBA to pay them a licensing fee to put the NBA name on the product. But the NBA sued Motorola and STATS instead, claiming they infringed the NBA's copyright on the broadcast of games and misappropriated the data presented on their pager.

Initially the NBA won the case, but it was overturned on appeal. Telscher did reference this case for CBC vs MLBAM, but the Motorola case turned on copyright issues, making it different than the CBC case.

CBS Interactive Sues NFLPI

CBS Interactive ran the website CBSSports.com, which had fantasy games. They had a license with NFL Players, Inc. (NFLPI), a subsidiary of the NFLPA, which handled all licensing for active NFL players. Their license expired in February 2008 and, based on the MLBAM case, CBS refused to renew. CBS had paid NFLPI $1.5 million the prior year, up from $1 million the year before that.

Even after the Supreme Court declined to hear the MLBAM case in June 2008, the NFL still insisted that CBS must pay licensing fees, claiming there were differences between them and the MLBAM case.

One day, Telscher received a call from Lou Briskman, the general counsel for CBS, and one of the top three executives in the entire company. He was considering acting against the NFLPI. They spoke for 30 minutes, during which Telscher gave him free advice. The next day, Briskman called and asked Telscher to come for a meeting in New York. Telscher agreed to the meeting, but was thinking, "I'm just little Rudy Telscher, at this point in my career I'm in my 40s—there's not a snowball's chance in hell that the general counsel of CBS is going to hire little Rudy Telscher, from St. Louis, Missouri, to represent CBS."

They met at Briskman's sprawling Manhattan office and Telscher told him all about the CBC case, strategies, and what Briskman should be thinking about. Briskman said, "I was following your case, and I thought you were going to lose. I didn't think there was any way you could beat Major League Baseball's lawyers. I was surprised you won, but you won, and that's great, and I want to hire you."

September 3, 2008, CBS sued the NFLPI in federal court in Minneapolis to seek judgment that names, stats, likenesses were free to use...

they sought declaratory judgement that the CBC case ruling extended to football. A week later, NFLPI countersued CBS in federal court in Miami, claiming CBS used names and stats without a license. NFLPI contended that there were several issues that distinguished this case from CBC's case.

According to Telscher, the only real difference with this case was that unlike CDM, CBS also had pictures of players on their website. Again, there was no trial, just a summary judgement. Telscher didn't need to get signed declarations from any "witnesses," since they already had the MLBAM precedent.

In April 2009, the court granted summary judgment in favor of CBS, finding the CBC case controlling on the issue. The court concluded that CBS used essentially the same information found allowable in the CBC case, and that they did not use players' names or likenesses in a manner that would lead the public to mistakenly believe that the players endorsed CBS's fantasy football service.

They wrote: "The court doubts that the 8th Circuit intended in *CBC Distribution* to articulate some special application of First Amendment jurisprudence to cases involving baseball only. Accordingly, the court declines to indulge in a philosophical debate about whether the public is more fascinated with baseball or football, or the statistics generated by each."

Yes, in a desperate argument, the NFLPI had claimed that people cared more about football than baseball, leading to the court's sarcastic comment.

Yahoo Sues NFLPI

Yahoo had a licensing agreement with the NFLPI that expired on March 1, 2009. After the CBS decision, Yahoo informed the NFLPI that they wouldn't be renewing, and wanted the NFLPI to acknowledge that they didn't need to. But the NFLPI refused, said they planned to appeal the CBS case, and threatened to sue Yahoo if they didn't renew.

However, on June 1, 2009, Yahoo sued the NFLPI first, claiming they should be able to use for free the names of players, statistics, pictures, photographs, voices, and biographical information. The case was settled in just five weeks. Terms of the settlement were not released. (NFLPI never did appeal the CBS decision.)

CDM After Lawsuit

CDM won their legal battle but was in debt after spending between $1.5-$2 million in legal fees. (Telscher guesses MLBAM and MLBPA combined racked up around $6 million in legal fees.)

During the lawsuit, Gannett had lost interest in acquiring CDM, but Toronto-based Fun Technologies emerged as an interested party. Within weeks of CBC winning the appeal—but before the Supreme Court declined to hear the case—FUN bought CDM in a deal worth $4.5 million up front, with earn-out potential that later resulted in another $3.5 million.

FUN Technologies—49% owned by Liberty Media—was a very successful online game company. Shortly before acquiring CDM, they had acquired Fanball.com, a company who had offered fantasy games since 1992. These acquisitions were FUN's first entry into the fantasy sports market. The CDM games were incorporated into the Fanball line. Fanball was relocated from Minneapolis to St. Louis. The Matthews, Wiegert and Brison all stayed on with Fanball.

In December 2007, Liberty Media bought Fanball, brought in new management, and let Wiegert go. Although CDM was operating successfully, Liberty had lumped them into a "division" that included some companies who weren't doing well. Liberty decided to close the division. Wiegert, Brison and a few others (but not the Matthews) bought the rights to the CDM games under a new company called RG Ventures. They opened a new office in St. Louis and, in March 2011, began operating the games under the trade name CDM Sports. Wiegert has said that this saved the Diamond Challenge, since he doesn't think anyone else at the time would have bought the rights from Liberty. A lot of loyal players would have been unhappy to lose the game.

In March 2016, SportsHub Technologies acquired RG Ventures. Wiegert explained that Daily Fantasy Sports and other competition had hurt their business, as well as draft style games overtaking salary cap. They could see the handwriting on the wall and took the offer to sell it when Sportshub wanted to buy it.

Wiegert was also a founding member of the FSTA and served as a board member and treasurer for over 15 years. He won the 2000 FSTA Lifetime Achievement Award and was inducted in the FSTA Hall Of Fame in 2001. Outside of work, he likes to garden and is very active with the Masonic Temple as a member and leader.

Brian Matthews no longer plays fantasy baseball. In 2012, he co-founded and is managing partner of Cultivation Capital, a venture capital firm that invests in technology and life science startups. Carol Matthews only played fantasy baseball when CDM started an office league—after Liberty, she worked in management for a technology company and, for a few years, was a partner in a company dedicated to helping women entrepreneurs succeed. She's now retired, plans the Matthews vacations, manages their wine collection, and spends time with family. Brison was still working in IT, for SportsHub, as of 2024.

The four partners co-founded 10 companies and sold four of them for a combined $175 million.

31 Years Later

I contacted Bill Topaz to request an interview and mentioned that I had already spoken to the Matthews and Wiegert. His response began with "I love those guys!"

Topaz told me that he did get inundated with sales pitches and only took the meeting with CDM as a favor to Gary Levy. He said the Matthews and Wiegert were very impressive. Topaz was unfamiliar with fantasy sports, so they needed to educate him. They convinced him it was the start of something big—they just needed the marketing help. Topaz could see there was a lot of money to be made, and it didn't really cost him anything to run their ads.

After receiving the first royalty check from CDM, for $102,000, Topaz had it blown up huge, like a Publishers Clearing House check. He brought it to the corporate board meeting in New York with the *Times-Mirror* and when it was his turn to issue a report, he held up the check. That was his entire report to the board.

Topaz told me, "After a few more quarters of success, I suggested to the president of The Sporting News Publishing Company, Nick Niles, that we should buy CDM. I knew it was going to be huge. But he didn't get it. He seemed to only understand advertising sales. My not being able to convince him to buy at least a major interest in CDM was a big factor why I left at the end of '93."

Clay Walker

It's a little-known fact that when CBC sued MLBAM, they stopped paying licensing fees to the other sports. Since their argument with MLBAM was that they didn't have to pay, it made sense not to pay anyone else. The NHLPA and NBAPA waited to see how the case played out. But the NFLPA sued CBC. At the first hearing in Manhattan, the judge asked, "Do you really want to go through with this?" She delayed the hearing until the afternoon, so they had a chance to talk. The NFLPA and CBC came to an immediate settlement that same day. Clay Walker then contacted Judy Heeter and told her, "We have settled. We strongly recommend that MLBPA do the same."

But Heeter and Bob Bowman, the head of MLBAM, said they would not settle. Walker said that as time went on, he repeatedly urged MLBAM to settle—many, many times—but "MLBAM was unreasonable," he said. "I can only speculate, but to me, there was no good business reason for them to go down this path unless they thought they could really monopolize the entire market and it would be just them. There would be no licensees and no competition. If someone wanted to play fantasy baseball, it would have to be on MLB.com."

Walker always preached to fantasy companies that being licensed and allowed to use the NFL name and logos was valuable and added legitimacy to their company. Many complied—some after getting a cease-and-desist letter, and a handful of others after ignoring a cease-and-desist letter and subsequently being sued by the NFLPA.

For years, the pro sports leagues were resistant to fantasy because they thought it was gambling.

But it was obvious to everyone who played fantasy that this was a great thing for the pro leagues.

Walker was probably ahead of everyone else in a position of authority with professional players or teams in realizing that fantasy was good for pro sports.

Bob Harris, from Football Diehards, explained, "About 1995, used to be if you used the word 'NFL' on your website you would get a letter from a lawyer. That building on Park Avenue is very big and it is filled with money and lawyers. Then a survey came out around 1996 that stated the obvious: Who's watching football games until the very last second even if the score is lopsided? Fantasy players. Who knows who the kicker is on every team? Fantasy players. Who spends money on football? Fantasy players. So, after that they started to accept fantasy as something other than the illegitimate bastardized child of gambling... and something that they could make money from."

Bruce Taylor, from *Fantasy Football Index* magazine, said, "It was funny to us that the NFL, for so many years, hated fantasy football and considered us the enemy. They were just so dumb, they had to be hit over the head with 2x4s...and then 4x8s...and then railroad ties...and then finally they figured out more people watched football because of this, and they were making more money. How dumb were they! It took them years to figure this out!"

CHAPTER 7

First Fantasy Sports Publications

In 1985, Kelly Grogan's co-workers invited him, and his older brother Dan, to join their fantasy football league. There was no internet, no fantasy magazines—all they could get to help was a *Street and Smith's Pro Football* magazine. They drafted Seattle wide receiver Paul Johns in the fourth round. Immediately one of the others at the draft said, "I guess you guys don't know, but Paul Johns retired."

After that blunder, they decided they needed to pay close attention during the year and track all developments so they wouldn't make a similar mistake next year. They kept notes during the year and during the following off-season. In June 1986, a guy in their league heard they were doing this and offered to pay them $10 to share their handwritten notes.

Kelly, 29, and Dan, 33, realized there must be others playing fantasy football that could benefit from this information, so they paid a woman to type up the information on a typewriter—they put it all on 11-by-17 legal paper, with a page for each team, a list of players stats by position, and basic information about fantasy football and the rules. They made 10 copies and stapled them together with a cover page calling it "Player Eval."

In August 1986, Dan went to Johnny's Newsstand, in Denver, and explained to Johnny what fantasy football was and that it was getting popular. Johnny agreed to take the 10 copies and said, "I'll call in a couple of weeks and let you know how it did." By the time Dan arrived home, Johnny had called to tell him, "It already sold out—bring more copies."

The Grogans subsequently enlisted the owner of Newsland to take copies at his five locations. They made copies as needed and sold a total of 80 copies through these six locations in the local Denver area. Their net profit for this work was $5. No, not $5 per magazine—a grand total of $5.

But they thought they were on to something good. Although they had no experience in publishing or distribution, they decided to do it again. The next year, they bought an Apple computer and worked on this at night after their day jobs. They went to press in May and printed 2,000 copies. It was 8.5 by 11, still all black and white, and looked only slightly more like a magazine.

Dan said, "We didn't know where we were going with this and weren't thinking in terms of a magazine, we just wanted to get information out to people."

They compiled stats, they read out-of-town newspapers, they even called teams to get information. Back in those days, they could sometimes even get a player on the phone to answer questions. And they compiled unique stats that would be helpful for fantasy players, such as a running back's frequency of 0-to-50-yard games, 51-to-99-yard games, and 100+ yard games.

The brothers both traveled for their jobs, and every time they were in a new city, they would look up newsstands in the Yellow Pages and ask if they would take 10 copies. They also started calling newsstands in other cities. They convinced Hudson Books to put them in all their stores. When calling to get magazines on newsstands and calling banks to get merchant credit card accounts, they had to explain that "fantasy football" was not X-rated and had nothing to do with porn.

The third year, they increased to 5,000 copies. A magazine distributor in Chicago saw it on a newsstand and called them. He said, "I think I can get you up to 100,000 copies, but you've got to make it look like a real magazine. You need to get a picture on the cover. You need to make it color."

For 1989, with the help of distributer H + S Media, they finally made it look like a real magazine, changed the name to *Grogan's Fantasy*

Football Analyst, and distributed 80,000 copies. This was also when they quit their day jobs and went full-time with the magazine. They took out a bank loan for $100,000, needing to put both their houses up as collateral, and opened an office with a small staff. They both had wives who worked and infant children.

Kelly said, "The second year, some people wanted to advertise, but we were so naïve, we turned them down because we thought having ads would take away from the content." They never took ads until the fifth year. At that point, they realized a well-known advertiser would lend credibility and help attract other advertisers, so they offered Charlie Wiegert a free ad for *The Sporting News*. At the start of 1989, they were offering a pre-season, four-week newsletter, with updated news since the magazine printed in May had some outdated information. These were sent by fax and mail. Their kids, some as young as 5 years old, would help folding, labeling, and stamping the newsletters. Some customers had leagues at work and would ask to have their fax sent at a precise time, so they could stand by the fax machine and prevent other guys in the league from stealing it.

The Grogans recruited people from around the country to watch their local pre-season games and take notes, after which Dan and Kelly would call them to get the information for their updates. In exchange, they were given a free newsletter subscription. They weren't always reliable. Dan recalls being told on one phone call "I was cutting the grass, so I didn't catch the first half."

In 1991, a friend who was in IT told them, "This internet thing is going to be really big—how about I build you a website?" The Grogan's agreed. Initially it only had a couple of pages of information. There were very few server companies at the time, but they found one in Seattle. And everything was written in code—not like today, where someone can just upload a Word document—so it took hours to make changes. Kelly taught himself how to write code.

It wasn't until the mid-'90s that the website became more useful for allowing customers to log in and see updates. And eventually pre-season updates were done online with no more mail or faxes. And they began offering subscribers in-season content. They both wrote content, but Dan was the head writer and was inducted in the Fantasy Sports Writers Association (FSWA) Hall of Fame.

A second magazine, *Fantasy Football Advisor*, was added in 1990. It was an abridged version of the main magazine, designed for casual players who didn't want to spend a lot of time studying for their drafts. It wasn't as successful as the primary magazine but did turn a profit. In 1994, *Grogan's Fantasy Baseball Analyst* was published, with a local sportswriter providing most of the content. It did sell enough to make a profit, but that year the World Series was canceled due to the MLBPA strike. The Grogans decided not to continue after just that one year because they were concerned there would be a decrease in fantasy baseball players angry about what had happened. They also looked at their competition, such as Ron Shandler's Baseball HQ and other analysts, and felt they couldn't compete with the great content already on the market.

By the late '90s, they outgrew H + S and signed with Time Warner. Their distribution grew to 200,000 for the primary magazine. In 2006, they sold the magazine to Athlon. The magazine business had gotten so competitive that they felt they needed to get a big partner. They were allowed to stay in Denver and run the magazine for Athlon. This worked well for a few years, until Athlon brought in a new person to help run it who didn't know fantasy, and the Grogan brothers quit in 2010, knowing it was going in a bad direction. As Kelly explained, "Athlon looked at it as a commodity—you just put a magazine together and throw it out there—but we put our heart and soul into it and felt that everything we put in had to have value to the fantasy player."

After leaving Athlon, both Grogan's briefly did a little freelance fantasy football writing, and then retired from the fantasy arena.

All-Pro Publishing

When Jack Pullman started playing fantasy football in 1977, points were awarded only for touchdowns and varied by length of the touchdown.

His first draft pick was OJ Simpson. OJ didn't score the first seven weeks and then he was hurt, so Pullman earned exactly zero points from his #1 pick.

Despite that, on the last Sunday of their regular season, Pullman went to bed one touchdown short of making the playoffs—but he still had 49ers running back Wilbur Jackson playing. Pullman was going to have to wait until the next morning's newspaper to get the 49ers box score. He bought a paper at a newsstand and took it into a stall in the men's room at his workplace. Flipping through the pages, he found Jackson had scored a touchdown, putting him into the playoffs. "YES!!! YES!!! YES!!!" he exclaimed quite loudly. He left the stall, and three men were standing there, staring at him.

One day in 1979, Pullman's wife asked, "Honey, do you need a kicker for your fantasy team?"

He replied, "Yes, why do you ask?"

She said, "Because you were muttering in your sleep all night, 'I need a kicker. I need a kicker.'"

By 1986, he was the commissioner of several leagues and people said, "Too bad you can't make a living doing this." He was recently divorced, had sold his house and was ready for something new. Pullman, who lived in Los Angeles, started to think, "Well, maybe somehow I can make a living with this?"

There were almost no publications for fantasy, so Pullman started All Pro Publications in 1986. He created a magazine with fantasy-relevant stats, write-ups about each team and player analysis by position. He didn't sell it on newsstands or bookstores, but by placing small ads in other magazines and mailing copies to his subscribers.

The first year, 300 people subscribed, then 500 in 1987 and 1,000 in 1988. By 1988, in addition to his annual guide, he had already added a guide on how to set up a fantasy league, an August preseason update issue, and a weekly update. People could buy everything individually or spend $44 for the whole package.

By 1988, he had also created his All-Pro Telephone Network. He enlisted subscribers (by offering a discount) in every city to feed him information they learned from their local media. His scouts, as he called them, would call in information constantly. Pullman even received calls from weddings, bar mitzvahs, and from someone visiting a sick relative in the hospital.

It became a year-long, full-time job. In February, Pullman would start working on next year's publications. Like most other early fantasy businesses, he later incorporated a fax option to replace USPS mail and launched a website in the mid-'90s. Pullman retired from the business in 2012.

Fantasy Football Index

One of the largest-ever fantasy sports magazines was created because Ian Allan's mother was kind to her children's piano teacher.

In 1986, Allan was a senior at the University of Washington. His good friend, Bruce Taylor, was a junior. One night, one of their roommates, Mike Yantis, told them about fantasy football. He pointed at Allan and said, "This game would be perfect for you—you're going to love this game!"

Allan did love the idea and organized two leagues before having ever played. One was with the staff of the student newspaper, and the other was with members of his family. Allan made himself commissioner of both. Before the drafts, he gave everyone an eight-page preview including rules of their game, schedules, stats, and notable players coming into the league from the USFL and college.

After the season, Allan and Taylor reflected on the missteps they had made and wondered why none of the football annuals had warned them about these mistakes. But these annuals had no content for fantasy football. That spring, 1987, Taylor was in a class called "Creativity and Innovation," which coincidentally was taught by Allan's father. The students were assigned a project: Think of a product or service they hadn't seen before, identify the first step toward executing it, and take that first step. Many students' idea was to be able to pay for gasoline with a charge card at the gas pump. Back then, people had to walk inside and pay cash. But Taylor's idea was to start a fantasy football magazine.

Allan agreed to work on this with Taylor. But they weren't just going to take the first step, they were going all the way. They were both journalism students, had worked on the campus newspaper, and figured if they could write, lay out and publish a newspaper, they could do a magazine. According to Allan, they arrogantly thought, "We had played for one year. We're now experts, ready to tell everybody else how to play." He added, "We didn't do any market research. We just assumed everybody was as interested in fantasy football as we were."

Taylor said, "We were lucky to go into business just as desktop publishing became reality. At the campus paper, we worked on typewriters. Cut-and-paste meant exactly that. I had never used a computer of any kind. As we began work on this project, a friend gave me a bootleg copy of Aldus PageMaker 1.2 and a Mac system disk. At night, Ian and I snuck into the computer lab in the chemical engineering building at the University of Washington. Ian wrote about teams, and I taught myself how to assemble pages. We ate pizza and worked late through the night, writing and assembling pages."

The content they wrote included instructions on how to play, schedules, player analysis and stats by position from the previous two seasons. The Miami Dolphins sent them a color slide of Dan Marino to put on the front cover. They named it *Fantasy Football 87* and published 5,000 copies.

And how did they pay to publish 5,000 copies? Ormond Mumaw, who taught Allan and his five siblings piano, had become a widower 10 years earlier. He had no children. After his wife died, Allan's mom invited him to have dinner every Sunday. He did so for a few years, until he passed away and left his house for Allan and his siblings. Allan had $5,000, which bankrolled the magazine.

Their next task was to get them on newsstands. There was a different wholesaler in every city. They had a code for a WATS line—which allowed users to make an unlimited number of long-distance calls for a flat, monthly rate—at the University of Washington and would sneak in and make calls to wholesalers. Most had never heard of fantasy football and weren't interested. But people in several cities agreed to take copies, and the boys went to UPS and shipped them.

Another friend of theirs worked for a publishing company that put out several sports preview magazines. He introduced Allan and Taylor to their distribution guy, and the man worked on the side for Allan and Taylor, pitching their fantasy football magazine when calling newsstands and bookstores about his company's magazines.

They were living in a rental house and published that as the address for the magazine, but moved out before the magazine hit stands. Taylor said, "Because we were 22-year-old morons, we didn't put in a forwarding address. I went back to the house in August and asked the new renters if they had any mail for us. The guy said, 'We just threw away a stack about this high,' and he held his thumb and forefinger about five inches apart."

They knew they were on to something good and decided to do it again the next year. But they needed to borrow money from Allan's siblings to make that happen, and borrowed more for the third year, 1989. That's when they hooked up with Curtis Circulation, one of the biggest nationwide wholesalers in the USA. They changed the magazine name to *Fantasy Football Index* and published 100,000 copies. Allan's brother Rob started working with them, and among other things, started selling advertising. Before 1989, they hadn't even had a phone.

With the magazine published in June, a lot of information was outdated by the time the NFL season began. So, they began offering pre-season updates. Allan said, "People say fantasy blew up with the advent of the internet—not for us. In 1989 the phone would ring and as soon as we'd hang up, we'd get another call in five seconds. Everyone wanted these updates. We had to figure out in early August how to get five more phone lines."

And they did get five more phone lines, in the basement of Allan's parents' home, where he was living. They hired students to work in the basement answering phones from 6 a.m. to 6 p.m. And they bought more computers and headsets so they could take orders. Some local people who couldn't get through on the phone—or just didn't want to wait for the mail—would come by in person and pay cash to get the updates. Allan's mom finally stopped this, saying, "The neighbors are going to think you guys are drug dealers."

Allan did most of the writing while Taylor handled most of the business tasks. Pre-season games were on Friday and Saturday, so Allan would stay up late Saturday night writing updates. He'd drop them off around 2 a.m. at a 24-hour Kinko's. Sometimes a Kinko's wouldn't have enough paper to print them all, so he'd need to go to a second Kinko's location. On Sunday nights, Allan, Taylor, and their girlfriends would sit at a dinner table folding and sealing, after which they brought trays and trays of mail to the post office. They had a parcel permit, so they didn't have to lick 6,000 stamps. In subsequent years, people started wanting updates by fax. It took forever to send out 400 or more faxes, until Rob figured out how to do broadcast faxing.

Allan said, "If people are paying me for advice, I needed to actually be an expert, not just claim I was." Back then, you could only watch your local team's game. So, they recruited someone from every NFL city to FedEx them a videotape of their team's pre-season games. The magazine paid for the FedEx and gave the person a free subscription.

Allan stopped answering the phone and doing other activities, since it took many hours to watch the games and do his writing. He is quite likely the only person to ever watch at least parts of every NFL pre-season game for years. By the late '90s, he stopped watching the NBA, the World Series, March Madness, and all other sports to focus 100% on football.

They were the first to have a "cheat sheet," which summarized all player projections on one page, such that people could take these to their drafts and cross off players as they were taken. Their slogan on the magazine cover became "Cheaters Always Prosper." In 1991, they were the first to ask writers from other fantasy companies—including magazines they were competing with—to provide their rankings for consensus experts rankings.

During the fourth year they broke even, and the fifth year they were able to pay back Allan's siblings. By the mid-'90s, they were selling 200,000 copies per year, had started a website—FantasyIndex.com—and debuted *Fantasy Baseball Index* magazine. Since they were only knowledgeable in football, they hired freelancers to write the baseball magazine. Like most fantasy baseball magazines, it never sold as well as the football magazines—perhaps only about 25% as much—but was still profitable until 2011, when Borders bookstore closed. Losing 800 stores selling an average of 25 copies each turned the magazine into a breakeven proposition, and they stopped publishing. As of 2024, they were still publishing baseball content on their website during the pre-season.

After peaking at a high of 225,000 football magazines sold, sales later declined due to the internet and more competition. Taylor remembers one year counting more than 30 fantasy annuals at newsstands. But theirs have remained profitable. Fantasy Football Index was the largest selling fantasy football magazine every year until 2011, when they—and most others—didn't publish due to an NFL lockout.

By 1992, Allan and Taylor were both working full-time for the magazine. Taylor had been working at a real estate shopper magazine. He remembers one of the co-owners making some unreasonable demand during a staff meeting, and he said, "George, every person in this room thinks you're full of shit, but I'm the only one who can say it out loud because I actually don't need this job." He said he felt like a hero and gave his notice the next day.

Allan was married and living in his own home, which served as their office for a few years until their office was moved to Taylor's house. There, they used three rooms, drilled holes through walls to connect computers, and bought an eight-line phone system with Category 5 wiring in the walls. Allan, Taylor, and Rob Allan were the only year-round staff, with typically eight to 10 temporary staff during the pre-season until everything was on the internet and they no longer needed extra pre-season help. They have also used a couple of freelancers to help with content and layout.

Allan has appeared on hundreds of radio shows. He is a member of both the FSTA Hall of Fame and the FSWA Hall of Fame. In his spare time, he runs marathons, swims, plays soccer and makes elaborate custom Jell-Os.

38 Years Later

In 1986, Mike Yantis pointed at Allan and said, "This game would be perfect for you—you're going to love this game!" And wow, was he ever right. But soon after that conversation, Allan never saw him again. Yantis may not know what Allan has done all these years. Allan has tried, unsuccessfully, to find him, to say "Thank you."

But the University of Washington campus newspaper fantasy league Allan started is still going, with him, Taylor and two of the other original eight guys still playing along with eight new guys. Taylor sold his 50% of the company in the summer of 2023 and retired. Allan still owns the other half and is not leaving. Rob Allan left in 2010 to pursue other ventures.

Taylor said that when they started, all their classmates said, "You're doing something really cool"—except for one guy who said, "You don't know what you are doing—this is a big mistake—you need to learn more about it first." And Taylor said he was closer to being right than the other people. "We were lucky we didn't know what we didn't know, or we wouldn't have done it."

Taylor added, "If you had asked me in 1987, would I still be doing this 35 years later, I would have said yes—because it seemed so obvious everyone would want to play and there was a need for this information."

Years later, Taylor ran into the phone company guy who did the Category 5 wiring, who told him, "I remember installing your system—I had assumed you were a bookie."

After our Zoom interview, Allan sent me this e-mail:

Somewhere in your book, you should address the issue of commissioners.

They've been diminished in the last 20 years. The commissioner nowadays is the guy who sets up the website and perhaps helps to resolve some disputes.

But back in the '80s and well into the '90s, the commissioner was the key guy, taking lineups via phone on Sunday morning, scoring games and putting out weekly reports. Reports that included updated rosters and standings and a list of the transactions. If you've got a good commissioner, maybe you've got some extras in there, such as the Player of the Week, Coach of the Week, Miss of the Week, etc.

(Thanks Ian, I just mentioned it.)

First Fantasy Baseball Magazine

At the University of Wisconsin-Platteville, Greg Ambrosius and seven dormmates played in a Strat-O-Matic league until one of them saw the Bantam Rotisserie Book and said, "We don't need to get together every night—we can just get together once a year to draft our players." In 1986, they started playing rotisserie baseball and fantasy football.

Ambrosius always wanted to be involved with sports. He went to college for journalism and photography, then got jobs as a newspaper sports editor of a twice-weekly and later a daily newspaper. After seven years, he was making $13,500 a year and living in his own mobile home. He loved it.

In 1989, he saw an ad looking for an editor of a debut rotisserie baseball magazine. Ambrosius drove 90 minutes north from his home in Baraboo, Wisconsin, to Iola—55 miles from Green Bay, population 1,310. He assumed some random guy wanted to start a magazine, and the interview would likely be in a barn. But he was shocked to see that in the middle of this tiny town was a huge building for Krause Publications, with basketball and tennis courts outside, a fitness center inside, and the best computers. Krause had been in business 35 years, with 200 employees, and called themselves "The World's Largest Hobby Publisher."

Ambrosius's experience in journalism and his three years of playing roto set him apart from the other five applicants. It didn't hurt that their softball team needed a third baseman, and he played third base. He was called and offered the job on his drive home.

His first day was June 5, 1989. The 29-year-old was told he was going to initially be the assistant editor for their *Baseball Cards* magazine, as they weren't sure if they'd be able to get enough advertising for a fantasy baseball magazine. While working on the baseball card magazine, he was to try and learn how many advertisers there might be for a fantasy magazine. He wasn't exactly happy with this news, since he had taken the job and moved to Iola specifically to be the editor of a fantasy baseball magazine, and now they were telling him it wasn't definite. Nevertheless, he contacted companies advertising fantasy products in *The Sporting News* and *Baseball America* to gauge interest, and by October had enough interest that Krause agreed to do it.

In the fall of 1989, Ambrosius, along with *Baseball Cards* editor Kit Kiefer, wrote player analysis, positional rankings, and players' projected dollar values. He also hired a couple of freelance writers. Ambrosius sent a letter to Glenn Waggoner asking him to write the foreword for their first issue. Waggoner replied, "Krause Publications is probably the right company to do this. We wish you the best of luck, but if you ever use the word 'Rotisserie' without including the trademark we will sue you."

Sure enough, they had planned to call it *Rotisserie Baseball* magazine... and they didn't want to have to show the trademark everywhere—so they changed the name to *Fantasy Baseball* magazine.

In December 1989, Ambrosius went to the MLB winter meetings in Nashville looking for additional freelancers. He put flyers in the writers room. An official from MLB put the flyers in a garbage can. Ambrosius snuck back in and put them back on the table. Again, the official put them in the garbage and again Ambrosius snuck back in. This happened several times until Ambrosius saw Rod Beaton, the USA *Today* beat writer for the National League, looking at a flyer. Ambrosius approached him and introduced himself. Beaton pulled a piece of paper from his pocket and showed Ambrosius his rotisserie team lineup. Beaton agreed to freelance.

Fantasy Baseball magazine debuted in January 1990. It bombed.

They sold only 25% of the 155,000 circulation. By contrast, *Baseball Cards* magazine, circulation 330,000, typically sold 75-80%. Two more pre-season issues didn't do any better, and two in-season magazines did even worse. Lucky for Ambrosius, not everything bombed in 1990—he met a fellow employee named Chris who became his wife in 1992.

Sales in 1991 weren't getting any better, and for the September issue they decided to try including football content as well as baseball. They put a picture of Randall Cunningham on the cover. That fall, the CFO told Ambrosius if they didn't average a 33% sell-through for 1992, the magazine would fold. The quarterly results subsequently came in, showing the Randall Cunningham issue had sold 47%. Ambrosius realized then that fantasy football was king and knew he had a good shot at averaging 33%.

Ambrosius bought airtime to host a fantasy baseball radio show to promote the magazine. This led to his being invited to talk fantasy on other sports radio shows, such as Norm Hitzges's show in Dallas.

Ambrosius examined the national distribution figures from the first two years and saw inefficiencies. For example, a store in Mississippi was given 80 magazines both years and hardly sold any. Apparently, people in Mississippi liked baseball cards, but not rotisserie baseball. Ambrosius corrected this wastefulness and slashed the circulation to 120,000. The 1992 baseball issues sold exactly 33% and football again topped 40%.

Kit Kiefer left Krause in 1992 and Ambrosius was the editor of both the baseball card magazine and the fantasy baseball magazine. In 1993, they went to two baseball and two football issues per year, and in 1998 changed the name to *Fantasy Sports* magazine. The internet caused the downfall of the magazine, and it was last published in 2010, never having expanded past that revised circulation of 120,000.

Ambrosius had an illustrious career in the fantasy industry. He founded the National Fantasy Baseball Championship (NFBC) and the National Fantasy Football Championship (NFFC), which are discussed in detail in Chapter 14.

In 1994, Ambrosius was interviewed on *Good Morning America* along with Dan Okrent about how big fantasy baseball was getting. And he was on ESPN's pay-per-view fantasy baseball special. In 1995, he was a regular panelist on the first year of Prime Sports' weekly fantasy TV show, flying weekly from Wisconsin to Dallas.

Ambrosius was a founding member of the FSTA and its president from 2003-2006. He is one of only five members of both the FSTA and FSWA halls of fame. He was an original member of USA *Today*'s LABR experts league, and, after the 2023 season, was the only person to have played all 30 years.

As of 2024, he was still running the NFBC and NFFC, with an eye on retiring one day to northern Wisconsin and spending time on a pontoon.

Emil Kadlec

During the first week of the 1981 NFL season, Emil Kadlec's good friend Bill Robertson told him about having just joined a fantasy football league. Kadlec had never heard of it before but liked the idea so much that he quickly recruited seven others in time to start a league for the third week of the season.

As the years went by, Kadlec realized there was a lack of information available and in 1990 decided to start a magazine. Unaware of *Grogan's* and *Fantasy Football Index*, which apparently hadn't made it to the Albuquerque newsstands and bookstores yet, he was under the impression that none existed.

Kadlec, 33, was a successful engineer at Sandia National Labs, with no journalistic experience, and was dyslexic. He quickly recruited Robertson—also with no journalistic experience—to become partners. Kadlec took vacation time from work, and they did all the writing themselves, using Word Perfect to build magazine pages. They had just a few hundred black-and-white issues printed that first year in 1990 and called it *Fantasy Football Pro Forecast*. They got them in local bookstores and newsstands on their own and ran ads in *Pro Football Weekly* and a couple other publications for mail order sales.

Kadlec proudly showed the magazine to his dad, saying "Dad, look what I created!"

His dad responded, "How much money did you lose?"

But he didn't lose money, it did well. So, the second year, they got a distributor. They published 16,000 copies—this time in color—and sold 9,000, which the distributor said was fantastic, so the following year increased to 100,000.

Kadlec and Robertson never knew other sports well enough to feel comfortable putting out a magazine, so they stuck with only football. In 1996, Kadlec quit his job to expand the magazine business. "My dad thought I was crazy when I left Sandia National Labs after 15 years to focus on a business not many people understood at the time," Kadlec said. "He may well have been right."

That year, they published a second football magazine, *DraftBook*, the success of which set them on the path to becoming the largest publisher of fantasy football magazines. They added *CheatSheets* magazine in 1998 and *Fantasy Football Experts Poll* (which later changed to *Football Diehards*) a couple of years later. Then they started publishing an updated version of *Pro Forecast* that was redistributed a month later each year, giving them five publications, with more than one million total issues in circulation.

They launched the FSPNET.com website in 1996 (later changed to FootballDiehards.com).

And they have had the *Football Diehards* radio show on SiriusXM Fantasy Sports Radio for many years, hosted by Bob Harris and Mike Dempsey. As of 2023, they still published three magazines, *Diehards* and *Pro Forecast* (still two distributions), with a total circulation of 350,000.

Robertson has always done this part-time, maintaining a full-time commercial real estate career. Kadlec also co-founded WCOFF, the first high-stakes fantasy contest, which is described in detail in Chapter 14.

And to think, if *Grogan's* or *Fantasy Football Index* had happened to get into a store in Albuquerque by 1990, perhaps none of this would have happened and Kadlec would have remained an engineer until retirement.

Kadlec co-founded the FSWA and is a member of the FSTA Hall

of Fame. He is very interested in the history of fantasy sports and did a series of Fantasy Sports Pioneer interviews which are available on FantasyNation.com and YouTube. Several are included in the bibliography for this book.

The fantasy league he started in 1981 still existed as of 2023. It started with eight people, some of whom are still members, and they've grown to 14 total. The entire scoring system is just 6 points for a touchdown—that's it, nothing else. Every couple of years, they have a meeting and Kadlec will suggest adding scoring for yardage, receptions and other things that are now common, but the other guys are like, "Why? We have the greatest league ever! Points per reception? What the hell is that?" So, Kadlec gives up every time.

Baseball Weekly

When Gannett Corporation launched *USA Today* in 1982, rotisserie baseball was an immediate factor in their success. Paul White, the USA Today baseball editor, said that by 1983 it became clear there was a demand from rotisserie players for baseball stats. They started publishing stats for the AL on Tuesdays and NL on Wednesdays because those were the papers' two weakest days, and it would boost circulation.

The statistics they published—as was the case with the ones *The Sporting News* had published every week—were always "year-to-date" stats. This meant that roto players would need to deduct the year-to-date stats from the prior week, to calculate the player's stats for the week that just ended. This made it even more cumbersome for commissioners who did their league's stats by hand. After a couple of years, *USA Today* started publishing stats from the prior week as well as year-to-date stats, which was fantastic for roto players.

In December 1990, *The Sporting News* announced it would be dropping baseball box scores. John Curley, the CEO of Gannett, and his brother Tom, the editor-in-chief of *USA Today*—both huge baseball fans—were horrified by this. But they also saw an opportunity to publish a weekly magazine dedicated solely to baseball, which would include all the prior week's box scores.

They launched the first issue of *Baseball Weekly* on April 4, 1991. White was moved to be the *Baseball Weekly* editor. They initially had limited fantasy content but did use a group of rotating columnists that included Glen Waggoner, Steve Mann (an early analytics guy), and former MLB player Billy Sample. These three were later replaced by John Benson, who took over writing the weekly fantasy column.

White said, "When we started *Baseball Weekly*, we assumed fantasy would be the driving force—and the first couple of years we did reader surveys and focus groups—and we were stunned to learn less than 50% of our readers played fantasy. There was even a backlash from some non-fantasy players. We got to the point where we knew what fantasy players wanted but we wouldn't label it all fantasy because it would turn off a lot of people."

In 1992, they published a fantasy draft guide contained inside a March issue of Baseball Weekly. A few years later, they started publishing a separate fantasy draft guide every March. In those early days, rotisserie players sometimes wanted to use other stats in addition to the normal roto stats, but they were limited to what was available in published box scores. The lone exception to this problem was the *USA Today* office roto league. They wanted to use "caught stealing" as a category. Any other league wouldn't have been able to do this, but they simply added it to their published box scores so they could use it for their own league.

John Hunt had been working at the *USA Today* agate desk since 1991, processing statistics and making sure all the box scores were included in the paper. In early 1993, he learned that John Benson might be leaving as their weekly columnist, and he volunteered for the job. Although he had played fantasy baseball and written for his college newspaper at Virginia Tech, he had no credentials as any type of expert, and had never written professionally. But they gave him a shot.

For the 1994 season, he created the first "experts" league, called LABR. It brought more attention to the game as it included celebrities such as Keith Olbermann (on ESPN's *Baseball Tonight*), Bill James, Glenn Waggoner, and Rod Beaton. The results of these auctions for their AL and NL leagues were published in the March fantasy baseball guide.

Baseball Weekly's circulation increased to 250,000 per week. And Hunt's column became a huge success. According to Ron Shandler, founder of *BaseballHQ*, "Whatever John Hunt wrote about was gospel."

The March draft guide peaked at more than 300,000 sold in a year. And the LABR results became a must-read for auction league players. A positive mention of a company or product by Hunt was a goldmine. Greg Ambrosius of *Fantasy Baseball* magazine said, "Everyone begged him to be mentioned. He once mentioned that our magazine had updated projections we would fax for $5, and we got 1,000 requests."

Lenny Melnick, co-host of a fantasy sports radio show, said, "If you got your name in John Hunt's column, that put you in the industry. And that's what John Hunt did for us. He put us in the industry."

White said, "We let the young guy on the staff take a shot at this and we were pleased at what a good job he did. But in essence it was like we just took this guy off the street and said, 'Go do it.' And the influence he had so quickly was both amusing and startling."

White once wanted to interview a back-up catcher at spring training and was told, "I'm not talking to you—my wife said not to talk to you because John Hunt wrote that I'm the worst catcher in the league."

The MLB work stoppage in August 1994, which ended the season and canceled the World Series, caused many advertisers to leave. And even when play resumed in 1995, they were slow to all come back. Gannett decided they should add football coverage and changed the name to *Sports Weekly*. They started with very little fantasy football content, but that increased over time.

While writing his column and being commissioner of LABR, Hunt had kept some of his agate desk duties as well as other aspects of Baseball Weekly. He married a copy editor at the USA Today. She was offered a great job in Portland, Oregon and in 1996 the two moved there. Hunt landed a job with the Oregonian but kept writing his Baseball Weekly column as a freelancer until 2006 and was replaced by Steve Gardner.

As of 2024, Gardner was still writing the weekly column and LABR was in its 31st season. Hunt was inducted into the FSTA Hall of Fame. Gardner said taking over the column from Hunt was akin to following Bear Bryant as the coach at Alabama.

Fantasy Football Weekly

Paul Charchian attended the University of Minnesota for journalism, but also had software training. He thought he'd never use the journalism degree because there was a lot more money in computer science. He got a job as a network administrator for an accounting company and became commissioner of the firm's fantasy football league. One day, Rob Pythian, a tax accountant and league member—who didn't know Charchian had a journalism degree—said, "There's nothing in print for fantasy football during the season, why don't we start an in-season magazine?"

The pair, both in their mid-20s, formed a company called Fanball, and in 1993 launched *Fantasy Football Weekly*. Indeed, it was the first ever in-season fantasy football magazine.

Charchian knew how to write but knew nothing about publishing or page layout. He bought a laptop and a program called Adobe PageMaker and learned how to do layout. "I was terrible at it," he said. "I didn't know how to make it look good." According to Charchian, the initial magazine "was printed in tabloid format, newsprint almost, 24 pages a week. There was no roadmap for how to talk fantasy football, how to break down games or predict games, or what people would even want—we just made it up."

They met with a local Twin Cities distribution company who agreed to carry it, but only locally. It sold very well. In fact, it sold more copies in those Minneapolis-St. Paul area stores than *Sports Illustrated* did. This success led them to get a national distributor for the following year. But this came with logistical problems. To get it on newsstands across the country early in the week, so that it had a few days to sell, they had to be done with the magazine by 9 p.m. on Sundays. They pre-wrote the magazine during the week, and then on Sunday changed things based on the games that they saw. Charchian said, "Back then you couldn't see all the games. We were at a massive disadvantage, but everyone was just so starved for content that we had an advantage just by being there."

And they had to FedEx heavy boxes. The overnight shipping costs were exorbitant, so it was difficult to make a profit. In fact, they lost money that year, since it turned out not all NFL cities were hotbeds for fantasy like the Twin Cities were. But after struggling for a few years, they had 50,000 subscribers in 1996, putting out 18 issues a year. There were three summer issues, followed by the weekly in-season magazines. The summer issues, since they were on sale for many weeks, eventually hit a circulation of 500,000.

Charchian's studio apartment was originally listed as the magazine address for people to subscribe. One day in 1994, there was a knock on the door. A man said, "Hi, my name's Rick. I love your magazine and was going to subscribe and realized we're in the same building. I live downstairs."

Rick also begged for a job. He said, "I'll work for free. I just want to be a part of this." They were able to give Rick a part-time job, with nominal pay, and were eventually able to offer him a full-time position. He quit his job at American Express, where he was working a corporate job that he hated, and took a pay cut to go full-time with Fanball. He wrote for Fanball for many years, articles with analysis, advice, and predictions, for both fantasy football and later fantasy basketball. It was the basketball articles that led to Rick—whose last name is Kamla—being discovered by NBA TV, where he was offered a job in 2003 as one of the first people on television talking about fantasy basketball. And he's been there ever since, becoming a studio commentator and calling hundreds of NBA games play-by-play. He's also been a radio talk show host on 92.9 in Atlanta as well as on SiriusXM.

Although the company was named Fanball since its inception, people only knew it as *Fantasy Football* magazine until it launched a website, Fanball.com. The idea was to make it a one-stop shop, with content for all major fantasy sports, news updates, advice, even offering their own games and commissioner tools.

At this time, the late '90s, the dot-com world was going crazy and it was easy to raise money. Charchian and Pythian found investors and raised $10 million in just two weeks. They added an office in Florida and one in London and had more than 50 employees. But revenue was slow, they burned through all the cash, and had to restructure around 2001. They gave up hopes of being successful with fantasy soccer in England, closed that office as well as the Florida office, and reduced staff to just 12 employees.

But then they became successful mostly due to their Fanball commissioner service and deals to run fantasy games for NASCAR.com and PGATour.com. They grew to be one of the largest fantasy destination websites on the internet in the 2000s. They also had partnerships with Turner Sports and AOL.

In 2005, Fanball was sold to FUN Technologies and then to Liberty Media, as mentioned in Chapter 6. Pythian and Charchian remained employees for a couple of years and then left. Charchian created new companies LeagueSafe and Guillotine Leagues and has been the host of the longest-running fantasy radio show. Meanwhile, Pythian has been a heavyweight in the industry— as of 2023, he was serving as CEO of both SportsHub Technologies and SharpLink. Both were inducted into the FSGA Hall of Fame.

CHAPTER 8

First Fantasy Sports Books

Cliff Charpentier and Tom Kane were friends since school in the Minneapolis-St. Paul area and played fantasy football. Charpentier got the idea of publishing a fantasy football book that would explain the rules, offer advice, show the previous years' player stats, and rate the players for the upcoming season to make it easy for the average NFL fan to play.

"I think this is going to be big," he told Kane. "I'm telling you, we're at the forefront of something."

Working out of Charpentier's mother's basement, they self-published their first paperback book, *Fantasy Football Digest*, in 1984. Charpentier wrote the book. Kane handled the business aspects. Kane had a connection with B Dalton books, who put their book into their local branches.

"The first year in the Twin Cities, we sold 3,000 books, and we knew we were on to something," Charpentier said. Then came a call from a prominent publisher and the Fantasy Football Digest became a nationally distributed, hugely successful annual publication. The *USA Today* called it the "bible of fantasy football."

Paul Charchian, who didn't launch Fanball until 1993, said, "In the early days there was almost nothing published about fantasy football. There was nothing on TV, nothing on radio, there was no internet. If you wanted any kind of advice, the only place to go was Cliff Charpentier's digest. For those of us playing back then, it's hard to overstate just how important that one book was."

By 1998, others had already started magazines, but Charpentier and Kane added their own, *Fantasy Football Draft Guide*. And they added subscription newsletters, a telephone hotline and fax updates. Kane said the fax machine was very lucrative.

The book and magazine were published annually until 2003. Due to increased competition—some of it free— and the rise of the internet, Charpentier and Kane saw the writing on the wall and called it a day. They also never played fantasy football again. "It burned us out," Charpentier said. "I just can't play ever again."

Other football books were out by 1990, such as *Rotisserie League Football*, by Peter Pascarelli, and *Danny Sheridan's Fantasy Football*.

Fantasy Baseball Books

After the original *Rotisserie League Baseball* book, first published in 1984, the next consequential book, *How to Win at Rotisserie Baseball*, by Peter Golenbock, came out in 1987 and sold 20,000 copies. Golenbock was already a best-selling author of several sports related books and played in the founders American League players game that had started in 1981.

David Rosenthal, a league mate who was an editor at Random House, asked Golenbock to write a book about winning. Although he hadn't been successful yet himself, Golenbock interviewed the successful players in the league. He asked league mate Alex Patton to write two chapters about player pricing. Ron Shandler, of *Baseball HQ*, has said, "The founders' book taught you how to play—Golenbock's book taught you how to win."

It also had humor and advice, with chapters such as: "Rotisserie Baseball: It's More than Life Itself," "The Joy and Pain of Having a Partner," "Emotional Involvement with Your Players," and "How to Keep Your Woman from Leaving You."

Bryant Gumbel wrote an introduction in which he mentioned he'd been playing roto for six years and was a little obsessive, having created team stationery and a team motto—he had even given serious thought to making a press guide.

How to Win at Rotisserie Baseball was published annually through 1996.

Patton Dollars

In the early years of Roto, participants generally had little idea of what players were worth. Mike Schmidt was obviously very valuable, but was he worth $10 at an auction? or $20? or $30? What about someone like Tony Gwynn, who had less power but a great batting average and stolen bases?

If anybody knew how to accurately place an auction price on hitters and pitchers, they weren't sharing it with the world—until Alex Patton. Patton, a Harvard English professor, created a system to calculate how much a player was worth in the context of a $260 auction based on the stats the player produced. He called them "Patton dollars."

"I started playing with algebra," he said. "I was amazed I even still remembered algebra...I started playing with basic equations and making assumptions." And this led to his invention of Standings Gain Points, a method for calculating dollar values.

As just mentioned, he first shared Patton dollars in Golenbock's 1987 book. Rather than making projections for what stats players would produce in the upcoming season, he was placing a dollar value on the stats they had produced in each of the previous three seasons. In 1988, he self-published his player values. It wasn't a book—it was more of a pamphlet run from a mimeograph machine and stapled together. He sold them mail order by placing ads in *Baseball America*, *The Sporting News*, and the *Baseball Forecaster*.

Patton was so sure everyone loved rotisserie baseball, he and his girlfriend drove to Florida with four big boxes of pamphlets to sell at spring training games. But they sold very few—most people didn't know about roto and didn't care.

Patton had written three novels, with an agent trying unsuccessfully to sell them. He gave his agent five pamphlets to send to editors, and that landed a book deal. Simon and Schuster published *Patton's 1989 Fantasy Baseball Price Guide*, with a foreword by Glenn Waggoner. It was published annually from 1989-1997. Patton then started selling a disk rather than a book, allowing people to manipulate projections to help with their own draft. He was still selling the software online as of 2024.

Many other annual books followed Golenbock and Patton, such as *The Fantasy Baseball Abstract* by Wayne Welch, Danny Sheridan's *Guide to Winning Rotisserie Baseball*, and the *Baseball Black Book* by Larry S. Meyers.

Three other very important people in the history of fantasy sports also had annual books out during this time, John Benson, Bill James, and Ron Shandler. But their stories include more than just publishing an annual book. Benson's story follows now, while James and Shandler are in the next chapter.

John Benson

John Benson was a CPA in Wilton, Connecticut, who had a BA from Princeton and an MBA from Columbia. In 1977, two years before Okrent started his game, Benson and a friend at work created a primitive version of rotisserie. They recruited six others at work and drafted players. Around 1985, he started another league, now working as a marketing executive for Emery Worldwide. Benson used the RLBA stat service for his league and went to their conventions.

Benson said, "I found that I had developed a knack for projecting what players would do the following season. And in 1987 I wrote a story for *The Sporting News* offering predictions on specific players for the next season."

The accuracy of his projections as well as his draft strategies and trading advice gave him a reputation as a savant. He started writing a roto column for *Baseball America* and published a book called *Winning Rotisserie Baseball 1989*, profiling players and predicting their stats for the following season. It became an annual book, with the name for the 1990 edition changed to *Rotisserie Baseball Analyst*.

He may have been the first to both project players stats and include a projected auction dollar value to the stats. (Patton, by comparison, was the first to put a dollar value with stats but was putting the value only on past seasons' stats, not projecting the upcoming year.)

By 1991, he was no longer with Emery Worldwide and was writing baseball full-time. In addition to his annual guide, he offered a $59-per-year monthly newsletter and a live, $1.99-per-minute 1-900 number. Benson would spend the month of March in Florida and Arizona, attending one or two spring training games per day, and talking to players, coaches, and managers to gather information. He also had a network of writers in most MLB cities who fed him information for nominal pay.

For a while he wrote the weekly fantasy column in the *USA Today Baseball Weekly*, as well as columns in many other major publications. In 1997, he wrote a weekly column for the *Sporting News* and held roto chats on AOL for the magazine.

While continuing his first annual book, he added a second annual, *Benson's A to Z Baseball Player Guide*, profiling more than 2,500 players. He later added an annual, *Future Stars*, profiling top minor league prospects. And he wrote one-time books *Rotisserie Baseball: Playing for Blood* and *Rotisserie Baseball: Playing for Fun*.

For most of these, he started having others help write and edit. For example, Lary Bump and Tony Blengino gathered most of the information for the *Future Stars* books and Benson edited it. There were several other contributing writers and editors, including Mark Bowman, Atlanta Braves beat writer since 2001.

For a few years, Benson published *Fantasy Football: Playing for Blood*, which was written mostly by others, although Benson did contribute some content himself. He adapted some of his fantasy baseball concepts to fantasy football. And for a while he published fantasy magazines for both baseball and football. He launched a website with articles and news, offered draft software, and ran his own fantasy contest with a $15,000 grand prize. With a loyal and massive following, he was widely regarded as the leading fantasy baseball guru.

Over the years, Benson appeared on ESPN, the *NBC News with Tom Brokaw*, and was cited in *The New York Times*, *The Wall Street Journal*, US

News & World Report, Business Week and dozens of other newspapers and magazines. He was also a frequent guest on radio shows.

In the late '90s, his son, James, took over running the business while Benson reduced his involvement to pursue other interests, primarily getting a Master of Divinity degree from Yale University. Their last annual was published in 2006. Benson was inducted into both the FSTA and FSWA halls of fame.

CHAPTER 9

Advanced Metrics

Before the 1978 MLB season—and before creating his rotisserie game—Dan Okrent saw a tiny ad in *The Sporting News* that read "an interesting way to look at baseball statistics, the *Baseball Abstract*." Okrent sent $4 to a post office box in Lawrence, Kansas. He received a mimeographed stack of papers from a guy named Bill James. "It was like a whole new world opening up to me," Okrent said. "This guy understood baseball at a level so profound, so revolutionary, and he wrote spectacularly well." Okrent has said that he may have been influenced by James's writings when creating the rules of roto baseball.

The Bill James Baseball Abstract had debuted in 1977, selling 75 copies. It became an annual publication, selling 750 copies in 1980. Okrent and James became long-distance friends, exchanging letters and phone calls. Okrent tried unsuccessfully to get James a book deal. Then Okrent proposed to write an article about James for *Sports Illustrated*. He flew to Kansas and spent a few days with James, who worked as a night watchman in a food packing plant. It was a perfect job for James, who said, "I spend five minutes an hour making sure the furnaces don't blow up and 55 minutes working on baseball numbers."

In those days, the Elias Sports Bureau had a contract with MLB and wouldn't release official stats to anybody. So, James had to do his own stats, and when Okrent submitted the article, the *SI* factchecker noticed a couple of mistakes, such as James listing Gene Tenace with a .401 on-base percentage while Elias had it as .399—the factchecker took James for a fraud and the article was killed. But a senior executive at *SI* suggested Okrent try again the next year with a revised article, and this time the article, "He Does It by the Numbers," was published in 1981.

James's writings turned much of the conventional wisdom of baseball on its head. He demonstrated how common statistics—such as batting average, RBIs, ERA, and wins—were inadequate to determine a player's true value. Jim Drucker (from Chapter 1) said that when he read the *SI* article, he felt like a physicist in the early 1900s reacting to Albert Einstein's theory of relativity: It was an "aha moment"—like, "He's right!"

The *SI* article led to a book contract with Ballantine, with Peter Gethers as the book's editor. It changed the 32-year-old James's life. He published the *Abstract* annually through 1988. From 1979 through 1984, he wrote annual MLB season previews for *Esquire* magazine. He went on to write many more baseball-related books and introduce new statistical concepts such as "runs created," "defensive efficiency rating," "win shares," and "Pythagorean winning percentage."

James named his work *sabermetrics* after the Society for American Baseball Research (SABR). SABR was formed in 1971 by Robert Davids, who recruited 15 other baseball researchers at the National Baseball Hall of Fame to form the organization. It's a membership organization dedicated to research and dissemination of the history of baseball, primarily using statistics. James had a huge following of people who appreciated his work, and sabermetrics began being used more and more over time. He inspired many others to work on sabermetrics.

James has said, "I didn't get into playing fantasy baseball, because I didn't want people to think I was writing about fantasy baseball. I was writing about the real game. And I didn't want people to confuse the two." However, sabermetrics became a great help to fantasy players for predicting baseball players' future stats.

Meanwhile, MLB executives and scouts initially mostly dissed his theories, but over time most came to realize the validity of his work. Oakland Athletics general manager Billy Beane began applying James's principles to running his team in the late 1990s, as chronicled in the book turned movie *Moneyball*. In 2003, James was hired by the Boston

Red Sox as a consultant and worked with them until 2019, mostly commuting from Lawrence, Kansas where he still lives.

In an essay in his 1984 Abstract, James vented his frustration about MLB's refusal to publish play-by-play accounts of every game. He proposed the creation of Project Scoresheet, a network of fans that would collect this information and distribute it for free. The resulting non-profit organization collected accounts of every game from 1984 through 1991.

In 1989, James collaborated with STATS, Inc. to launch a fantasy baseball game, which is discussed in Chapter 10. From 1993-1995, he published the *Bill James Player Ratings Book*, which contained profiles and statistics. Although he didn't specifically market this as a fantasy book, it was used by many to help for fantasy drafts. And in 2003, he launched an annual called *The Bill James Handbook* which again provided upcoming season projections for MLB players. It is still published annually.

Ron Shandler

When Ron Shandler was 8 years old, he went to his first ball game at Yankee Stadium. Shandler didn't understand what was happening, he just wanted to get another hot dog. But the native New Yorker grew to love baseball and became a die-hard Mets fan. After getting an MBA from Hofstra University, he moved to New Hampshire and worked as a forecasting analyst for a publishing company. One day in July 1984, he walked into a B Dalton bookstore, and it changed his life. He purchased two books: the 1984 *Bill James Baseball Abstract* and *Bantam Rotisserie League Baseball*.

The 26-year-old Shandler had played Cadaco-Ellis All-Star Baseball, then APBA, and loved baseball statistics. He was so excited by the Rotisserie concept that he didn't want to wait until the next spring to play, so he recruited some friends and, that fall, they started a fantasy hockey league. They used the Rotisserie book as a guide to make up rules and a scoring system. The first player Shandler bought in their auction was Pittsburgh Penguins rookie Mario Lemieux.

The next spring, they started a baseball league, using teams from only the AL East and NL East divisions. Shandler finished in fourth place and was not satisfied with that. That winter he thought about how he could do better in fantasy. He loved the work of Bill James, had joined the SABR organization and discovered other writers who were using new methods of evaluating baseball players' skills, including Pete Palmer and Thomas Boswell. Shandler was convinced that the key to doing better at Rotisserie was somewhere in their work. He thought it would be helpful to create a spreadsheet with all relevant baseball players listed, and columns showing how the primary new metric used by each of the three writers rated the player.

He also realized that if he found that useful, so might others. He had been a writer and the editor-in-chief for his college newspaper, had worked for several publishing companies, and had learned direct marketing—so he decided to write a book.

It took a year before he could execute his idea. In the fall 1986, working from his kitchen table, he launched Shandler Enterprises. He created LOTUS spreadsheets showing the players with their standard stats and the three metrics he wanted to compare: Bill James's Runs Created, Boswell's Total Average and Palmer's Linear Weights. He also added two new pitching metrics he invented himself. He designed a cover and had Kinko's make 100 copies. He placed a small ad in *The Sporting News*, with the header "Baseball SuperStats!!" To pay for all of this, he gave up coffee for a month. By opening day of 1987, he had sold 67 copies at $9.95 each. Too impatient to wait a year to do it again, he started a monthly newsletter that debuted in June 1987. Later, the second edition of SuperStats!! sold 120 copies.

The next year, he started sending *Boston Globe* sports columnist Dan Shaughnessy complementary issues of his newsletter, and Shaughnessy printed a few items from it, one of which was picked up by the national wires and mentioned in several national newspapers. Several readers of *SuperStats!!* sent Shandler letters explaining they played fantasy and would like him to include player projections. In the fall, he changed the name to the *Baseball Forecaster*. In addition to all the stats and metrics, this time he included a player ratings section with projections for 1989. The book provided a single source for comprehensive sabermetric information as well as fantasy projections. After he placed a quarter-page ad in *Baseball America*, at a cost of $300, and it brought in more than $3,000 in book sales, Shandler realized he was on to something good. He was the first to combine sabermetrics with fantasy projections, and it had a market.

In these early days, he and his wife Sue worked day jobs, had dinner, then ran Shandler Enterprises from their one-bedroom apartment at night. Sue became the customer service rep, answering the phone at the kitchen table and stuffing envelopes while Shandler crunched numbers. As they grew, they needed help. Thanksgiving became a work party, with family and friends spread out on the living room floor, stuffing books into envelopes, attaching labels and postage. In 1991, he sold 1,000 books and had to find a fulfillment house for shipping. Thanks to an unreliable US Postal Service, he would sometimes get messages like "You asshole, it's draft day and I didn't get my book!"

Sales of both the *Forecaster* and newsletter continued to grow, but Shandler kept his day job with publishing companies until 1994. Rather than quitting because his business was starting to take off, he ended up being fired. By his own admission, Shandler was a bad employee. He didn't like working for others, bureaucracy, and corporate politics. During his career, he had eight jobs and was fired from six.

When he was fired on August 5, 1994, Sue was no longer working, and the MLB players were threatening to strike. But Shandler assured his wife, "Don't worry, our baseball income is safe...there's no chance the players will actually strike." A week later, the players went on strike. And in September, with no end to the strike in sight, the rest of the season and playoffs were canceled.

Shandler wanted to avoid going back to corporate work if possible. He said, "We rifled through our savings over the next year as we looked for a place to move to that had a lower cost of living, was warmer than

New Hampshire and would be a good place to raise our two toddler girls." They moved to Roanoke, Virginia in January 1996, when baseball was back and lucrative enough for Shandler to stay away from a corporate job. He spent two months that summer learning to code in HTML and launched a website BaseballHQ.com. Within nine months, the paid subscribers to the website surpassed his newsletter's volume. And it kept growing, quickly reaching the top of lists of best baseball websites. The *Forecaster* book sales skyrocketed, requiring Shandler to find a larger fulfillment house, and hire an accountant and a customer service rep. The business became very profitable.

Shandler kept creating his own new metrics for evaluating player performance as well as new ideas for fantasy baseball strategy. Among the stats he invented was Base Performance Value (BPV), which combined a pitcher's strikeout rate, strikeout-to-walk ratio, and opponents' batting average. Traditional stats for measuring pitcher performance, such as ERA and WHIP, don't account for good luck or bad luck. BPV helped fantasy players judge the true skills of pitchers.

"This type of analysis was a revelation at the time," Shandler said. "Traditional Roto stats supported the common wisdom that pitching was a crapshoot. But sabermetricians had shown that those flawed stats were highly influenced by team offense, team defense, and the quality of a pitcher's bullpen. No other fantasy writers were doing this type of analysis at the time and presenting it in a way that fantasy leaguers could connect to."

In the late 90s, many websites were free, relying on advertising to make money. Shandler believed good content was worth paying for, and never changed his business model. Instead, he was determined to make his product even more valuable, and added more writers, analysts, and support staff. This hurt his profits, but he thought it would pay off in the long run.

Shandler was vindicated, as around 2001 the dot-com bubble burst and most of the free sites went bankrupt or switched to pay models.

According to Shandler, one key to his success was that "unlike other organizations that hired professional writers who played fantasy baseball,

I hired successful fantasy leaguers who knew how to write." Another key was that his direct marketing experience led to very successful campaigns. "You need a valuable product, but you also need to market it," he said.

BaseballHQ and the *Forecaster* continued to grow. By 2007, six editors managed more than 50 writers and analysts. Ray Murphy and Brent Hershey, who had been working as editors for several years, were taking on managerial tasks. And the *Forecaster* could be found in half of MLB front offices. But even with all these people, Shandler never opened an office. He and everyone else all worked from home.

In addition to the *Baseball Forecaster*, Shandler has published *The Minor League Baseball Analyst* every year since 2006. Patrick Davitt has hosted a BaseballHQ podcast that started in 2006 and was still active as of 2024.

First Pitch

Rick Wilton and Jim Dressel ran the *Fantasy Baseball Journal* (FBJ) and decided to hold an event called the First Annual Arizona Fall League (AFL) Scouting Trip. The AFL was held in October and November in the Phoenix area, where MLB teams would each send six of their top minor league prospects to get more development time.

For $345, participants would be able to attend a conference with top fantasy writers, have tickets to ballgames, a barbecue with AFL players and coaches, and accommodations at the Marriott Courtyard in Mesa, Arizona. What was surprising, and probably not a great business decision, is that they held it in November 1994, during the baseball strike. Many fans were angry and wanted nothing to do with baseball. The event was a flop, with 13 speakers and eight attendees. No, that's not a misprint—there were more speakers than attendees.

But Shandler was one of the speakers, and despite the horrible attendance, he felt excited just to be there. "We were 21 baseball-obsessed fantasy leaguers," he said. "Some of us happened to be writers, but we all had stories and experiences to share."

Six months later FBJ went under. Shandler had loved one of their products, which was a report called the Hot Sheet that was faxed three times a week to subscribers containing news and the "MASH" report with injury information. Shandler offered to bring the Hot Sheet and the AFL conference under the *Baseball Forecaster* umbrella. Dressel wasn't interested in staying on, but Wilton agreed. Working remotely from his home in Racine, Wisconsin, Wilton became the *BaseballHQ* news director as well as "Dr. HQ," the *BaseballHQ* injury analyst.

They didn't try another fall conference until 1996. Shandler's goal was to just break even and build from there. This time, they didn't include hotel accommodations, had only five speakers (including Shandler and Wilton) and there were 18 paid attendees—resulting in a bit of profit.

The conference was later renamed First Pitch Arizona, and attendance grew. In addition to the weekend event in November, they started running a series of three-hour-long First Pitch events in February and March throughout the country. By 2007, they offered First Pitch in 15 cities.

The Arizona weekend had become an industry destination event drawing hundreds. It was a place where industry people could network, and attendees could meet their favorite writers—maybe even sit with them at AFL games. Seminars included draft strategies, sleepers, sabermetrics, and many other topics. The local events stopped after 2019 due to declining attendance, but First Pitch Arizona has continued every year (except for 2020, due to Covid.) The 2023 event drew about 200 attendees.

Shandler sold his company to Fantasy Sports Ventures in 2008, remaining as an employee overseeing editorial and marketing. He said, "I felt that I had taken it as far as I could and needed a bigger company behind it to grow." He had also been starting to get burned out and wanted to spend more time with his family.

Fantasy Sports Ventures later sold to the *USA Today*. As of 2024, Shandler was still working in a limited capacity, primarily just writing the introduction for the *Forecaster* and having the final edit—as well as attending First Pitch events. Brent Hershey and Ray Murphy have been co-general managers since 2015. As of 2024, the *Forecaster* was still thriving as fantasy baseball's longest-running publication. More than 500,000 people have read it over the years.

Shandler's illustrious career also includes being an advisor for the St. Louis Cardinals during their 2004 season and leading the creation of the fantasy baseball experts league Tout Wars. Shandler was inducted into the FSTA and FSWA halls of fame and given an FSTA lifetime achievement award. In addition to the new metrics he invented, some of his philosophies—such as "Draft skills, not stats," and "Once you display a skill, you own it"—became common phrases used by fantasy players.

"Working with Ron has been a pleasure," Rick Wilton said. "He is one of the most sincere, caring, honest and hard-working people I've ever met. My life is so much better for having met and worked with him."

Shandler says what he enjoys the most is writing, so since selling the company and cutting back on his duties, he has done a lot of freelance work, first with a regular column in the USA *Today* from 2008-2014, then freelancing for ESPN.com until 2019 when he began writing for The Athletic. He also wrote a book, *Fantasy Expert,* released in 2024, which is partly his personal memoir and tells some of the history of the early fantasy baseball analysts who helped build the industry.

Baseball Prospectus

The work started by Shandler of connecting sabermetrics with fantasy baseball was continued by others. Baseball Prospectus (BP) launched an annual book in 1996, followed by a website in 1997. They provide original sabermetric analysis that appeals to both regular MLB fans and fantasy players. Since the beginning they have included analysis and projections for players to help with fantasy drafts. In 2000, John Hunt called it the "best book overall for preparing for a rotisserie draft." BP has a staff of columnists who provide content for the website, and BP has published other books about baseball analysis and history as well as offering podcasts.

BP was founded by Gary Huckabay, then an MBA student at the University of California, Davis. The first annual was produced on a photocopier and sold about 170 copies even though they omitted the St. Louis Cardinals. But by 2007, it reached the *New York Times* bestseller list, topping 70,000 sold. BP was still very successful as of 2024.

Fangraphs

David Appelman was in his early 20s, obsessed with fantasy baseball, and not happy with his job as an analyst for AOL. An avid reader of BaseballHQ.com, David thought he could apply his skills to fantasy. He launched FanGraphs in August 2005. The website has a mix of sabermetrics, general baseball information, and fantasy content.

The website contains statistics for every major and minor league baseball player in history. Want to see Stan Musial's statistics for every year he played, from 1941-1963? It's all there—all standard baseball stats and lots of advanced metrics. And for current MLB players, there are projections from several sources for the upcoming season, appealing to fantasy players preparing for their drafts.

After Appelman launched, traffic grew enough that he quit his day job the next summer. Over time, he started hiring writers and the website grew steadily for many years, becoming quite popular. But when Covid hit, there was a sharp decline in visitors and thus advertising revenue. Appelman cut the salaries of 10 full-time employees, including himself, and laid off more than 20 freelancers. "It was a real disaster," he said. But enough customers continued to pay for their membership, some even made donations. Appelman got a PPP loan, and FanGraphs survived. It was still as popular as ever as of 2024.

Football Sabermetrics

Long before Bill James started his baseball work, Virgil Carter, who had a master's degree from Northwestern University, was working part-time at Xavier University as a math and statistics instructor. In the spring of

1970, he called every NFL team and asked for their play-by-play logs. He spent hours and hours, helped by his wife, coding 8,373 punch cards—one for every play from the first half of the 1969 season—into an enormous computer. His goal was to get a better understanding of his day job, which was as quarterback for the Cincinnati Bengals.

Among his remarkable findings were that a team's field position was often more important than ball possession and that the position on the field helped determine the probability of a team's scoring chances. This eventually led to the football metric now known as "expected points."

And he disproved much conventional wisdom, such as why coaches should not be too conservative with play calling on their side of the field, when to go for it on fourth down, and more.

An interesting side note is that when Carter took over as their starting quarterback in 1970, assistant coach Bill Walsh completely changed the Bengals playbook to take advantage of Carter's ability to connect on short to medium passes. Walsh later became the head coach for San Francisco, and this became known as Walsh's famous "West Coast" offense.

The next crack at advanced analytics for football was a 1988 book called *The Hidden Game of Football*. It was written by Bob Carroll, John Thorn, and Pete Palmer (the same Pete Palmer who wrote about baseball sabermetrics.) In 2002 and 2003, the parent company of Baseball Prospectus worked with FootballProject.com to publish *Pro Football Prospectus*, but the books didn't contain many analytics and didn't sell well.

The Bill James of Football

Aaron Schatz grew up in Framingham, Massachusetts, a suburb of Boston, and idolized Bill James. Ironically, while earning an economics degree at Brown University, he generally skipped the one college statistics class he took because it interfered with lunch time.

In 2002, Boston sportswriter Ron Borges claimed the Patriots were losing games because they couldn't establish the run. Schatz wondered if this was true. Over Christmas vacation, he cut and pasted into a spreadsheet the play by play from ESPN.com for every single play of the entire 2002 NFL season. He found no correlation between teams winning games and how much they ran in the first quarter. Thus, the Patriots were not hurting themselves by running less often early in games.

He then wondered what he could do with all this information he had compiled. He said, "I sent it to some people I knew who had sports websites and they said this is good, but it's pretty niche, so we aren't interested. So, I decided to start my own website."

He enlisted the help of some of his former Brown University frat brothers, most of whom still played with Schatz in the fantasy football league they'd started in college, and they launched FootballOutsiders.com (FO) in July 2003. The website had a staff of writers, and offered stats, new metrics, commentary, and discussion threads.

Schatz said, "*Moneyball* came out that year and we advertised ourselves as '*Moneyball* for Football.' My timing was very lucky, because people would search the internet for '*Moneyball* for football' and we had no competitors."

But the website wasn't producing much income when the 29-year-old was laid off from his day job in February 2004. He started collecting unemployment, searching for a job, and had a 6-month-old daughter and a worried wife who was "scared as hell." But thanks to the website, Schatz started getting work writing for the *New York Sun*, *New York Times*, ESPN, AOL, and Fox. By September 2004 he was able to stop looking for another job and was off unemployment.

He was quite aware that he was trying to do for football what Bill James had done for baseball. A colleague called their system "SAFR" and "safermetrics," changing the "B" for baseball in SABR and sabermetrics to an "F" for football. Schatz however preferred to call it "my giant time-sucking hobby."

His work wasn't intended for fantasy—his objective was to look through the conventional wisdom and know why teams were winning and losing. And he made team projections. But many people asked him to do player projections and he realized he could market this to fantasy players, so in 2005 he added player projections. Although it wasn't his purpose, gamblers also found the information helpful.

His system ranks teams and players based on charting every play in every game. And he analyzes them through a complex system of situational factors. Some of his early assertions that clashed with conventional wisdom were that star running backs were overpaid and overhyped and passing was twice as important to winning as was running.

FO invented many new metrics, mostly by Schatz but some also by his staff members. One of the most important new metrics Schatz invented right away he called DVOA (defense-adjusted value over average). He looked at a concept from the *Hidden Game of Football* called "success rate" and realized it was flawed. He fixed the flaw and then adjusted it for defenses. Other new metrics include Adjusted Line Yards, DYAR (defense-adjusted yards above replacement), and the KUBIAK fantasy football projection system. By 2006 the website had gone from 30 daily readers to 10,000.

Schatz sold the company in 2018, staying on as editor-in-chief. Everything operated normally until 2023, when the new owners ran out of money and stopped paying Schatz and several writers. Schatz left FO and joined the FTN network. The FO website became inaccessible by September of 2023.

Many people have followed in Schatz's footsteps with advanced analytics, as have companies such as Pro Football Focus and Sumer-Sports.com.

21 Years Later

Schatz said, "It's amazing what's happened with the thing I still think of as my goofy little hobby—that last week of 2002 I just sat at home and did this all day. And what has happened to this in the last 20 years is astonishing."

Cynthia Frelund

Others have added new elements to even advanced metrics, such as Cynthia Frelund. After working for ESPN for four years, she joined NFL Network in 2016 as their predictive analytics expert and was still there as of 2024. She is often on such shows as NFL Fantasy Live and NFL GameDay Morning.

Frelund looks at questions such as "Tom Brady is a pocket passer, how has he done in the past against defenses like what he's going to face this week?" She will offer insights such as "The Eagles are the #1 defense against third downs. This week, they're playing the team with the league's best third-down offense. History shows that 60% of the time the team with the better third-down defense will win."

In short, she uses every bit of information she can gather, including statistics, individual matchups, coach tendencies, injuries, weather, etc., and writes her own code to generate about 10,000 computer simulations of each game. From this she can make predictions that are helpful for fantasy players, gamblers, and general NFL fans.

There are also now advanced metrics for most other sports, some of which are used by fantasy players to evaluate talent. For example, hockey's most important metric is "expected goals."

Andy Andres started teaching the first college course in baseball analytics at Tufts University in 2004, which has evolved into a large online free course offered by Boston University called "Sabermetrics 101."

CHAPTER 10

Commissioner Services

As mentioned, it was very time consuming for early roto players to calculate team stats and league standings by hand. One of the most bizarre stories to that effect comes from Dan Okrent, who during the summer of 1982 vacationed on Cuttyhunk Island, Massachusetts, for a few weeks. Every morning, he got in a rowboat and rowed himself across the harbor to the only phone on Cuttyhunk Island. He called league mate Robert Sklar who would read him all the box scores, line by line, so Okrent could compute the league stats.

As computer capabilities grew, many services sprang up in the 1980s to compute statistics and standings for fantasy leagues. They were commonly referred to as a "stat service" but over time this was generally replaced by "commissioner service." This chapter will highlight a few of the early services. One of them also created one of the largest fantasy news websites and then became the basis for NBC Sports fantasy. Another helped CBS Sports fantasy explode.

One of the earliest services was run by Jim Burger, with some help from his wife Gloria. Working from their home in Chester, Pennsylvania, they started Fastats in 1986. Initially just wanting to supplement his day job as a writing consultant, Jim went full-time in 1988. They peaked with about 120 leagues and a little over $100,000 in revenue.

On April 29, 1987, Gloria went into labor. They had planned a home birth and had a doctor and a midwife there. Unfortunately, it was a Wednesday, the day they would enter the NL stats from USA Today. But a little thing like giving birth didn't stop them. Jim recalls, "Between contractions, she was reading the stats from *USA Today*. She'd say, 'Hold on, hold on, here comes another one...'" When the momentary muscle constriction would pass, they'd continue and do another team. "We were able to get through the whole National League by 10:30 am," he said. "Brigitte was born at 3:30 in the afternoon."

Fastats never did football statistics, but they were one of the first to do the NBA. Burger started phasing out the company after the '94 World Series was canceled and the '95 season appeared to be in jeopardy. They closed in 1996.

37 Years Later

Brigitte now has a 1-year-old son and plays in a fantasy football league with her dad.

All-Star Stats

Rich Pike and Mike Oliveto were friends since high school in Westchester County, New York, just an hour north of Manhattan. After college, Pike worked in Prodigy's marketing department, and Oliveto was a systems developer for a software company.

Pike was in a roto league at Prodigy, and the two co-managed a team in a different roto league. Their league used Heath Research, one of the first large stat services. While Heath generally had a good reputation, Oliveto thought it was lacking. For one thing, it only gave customers weekly results for their team. There were no year-to-date totals for the individual players. And he thought it could be more visually appealing. He thought he could do better. So, Pike and Oliveto co-founded All-Star Stats in 1989.

The pair, in their late 20s, worked part-time at night, placed one ad in a baseball magazine, and signed 10 leagues. That winter, they decided to throw caution to the wind, quitting their jobs and going full-time for the second year, thinking, "Let's outdo everybody—let's get the biggest ads in all the major baseball publications."

Pike's mom was married to her second husband, Doug, the CEO of a large corporation. Pike got together with them to explain what he was doing, told them he and Oliveto were going to spend $10,000 on advertising, quit their jobs, and he'd like to move back into their house to save money. They said "Okay, sounds great."

(Years later, Pike's mom told him that after he left, she asked Doug, "Do you understand what he's saying?" Doug replied, "No, but he seems to know what he's talking about, so I think they'll be okay.")

Pike said, "We crossed the river and burned the boat. We weren't going back."

What they didn't anticipate was the 1990 MLB lockout. Oliveto said, "Oh my God, we just quit our jobs and baseball went on strike." Adding to the concern, Pike's wife had just become pregnant with their first child. They knew baseball would resume, but didn't know how long it would be, or how many upset fans would stop playing roto. But when MLB announced the strike was settled and the season would only be delayed by one week, they were inundated with orders. A total of 210 leagues, paying in full up front an average of $500 per league, brought in $105,000. This allowed them to buy more equipment and earn a profit.

Their office was in Pike's parents' house, taking up the family room and basement. Pike's wife, Andrea, and their new baby girl were there. Andrea worked in customer service for All-Star. (It wasn't as crowded as it sounds, since Pike's parents had a second home in Oregon where they spent most of their time.)

The third year, they moved into a real office, hired staff, and continued to grow. In 1994, they served 650 baseball leagues, with Pike, Oliveto, three other full-timers and a dozen part-timers during peak season. But the 1994 baseball strike canceled the end of the season, the playoffs, and lasted until April 1995. During that time, Pike and Oliveto had to lay off all employees.

During the '90s, some of the other big stat services were USA Stats, Roti-Stats and My Fantasy League. And there were dozens of smaller services.

John Wallwork, of Fountain Valley, California, had left his computer consulting business to start Roti-Stats. Bill Meyer, a federal prosecutor started Baltimore-based USA Stats with a partner in 1988. Three years later, his boss made him choose between being a prosecutor or running a stat service. He chose stats.

My Fantasy League (MFL) was launched in 1995 by Kevin Austin. He soon teamed up with Mike Hall and they turned MFL into a powerhouse. By 1999, they had 20,000 leagues with three employees, all in different cities. As of 2024, they were still one of the leading commissioner services.

When some of the smaller companies wanted to leave the industry, Pike and Oliveto bought their subscriber lists helping to grow All-Star. They added services for football, basketball, and hockey. At their peak, they had more than 1,000 baseball leagues per year.

By the late '90s, most leagues had transitioned from mailed and faxed reports to the internet. And they were making their own lineup changes online. This greatly lowered All-Star's production costs (while keeping their fees the same) and increased profits. The first hiccup in their growth was when SportsLine bought Commissioner.COM in 1999 and started offering a free service. This hurt All-Star's business. For the first time in 10 years, their volume decreased rather than growing. But they still had enough leagues to be profitable.

In 1997, RotoNews (which later became RotoWire) launched, quickly becoming the largest provider of online fantasy news. Pike and Oliveto thought they'd make great partners for a joint venture. All-Star could offer news to their clients and RotoNews could offer a stat service. They proposed the idea to RotoNews president Peter Schoenke. When Schoenke replied he wasn't interested, they were astonished. They thought they had a perfect match. They hung up the phone and Oliveto said, "Well, I guess that's the end of that." But Pike replied, "Fuck them, we'll do it ourselves."

Pike's dad, Charlie, about 65 and retired, had always been a huge Yankee fan and statistics fan. When he was young, he would listen to Yankee games on the radio, score the game, and check the newspaper the next day to make sure the paper had the accurate box score. He had also been playing rotisserie for several years in his son's two leagues.

Pike told his dad they were starting a news service and were looking for someone to write player blurbs. Charlie volunteered. They launched RotoWorld.com, in 1998. Charlie wrote most of the player notes, with Pike and Oliveto also helping. The news was also displayed on the All-Star stats pages and provided subscribers with a link to get news on players on their team.

In 1999, they hired Matthew Pouliot to write columns, working remotely from his home in Pensacola, Florida. In January 2000, Pouliot took over writing all player notes by himself. He was at his computer all day, watching games on TV, looking at box scores online and scouring news services, local papers, everything he could find. Oliveto said Pouliot loved it and never wanted to leave his keyboard.

Typically working 14-to-16-hour days, seven days a week, Pouliot wrote about 100 player updates per day, covering the NFL, MLB, and NBA, including how a player did in a game that day, injury news, trades, etc.

"It was just my life," Pouliot explained. "I was a 21-year-old college dropout, living with my father, when I started. I usually went to bed around 3 a.m. On a good night, I'd watch a movie to unwind after the final MLB recaps were out. From 2000 to spring 2004, I had one day off when I was moving. Finally, by 2004-05, I had quite a bit more help and was mostly focusing on baseball. The saving grace is that sports news wasn't as much of a 24/7 thing back then. This was both pre-Twitter and pre-blogs. So, you didn't need to monitor Twitter all day long. It allowed me to both do news and continue to put out columns or work on a draft guide—I don't think that'd be possible today."

RotoWorld exploded very quickly, organically, without promoting the website. They initially had just wanted to provide news for their subscribers, but it became so popular they started selling advertising and it was extremely profitable. In 2003, they added Gregg Rosenthal to handle the NFL notes. (Rosenthal went on to become a star on the NFL Network.) Rick Cordella was hired as general manager in 2003 and helped grow RotoWorld. As time went on, they added more columnists, draft guides, depth charts, and more.

When Pike had worked for Prodigy, he became friends with co-worker Rick Wolf, who joined Pike's Roto league. This was Wolf's first experience in fantasy sports. Wolf had left Prodigy and became CBS Sportslines general manager of fantasy sports. He hadn't spoken to Pike in quite a while, but when Wolf left SportsLine in 2001 he contacted Pike and that led to Wolf joining All-Star. Pike and Oliveto appointed him their Executive Vice President of Strategic Partnerships.

Wolf created more than 20 partnerships, including with USA Today, FOX Sports, NHL, MLB, Head2Head Sports, and many others. They white-labeled games and provided content for all of them. Among other things, they built the software for MLB's Beat the Streak game. All-Star also began a partnership with Sandbox.com, which included a triggered buyout. By 2006, their office in Somers, New York, an hour north of Manhattan, had Pike, Oliveto, Wolf, Cordella, six customer service reps, and four programmers. Another 20 or so worked remotely, part-time or full-time, writing player notes, columns, and other content.

That year, NBC bought the rights to broadcast NFL games, and they didn't have a digital fantasy strategy. Some of the NBC executives knew people at the Arena Football League (AFL) and asked for recommendations on who could do their fantasy football. Sandbox had been running the AFL fantasy games, so they put NBC in touch with Wolf.

All-Star got the contract to build the NBC fantasy website, but before the 2006 football season even started, NBC decided to buy All-Star, which included RotoWorld and Sandbox. The buyout for Sandbox was triggered, and All-Star bought Sandbox the same day they sold everything to NBC. Sandbox offered 25 games in nine sports. According to Wolf, "NBC loved the RotoWorld web traffic."

Their offices were moved to an NBC sports office in Stanford, Connecticut. Since it wasn't far from Somers, all employees stayed on. All-Star, Sandbox and RotoWorld became the fantasy department for NBC. Pike and Oliveto worked for NBC for one year, and then left the fantasy industry.

Wolf ran NBC's digital business development until 2011. Pouliot, still working from Florida, and a couple of programmers were still with RotoWorld as of 2024. Cordella worked his way up to become the President of Sports Programming for NBC Sports and Peacock. NBC later shut down All-Star Stats, since the industry was shifting more and more to free services being offered by the likes of ESPN, SportsLine and Yahoo. They also quickly closed Sandbox, whose revenues had been declining. In 2021, they briefly changed the name from RotoWorld to NBC Sports Edge, later changing to simply NBC Sports.

35 Years Later

According to Oliveto, soon after the sale to NBC, there was a Jeopardy question "If you play fantasy sports, you use this website" and the answer "What is RotoWorld?" Oliveto said, "You know you hit the big time if you're a Jeopardy question."

"Looking back, we were in the right place at the right time," said Pike. "We were lucky to get in early, just when roto was taking off."

Pike and Oliveto have been best friends since high school. They still talk almost every day. As of 2024, Pike's Prodigy roto league was still going, with five of the original owners still playing. Ironically their league now uses the free ESPN commissioner service.

Pike's dad, Charlie, is 91 and still plays in those two roto leagues. He is obsessed with Shohei Ohtani, who is on his AL-only team, and stays up until 2 a.m. watching the Angels' West Coast games. He won the 2023 league title, despite Ohtani being on the injured list for the last month.

Real Time Fantasy Sports

After graduating from Ohio State University, Mark Hanna moved to St. Louis and started a job as a software engineer at McDonnell

Douglass (now Boeing) in 1987. He also joined the company's fantasy football league. (Meanwhile, a co-worker he didn't know, Brian Matthews, was playing in the company fantasy baseball league and then co-founded CDM.)

In 1993, he was learning an internet program and started posting league results on the company intranet so everyone could see them. The next year, he added more to the software and made it flexible so different leagues could use it, they could change rules, and he added different report options. He put this on the regular internet. He didn't advertise, but people found it through searches, asked him questions and made requests to add things.

Hanna researched fantasy football and realized it was already around the world with thousands of leagues. He searched and couldn't find any commissioner services. Realizing with the internet this could be a goldmine, he decided to start a business. In 1995, he launched Real Time Fantasy Sports. (His brother was a 50% owner, but he wasn't involved except as an investor.)

They quickly needed another engineer, more servers, and customer support. They doubled or tripled their customer base each year until 1999, when SportsLine went free with their commissioner service. They still grew, but only at a 30% rate. When SportsLine announced in 2001 that they were going back to a paid service, Hanna ran out and bought more servers.

In 2007, after the UIGEA deemed fantasy games legal (Chapter 17), RT Sports started offering their own games. They also added fantasy baseball and later basketball. As of 2024, they were still very successful almost 30 years later, offering games and commissioner services for thousands of customers.

"Now 75-80% of commissioner services are free," Hanna noted. "We were lucky to get into the business just in time."

Commissioner.COM

Peter Pezaris, Michael Gersh, James Price, and Scott Harger were frater-
nity brothers who had graduated from Carnegie Mellon University, and
later all got jobs in Manhattan. One night in August 1995, they were at
a local bar talking about what they would do if they had as much money
as Bill Gates. They realized instead of just talking about it, they should
do it. So that night they decided to start a business while keeping their
day jobs. They called it Daedalus Worldwide Corporation.

They created an online restaurant guide that wasn't successful. Next
came a Java-based billing system. Didn't work, either. By then, more
than a year had passed. A fifth partner, attorney Matt Fortnow, had
joined them. During this year, they also consulted and built websites
for anyone who wanted to have an online presence. A fantasy baseball
player contacted them to build a website that would make it easier for
him to share the standings with league mates. He said he would still
calculate results himself.

Pezaris had played one year of fantasy football and asked his commissioner how long he spent doing everything. The commissioner said
it took him about eight hours per week. So Pezaris and his buddies
thought, "What if we do all that work for the commissioner? Owners
can set their own lineups rather than having to call the commissioner.
We can calculate the stats and put up the standings. And this can all
be done online."

The five partners planned all this in one night, November 25, 1996.
After a year of failed attempts, they were feeling virtually certain this
would work. It would be a valuable commodity to offer fantasy players.
At the time, there were already fantasy stat services that charged about
$300 per season. The partners decided to also charge $300 per season,
but they would make it much better than what was currently available,
and it would be the first online.

They assumed they had a few months to prepare before the baseball
season, but two days later learned the back page of *Fantasy Sports* magazine—the largest circulating fantasy magazine—was available. Although

they had just gotten the idea, and hadn't written a line of code, they were so confident they took it. Not only that, but the ad needed to be submitted in 24 hours. They had to create the name of the company, artwork, and ad copy. They designed the ad stating they would update stats daily—they accepted American Express, Visa and Mastercard—and promised other things they hadn't set up yet.

With each contributing $2,000, they had a total budget of $10,000. This ad cost $5,400. Then they put an ad on Yahoo, which was the dominant search engine at the time. For $1,500, anytime someone typed in "fantasy baseball" their ad would come up. They grabbed it. But this ad started January 1, meaning they only had one month to build everything.

They launched Commissioner.COM as the ball dropped in Times Square to ring in 1997. To accomplish this in just one month, Pezaris—while still working his day job at Banker's Trust—slept only one hour a night. Pezaris said, "This sounds like hyperbole, but it isn't—I worked all day, every day, about 23 hours. Once we launched, I allowed myself three hours of sleep a night, because we had to get ready for the baseball season."

The first week that the Yahoo ad came out only brought two visitors to their website. But there was a day in late February when they sold five leagues, and that's when Pezaris became confident they would succeed. Soon after that, Pezaris was walking to his desk at Banker's Trust one day and collapsed, just from sheer exhaustion. He said, "It was a struggle for me to get up and get back to my desk, and that's when I knew I couldn't do this anymore."

Gersh, who had also been working extreme hours, suggested Pezaris go to the bathroom at work and take a power nap. Pezaris tried this. He sat in a stall, leaning his head against the toilet paper holder. After a 20-minute nap, he felt great. He went to the sink to wash his hands, and saw in the mirror, imprinted in his forehead "If roll is empty, slide cover to right." Knowing he couldn't keep doing this, and confident after having gotten five sales in one day, he gave his boss two weeks' notice.

Many tried to talk him out of it. His mom couldn't believe his "crazy decision" to quit his high-paying job for a start-up with no money and no investors. And it *was* incredibly risky. Pezaris couldn't afford to pay his rent if he quit his job. The partners made a deal: James Price would keep working and would pay to rent an office. Gersh and Pezaris would quit their jobs, give up their apartments and move into the office. And Price gave them each $1,000 per month to live on.

Pezaris was the software developer while Gersh handled business aspects such as vendors and marketing. The office was in a building that probably should have been condemned. There was no heat, no hot water. Every day, they each took a 30-second freezing-cold shower. They slept next to their computers as it was the only source of heat, sometimes being woken up by a mouse scurrying across their face. They ate 99-cent Whoppers to make their $1,000-per-month stipend work.

But it paid off. That first baseball season, there were 200 paid customers, at $300 each. And then 100 subscribers for football. The following year, baseball increased to 800 leagues. Whatever requests were made by customers, they built. This set them apart from competitors such as ESPN and SportsLine, who only had one set of rules that people could play. They were able to move to a new office that was small, but in good condition.

Pezaris had quit his day job to get more sleep, but that didn't happen. "It was three hours of sleep a night for the first three years of Commissioner.COM—and no weekends off," he said. He had no social life and only took a day off for Christmas.

During the second year, Harger left the company, but another friend from Carnegie Mellon, David Hersh, joined them. During that second year, they realized the big companies such as ESPN and SportsLine—despite having inferior software— would be able to dominate the industry due to their ability to get huge advertising. They decided to try and get a partnership with someone big. They contacted all the major networks and sports sites. CBS SportsLine was the only one to respond with any interest.

Rick Wolf was the SportsLine GM of fantasy sports then, and explains, "One day Gersh sent me a note basically telling me how bad our commissioner stinks and how we need his. We looked and realized he was right."

Commissioner.COM allowed users to create a new league—complete with its own website, chat room, and news ticker—in just a few minutes. The program would automatically update each team's statistics, e-mail them to each owner, and post them on the league's unique website. Leagues could be customized to adapt to any set of league rules and included unique features such as a scrolling news ticker. Leagues could also conduct their entire draft live online. (When the Kings X league looked for a service, they chose Commissioner.COM because they could adapt to their unique rules.)

Wolf came to their office for a meeting. SportsLine.com was about to relaunch their website with a new look and feel. Wolf showed them a sneak peek of what it was going to look like. When Wolf and Gersh went into a conference room to talk, Pezaris changed the design of Commissioner.COM to make it look like the new SportsLine. When Wolf came back out, Pezaris showed him and Wolf asked, "How'd you get access to SportsLine?" Pezaris said, "No, this is Commissioner.COM. This is what it would look like if we did a deal. We could make it look like this." Wolf was impressed.

They created a partnership. Starting with the 1998 fantasy football season, CBS SportsLine Commissioner.COM was born. They used the Commissioner.COM software over the SportsLine infrastructure. Their deal called for the price to drop from $300 to $100 per league. And there was a revenue share on subscriptions and advertising income. (Commissioner.COM had never had advertising on their own website.) With the added exposure from SportsLine, their second year of football brought in about 1,000 leagues.

The following year, they dropped the $100 charge, made it free, and it exploded. They had 10,000 football leagues. It became the dominant business for CBSSportsline.com. One month, their check was for $500,000, at which point SportsLine wanted to buy them. On December 7, 1999, CBSSportsline.com bought Commissioner.COM for $46 million. It was a life-changing moment. Pezaris said, "When

I checked my bank balance that day, I half expected to see $12, or whatever, in my checking account. But there were a lot of zeros. It was the most surreal thing."

The five co-owners all went to work for SportsLine. They were allowed to remain in their Manhattan offices, but later SportsLine CEO Mike Levy tried to convince them to move to Florida. Pezaris assumed everyone liked living in Manhattan, but to his surprise 14 of the 16 staff members wanted to go to Florida. They moved into the SportsLine building in Fort Lauderdale. (Fortnow stayed in Manhattan and stopped working for SportsLine.)

After offering the service free for two years, advertising revenue slowed, and they began charging again. (This was happening all over the industry as advertising slowdowns caused many companies to change from free to a paid model.) Customers had experienced how superior their commissioner service was and they converted about 30% to paying customers. The change netted $9 million from fantasy football and $11 million in overall fantasy revenue. By 2003, it increased to about $15 million in subscription revenue.

SportsLine was one of the leaders in the industry, offering fantasy products for MLB.com, NFL.com, NBA.com, AOL, Excite (a search engine at the time), Netscape and others. They worked with India-based Cric Info to offer fantasy cricket. Although people could only play this game if they lived in the US, 55,000 people signed up the first day. And they worked with a company in the United Kingdom to offer fantasy soccer.

Elias Sports and STATS were the two sources at the time for statistics, but SportsLine thought they were slow and had limited detail. So around 2000, SportsLine hired dozens of people to watch the games on DirecTV in their Fort Lauderdale headquarters and built software that allowed them to key in what happened, and they published the stats. They were able to have fantasy games and league stats update in as little as six seconds after a play was completed on the field. This was ground-breaking. While you once had to wait several days to get a report in the mail, or for your commissioner to calculate everything, now you could see your league standings updated in real time. They used two people per game to make sure they agreed with each other. This started with the NFL, then MLB, college football, the NBA and NHL.

Tony Fernandez was SportsLine's lead software developer for several years and was the one primarily responsible for inventing this live scoring. In 2019, he (and Sportsline) was given the FSTA's Matthew Berry Game Changer Award for this. He has continued to have a brilliant career and as of 2024 had been the lead software engineer for My Fantasy League since 2015.

At one point, the website had 3.5 billion page views, with most coming from the live scoring during the football season. Wolf said gamblers and fantasy players would spend 10 straight hours online on Sundays. Wolf also said, "Our research showed that 54% of the surfers on our site were fantasy players."

Pezaris, Price, Gersh, and Hersh stayed with SportsLine, having fun, until 2003 when they got the itch to start something new and left. In 2004, they were inducted into the FSTA Hall of Fame.

The new venture they started in 2003 was Multiply, a social networking site Pezaris refers to as "Facebook meeting Etsy." It became very popular, particularly in southeast Asia. By 2009, more than 20 million visited per month. They sold it in 2010 for about $100 million. Two more successful start-ups followed. Pezaris, Price, Gersh and Hersh met at Carnegie Mellon in 1986. For 37 years, they worked together in these four start-up companies.

"The biggest key to my success was the team," Pezaris said. "We couldn't have done it without each other." Looking back, Pezaris says the early years launching Commissioner.COM "was the most intense period of my life and the most satisfying. And I could not have done it without my partners being shoulder to shoulder, in the trenches. We felt like we were going through war together."

Just prior to getting the idea for Commissioner.COM, Pezaris and Gersh took a vacation to Greece. Gersh took a picture of a large yacht off the coast, and they put this as the desktop image on their computers for motivation, thinking, "One day we will be on a yacht in Greece."

After Commissioner.COM was sold, Pezaris took his first vacation since launching it. He went back to Greece and rented a yacht. When Multiply sold, he took another vacation to Greece and was able to locate and rent the exact yacht in the picture. He continued the tradition of the Greece vacation and renting a yacht after selling the third and fourth start-ups, and now owns a vacation home in Mykonos.

How Stat Services Get the Stats

When the very first stat services started, they had to input stats from *USA Today*, or other newspapers. With the advent of technology, the stat services could start buying the information from sources such as the Elias Sports Bureau and later STATS, Inc.

STATS, Inc.

John Dewan grew up on the South Side of Chicago, becoming interested in baseball and statistics while listening to White Sox games on the radio and playing Strat-O-Matic with friends. He also attended White Sox games. "We never missed a bat-day doubleheader," he said. "It was the main source of my baseball equipment growing up."

Dewan graduated from Loyola University, went on a mission in Central America for three months and then settled into a career as an actuary. He played Strat-O-Matic at lunch with a co-worker. One day, the co-worker gave Dewan the *Bill James Baseball Abstract*, and everything changed. "Bill James was doing baseball analytics with baseball statistics in the same way that I was doing insurance analytics with insurance statistics," Dewan recalled. "That was the turning point of my career. I knew that I could have much more fun working with baseball numbers than I could working with insurance numbers."

A couple years later, when Bill James announced the creation of Project Scoresheet, Dewan said "It was like I was in a trance...I knew I had to do this." He immediately called directory assistance in Lawrence, Kansas, to get James's number. Within a week, he was a volunteer scoring games, and within a month, he was the designated programmer writing the code to input the scoresheets. Within a few months, he was the executive director of the entire project and coordinated the effort around the country. "It was like having a second full-time job," Dewan said. "Fortunately, I had passed all my actuarial exams. So, instead of studying for exams in my spare time, I started coordinating the computerization of baseball data."

A company called Sports Team Analysis and Tracking Systems, Inc (STATS) was the first company that provided advanced, play-by-play-based data to MLB teams, but they folded in 1984. Dick Cramer was the guy who created their software and still had it. He contacted Bill James, who set up a meeting that included Dewan. Dewan and his wife, Sue, along with James, invested cash and they co-founded and relaunched STATS in 1985. Dewan became its president.

Their first two clients were the White Sox and Yankees. Sue was an IT manager at a bank and had great computer skills. After starting part-time for STATS, she quit her job in 1986 to go full-time. The next year Dewan quit his day job. He and Sue would stop at Dunkin Donuts to pick up breakfast, go to the office, eat a lunch they had brought with them, go home for dinner, then return to the office until it was time to go to bed. "It was 24/7, getting STATS going," Dewan said. He and James resigned from Project Scoresheet that year.

When 33-year-old Dewan had started as an actuary in 1976, he made $11,000. With raises, his salary was $85,000 when he quit in 1987. That year, they made a deal between STATS, Project Scoresheet, and a Florida company called Sports News Network. In October, there was a Black Monday stock market crash. The owner of Sports News Network disappeared and didn't pay what they owed. Dewan called the owners' secretary and she said, "I don't know where he is. He owes me money, too." That ruined what would have been a somewhat profitable year, and Dewan's 1987 income was $11,000—the same as when he started in 1976.

It was times of uncertainty like this when Sue would tell Dewan, "Keep paying your actuarial club dues—keep your status as an actuary, in case this doesn't go well."

In 1987, Dewan had a conversation with his first employee, Carmen Corica, that went something like this:

Corica: "John, you gotta play fantasy baseball, it's so much fun!"

Dewan: "Our mission is to provide professional information. We can't be playing games."

Corica: "I'm gonna make you co-owner of my team!"

After two months of running the team with Corica, Dewan said, "It was a revelation. Not only was it fun, but it was good because it made me aware of the individual players, not just the teams." In 1988, Dewan ran his own fantasy team. STATS started providing statistics to fantasy game operators and, before long, had 20 clients.

Dewan decided to create his own fantasy game. He spoke to Bill James and said, "I've been playing fantasy baseball. It's really cool, but it's not very realistic because stolen bases are overvalued and other things—but we could make something more realistic, would you be interested in helping us develop a game?" James replied, "Yeah, I think so." A few weeks later, he sent Dewan a 40-page dissertation on how every aspect of the game would work. Dewan said, "He came up with a game that was as realistic as could be based on the stats that existed at that time."

Changes from standard roto included drafting two players from each position, one multi-position player, five starting pitchers and three relievers. Of these 25 players, 20 would be active. The scoring system awarded points for runs, RBIs, etc. rather than ranking teams in each category. Defensive stats counted and there were daily transactions.

Dewan launched Bill James Fantasy Baseball in 1989. They set up a call center for players to call in transactions every night of the season. The game had some success for several years, peaking at about 1,000 participants, but wasn't the type of format most people liked and eventually folded.

In 1989, STATS landed a deal to provide information to USA Today, and the Associated Press a year later. STATS started having people in press boxes at every MLB game to collect data. For football, basketball, and hockey, most of the information was collected by people watching games on TV at home. They later added college sports.

STATS started in a spare bedroom office in the Dewan's home, and the next year a small office outside the home—every year as they kept growing, they added more office space. Sue stopped working after having her second child in 1993. Cramer worked part-time until about 1996. It took almost 10 years for Dewan to get back to the $85,000 salary he had when he left his job. In 1997 Steve Byrd was hired to oversee their fantasy business, and later became the Co-COO of STATS.

STATS became the leading producer of real-time and advanced statistics, providing data to every major media outlet, such as the AP, ESPN, Fox Sports, and others. They powered new, exotic box-score presentations and provided detailed pitch-by-pitch accounts of every event on the field. By 2000, STATS had about 100 employees and was sold to Rupert Murdoch and Fox News. Dewan stayed on for a year. It has continued to grow, acquiring many companies, such as SportVU, PA Sportsticker, NFFC/NFBC, Bloomberg Sports, The Sports Network and Automated Insights.

As of 2024, it was truly a global giant. STATS collects and processes massive amounts of sports data that covers over 300 leagues across the world, including the NBA, FIFA, the NFL, and MLB. It distributes the information to more than 500 clients, such as the NBA, Google, Yahoo, Duke University and NBC. It's all collected in real-time for approximately 83,000 games annually.

After a brief stint with Fox, and after his no-compete expired, Dewan subsequently co-founded another company, Sports Info Solutions, specializing in analytical services for most of the 30 MLB teams. Dewan is also the author of four editions of *The Fielding Bible*, which revolutionized defensive baseball analytics. It resulted in defensive changes on the field, such as "the shift," and evaluation of players with new metrics such as Defensive Runs Saved. Dewan is also a board member of Strat-O-Matic.

37 Years Later

"Probably the biggest thing we did was to make a major investment in gathering data on a live basis," Dewan explained. "Now, when you go on the internet, you can see box scores in progress. You can look at any game in any sport and see statistically what's going on in the game up to the minute. That was something we invented back in the early '90s."

CHAPTER 11

Fantasy Radio and TV Shows

It has been reported that the first ever fantasy sports radio show was started by Lenny Melnick and Irwin Zwilling in 1993. And this chapter was originally going to begin with that statement. However, in my interviews with Greg Ambrosius (Chapter 7) he mentioned that his company bought airtime in 1992 to promote their new Fantasy Baseball magazine.

For $16,000, they bought one-hour shows, twice a week, for eight weeks, on the American Radio Network. It ran from January to March 1992. Ambrosius hosted the show from his mobile home in Wisconsin, had no guests on the show, and took calls from all over the country about fantasy baseball.

And interviewing Emil Kadlec (also Chapter 7), I learned that he and his partner, Bill Robertson, asked a local radio station called the Sports Animal if they could do a fantasy football show. Starting September 1992, it aired every Sunday night at 9 p.m. for the NFL season, just in their local Albuquerque area. They took calls, and occasionally had beat writers from various cities as guests. Being at a sports radio station, they had access to the ticker. Many people would call to ask how their players did. It took too much of their time, so they only did it for the one year.

If you want to add qualifiers such as "first radio show that lasted more than 16 weeks" or "first show that covered all fantasy sports," then Melnick and Zwilling would qualify as the first. Regardless, they had an illustrious career that also included television.

When Melnick was 9 years old, he loved baseball and decided "nobody's going to ever know more about baseball than me." As an adult, he started a company that manufactured corrugated boxes on Long Island. Once a year, he would travel to Manhattan to see his CPA, Irwin Zwilling, and get his taxes done. They also talked baseball. During the 1984 visit, Zwilling told Melnick about an article he had read in *The New York Times* about Rotisserie baseball. The following spring, Zwilling found someone he knew who had a league, and Melnick and Zwilling partnered on a team.

They started speaking on the phone every night, going through the box scores, looking at who was batting second, who was batting fifth, who was stealing bases, how many pitches guys threw. And they always said, quite seriously, their conversations should be a radio show. They would go to a newsstand in Manhattan two or three times a week, buy all the newspapers from across America, take out the sports sections, throw the rest out—and load them into a pick-up truck. They read every paper looking for any information that might help them.

As mentioned elsewhere in this book, back in those days Roto players would call clubs' PR offices for info, and often were hung up on because it was assumed they were bookies, or fantasy geeks. But Melnick outsmarted them. He said, "I had a secretary, Rosalee, she would call and tell them, 'I'm going to the game Saturday, and I noticed Jerome Kersey's name wasn't in the box score yesterday. I was wondering if he's going to play, because I don't want to go to the game if he's not going to play.' And they would say, 'Hold on, Sweetie,' and come back with the answer. Not only did they give her the information, but they even called her Sweetie—whereas they would have hung up on me."

For eight years, Melnick and Zwilling continued to speak on the phone every night—even in the off-seasons—talking baseball and managing their team. Melnick also joined as many other leagues as he could find—about 20 total, mostly baseball, but also a few football, hockey, and basketball leagues. It's not that he was that fanatical about fantasy sports, it's that he realized it was good for business. There was a common bond with league mates, so when they found out he sold boxes, many would become customers.

One year, Zwilling went to spring training in Florida. The White Sox trainer, Herm Schneider, was a friend of Zwilling's. Zwilling was a racquetball player but had terrible tendonitis. He asked Schneider for help, and Schnieder said, "Sure, come to my office at the stadium around 7 o'clock, nobody will be here."

Zwilling was on the trainer's table, face down, Schneider working on him, and someone burst through the door, shouting, "Where's Zwilling?! Where's Zwilling?!

It was White Sox first baseman Greg Walker, and he was very angry. He told Zwilling, "Herm told me I only went for $1 in your league!"

Zwilling, a bit stunned, replied meekly, "Well, Greg...you didn't have the best year last year."

Still angry, Walker said, "Well, they're gonna regret it!"

Except for that brief show by Ambrosius and the one-year-only football show in Albuquerque by Kadlec and Robertson, there were no radio shows dedicated to fantasy sports at the time. Some shows might mention fantasy sports, such as Jody MacDonald's show on WFAN in the late '80s, which included a fantasy baseball segment, but it was primarily just his reading the late-night box scores at 1 a.m. (Melnick would set his alarm to listen.)

Melnick saw an ad in his local newspaper where WGBB 1240AM offered "Do your own radio show." Melnick, 46, and Zwilling, 44, along with friend and league mate Sandy Stolle, signed up for 16 weeks, at a cost of $200 per week for a one-hour show. In August 1993, with no prior radio experience or training, they launched The Rotisserie Hour. And they found the perfect sponsor—Roto Rooter—who paid them $300 a week.

Just four minutes into their first show, they got their first call. Mike, from Valley Stream, asked, "Who will be the starting quarterback for the Atlanta Falcons, Bobby Hebert or Chris Miller?"

Then Nick, in West Hempstead, wanted to know if they thought Billy Swift would win the NL Cy Young award.

And the calls kept coming: A question about Barry Bonds...a woman who wanted sleeper picks for her fantasy football draft...about the

Astros closer situation...what software to buy to run a roto baseball league...and more. And the three hosts had the answers and opinions for everything.

The commercial breaks included ads from Strat-O-Matic, a fantasy sports stats service, local restaurants, and, of course, Roto Rooter. (Hal Richman, owner of Strat-O-Matic, was already a customer of Melnick's box business. Melnick would often hang out with the guys at Richman's office and play Strat-O-Matic with them.)

Melnick's business was 20 minutes from the studio, and he had a 1-800 number. He would forward calls to the radio station, providing listeners with a toll-free number. Zwilling knew Phil Mushnick, sports columnist for the New York Post, and told him about the show. Mushnick said he'd listen and write about it. But Zwilling was concerned about his professional reputation, and told him, "I'm an accountant, do me a favor—if you have something bad to say, don't write it, just tell me and I'll quit the show."

Mushnick subsequently called Zwilling and said, "You guys are terrific! It's so much fun listening to three men talking about baseball like kids." He wrote a very positive column about the show. And they were mentioned by other columnists such as Bob Raissman of the Daily News and Steve Zipay of Newsday. Zipay subsequently became a frequent guest on the show.

Stolle was only on the show briefly, as it took up too much of his time. So, it became just Melnick and Zwilling. They invited John Hunt, the USA Today Baseball Weekly columnist, to be a guest. He mentioned the show in his column several times, and it was a huge boost to their listenership. Hunt also invited Melnick and Zwilling to be in the 1994 inaugural USA Today LABR experts league. They invited other writers on the show, knowing they would probably mention it in their columns. People called in from all over the country, even though most couldn't even hear the station. A few people called just to be able to hear the show while waiting on hold.

Melnick and Zwilling were having fun hosting the show. And it was good for Melnick's business, since he would invite his customers' kids on the show to make football picks. The kids would call him "Uncle Lenny." It solidified relationships with his customers.

One night, Melnick forgot to go back to his office after the show and cancel the call forwarding. The next day's morning show was full of calls like "Joe from Staten Island, you're on the air!"

"Yeah, where are my boxes?"

Ann Liguori hosted a call-in sports show on WFAN, the nation's first sports talk radio channel, that reached to Florida, Canada, and the Midwest. She invited Melnick and Zwilling to be on her Friday overnight show and they became frequent guests for two years. "They were incredibly passionate and enthusiastic about baseball," Liguori said.

For Melnick, it was a "dream come true. I listened to WFAN all the time, and now I was sitting in Don Imus's seat."

Zwilling compared it to "just beginning to learn how to play the piano and then going straight to Carnegie Hall."

Zwilling had many clients in the sports and entertainment industries and thus was an active member of the National Association for Television Program Executives. At one of their conventions, Jeff Belafonte, the president of Phoenix Communications, told Zwilling he'd heard them on the radio and was intrigued by fantasy baseball. Zwilling said, totally joking, "You guys are the production company for MLB, why don't you put us on TV?"

Belafonte replied, "You know, that's not a bad idea."

Several weeks later, Zwilling's wife thought he was joking when he told her a camera crew was coming to their house to do a screen test in their basement. After passing their screen test, Melnick recalls, "They set up a meeting in Manhattan at this fancy restaurant, and their lawyers are there, and Irwin and I are two schmucks from New York who don't even know what we are doing on the radio—all we know is we love baseball..."

This resulted in their being given weekly three-minute segments on Pennant Chase with Fran Healy in 1997. Healy would introduce them with "And now for the fantasy baseball report, we welcome Lenny Melnick and Irwin Zwilling." The segments were pre-recorded—sometimes in Zwilling's basement—but mostly at locations such as Yankee Stadium, Shea Stadium, and the All-Star Café. They were on every week for a couple of years.

In 1997, MLB sent them to the All-Star game in Cleveland to do a fantasy baseball seminar at Fan Fest. They were billed as the featured event. Chairs were set up for 500 people. More than 1,000 attended. They expected to get questions about how to play fantasy baseball, but these people apparently knew how to play because they asked questions like "Who's the back-up second baseman for the Reds?" and "Is anyone good coming up from AAA?"

Zwilling said everyone in the audience had their heads down, writing notes. Afterwards many stood in line to take pictures and get their autographs. "Half of them probably had no idea who we were," Zwilling said. "The more we did this, the more we realized Rotisserie is not something that is going to go away."

Pennant Chase's sister show was This Week in Baseball with Ozzie Smith. Melnick and Zwilling did a few fantasy segments for the show while in Cleveland.

During this time, they stopped the WGBB show. Coming up with new information every week for both TV and radio proved to be too much to handle. And for Zwilling, it was very difficult getting from Manhattan to Long Island for WGBB, especially during tax season and the bad weather winter.

They were asked to consult for an episode of the HBO series *Arliss*, starring Robert Wuhl. In the episode, one of Arliss's friends, a surgeon, would take breaks and make fantasy baseball trades from his operating room. Wuhl loved fantasy baseball and came on their radio show once.

The next stop on Melnick and Zwilling's fantastic journey came in 2001 when MLB.com was ready to launch a fantasy baseball radio show, to be called Fantasy 411, and they wanted the pair to host. But at a meeting to discuss the opportunity, they learned the show would be broadcast from Manhattan on Mondays, Wednesdays, and Fridays at noon. A dejected Melnick returned to his office and informed his three female employees he couldn't do the show because he'd have to travel from Long Island to Manhattan three days a week in the middle of the workday.

The ladies went to lunch and returned with a message: "You do the show, we will handle the office—if you turn this down it will haunt you for the rest of your life."

Melnick said, "It was one the nicest things anyone ever did for me."

They did the show from 2001-2002.

In 2009, SiriusXM started a fantasy sports channel and hired Melnick and Zwilling to host a show. "That was a pretty amazing experience," Zwilling said, "watching calls come in from Germany and everywhere."

Melnick had sold his box business in the early 2000s, but Zwilling was still a CPA. It became too much for Zwilling to handle and he retired after a couple of years. Melnick remained on SiriusXM for 13 years. The final two years, he co-hosted a show with his girlfriend Andrea Lamont, called Lady and the Legend. Melnick also started his own podcast on BlogTalkRadio in 2005 and has had a podcast ever since. Listeners think he's in a studio somewhere, but he's usually sitting in his living room in his underwear.

Melnick started radio with no experience or formal training, but he learned how to be successful. Among his keys to success: Begin with an attention grabber, no chitchat about "How was your weekend?"; have energy; and talk about things others don't talk about (he finds those things by continuing to read the out-of-town papers). And most importantly, he has always had a lot of fun.

ESPN Pay-Per-View Special

On March 29, 1994, ESPN, and Time Warner Sports partnered to air *ESPN Baseball Tonight's Great Rotisserie Pay-Per-View Special*. The two-hour show was hosted by Keith Olbermann and Peter Gammons. Some 25,000 people paid $20 to hear an array of experts discuss players and the upcoming season for two hours. Included were John Benson, Alex

Patton, Paul White, Rod Beaton, Glen Waggoner, Bill James, Greg Ambrosius, and several others.

The show wasn't repeated in 1995, since MLB had gone on strike at the end of 1994 and it wasn't settled until April 2, 1995.

First National Fantasy TV Show

Prime Sports Network (PSN) was a group of regional sports networks owned by Liberty Media. In the early 1990s, Brad Mumm joined their R+D team and was asked to develop an interactive television show. His task was to create a show such that Prime Sports regionals would be one of the few channel's viewers would want to keep coming back to.

He started to hear more and more people talk about fantasy sports and noticed how passionate they were about it. Mumm had always believed that where there's passion, there's opportunity. He got the idea of starting a fantasy game and complimenting it with a TV show. He recruited help to develop fantasy games for football and baseball and advertised on the back covers of many sports magazines.

Debuting in 1994, the TV show was co-hosted by Norm Hitzges, a Dallas area radio icon, and Rick Korch, of *Pro Football Weekly*. It was produced at PSN's studio in Irving, Texas, and aired to 12 million homes on affiliates all over the country. In 1995, they started weekly 30-minute shows, with Steve Silverman, a senior editor for *Pro Football Weekly* replacing Korch as co-host. The shows would recap the prior week's fantasy action and help prepare people for the next week's lineup decisions. PSN also used the shows to pitch its own games.

In 1996, Fox entered a joint venture with Liberty, acquiring 50% of PSN and the network was rebranded as Fox Sports Net. They added other affiliates and the viewership increased from 12 million to 54 million homes. The shows aired twice a week, with two additional replays per show per week.

Brady Tinker had been working for PSN selling advertising. He had always wanted to be on television, for anything sports related. Being the great salesman that he was, the 31-year-old convinced management to give him a shot on the show as a panelist in 1997.

Tinker had no TV experience, and was not at all a fantasy expert, having played only two years of fantasy football and no fantasy baseball. He practiced with teleprompters and earpieces and read everything he could to learn about fantasy football and fantasy baseball. In 1998, Tinker took over as the show's host. The show continued through 2001.

The shows' co-hosts and panelists at times included former NFL greats Bob Golic, James Lofton, Tony Dorsett, Gil Brant, and Hank Stram; former MLB players Goose Gossage and John Kruk; fantasy analysts Paul White, Ian Allan, Cliff Charpentier, and Greg Ambrosius; and NFL writer Larry Weisman. Terry Bradshaw was a guest on their very first one-hour pre-season fantasy football kickoff special. Kruk and Lofton— having no prior TV experience—went on to have great broadcasting careers.

Mumm was shocked by how many entries their salary cap games received and the amount of revenue they generated. At the height, around 1996-97, almost 50,000 were playing football. MLB, NBA, and NHL games were also quite successful. NASCAR and PGA not so much. At one point, they were making $90,000 per week from people calling in transactions to their call center. These calls included five nuns from a Chicago convent who co-managed a team for several years.

The football show was sponsored and co-produced by the NFLPA, who helped get sponsors and talent, and underwrote some costs. They had a 10'-by-10' neon "NFPLA" sign on the set. Clay Walker of the NFLPA said, "We were investing in the future of fantasy sports—evangelizing any way we could—at a time when nobody else was. Not the NFL, MLB, MLBPA, NBA, NHL...nobody." At a time when most professional sports were still resistant to fantasy, Walker was one of the few who saw how big and helpful fantasy could be for professional sports and their players.

Longest-Running Fantasy Program

As mentioned in Chapter 7, Paul Charchian and Rob Pythian started *Fantasy Football Weekly* magazine in 1993. Charchian started doing occasional guest spots on a local sports radio show to talk fantasy. But even when he wasn't a guest, people would constantly call the sports shows and ask fantasy questions, often trying to pretend they weren't fantasy questions, such as "Who do you think will get the goal line carries this week for the Buccaneers?" The hosts were sick of it.

One day, the program director said to Charchian, "Why don't you do your own Saturday fantasy football show? And then we can tell all these idiots to stop calling our regular programming and call you."

And thus, in 1995, Charchian started hosting the *Fantasy Football Weekly* radio show. That show was still airing weekly as of 2024, making it the longest-running fantasy sports program ever. Originally it was on AM radio and didn't reach much beyond the Minneapolis-St. Paul area. But later, the station became part of a network and was heard on stations throughout Minnesota, the Dakotas, a bit of Wisconsin and a bit of Canada. Still later, it was switched to an FM station, KFAN, and then it was nationally syndicated, and could be heard throughout much of the United States. Since 2019, the show has also been a nationally promoted podcast produced by iHeartRadio, which owns KFAN. The podcast is usually among the top 10 sports programs in iTunes each week during the football season.

Charchian has always been the host, with some various co-hosts over the years. He said one of the keys to his success is to be entertaining as well as informative. "People will tell you they want to be informed, but in reality, they want to be entertained," he said.

In the late '90s, Charchian also hosted a TV show, *Fantasy Football Weekly*, that aired on Sunday mornings on a local Twin Cities station. And it became nationally syndicated for 1999-2000, with Charchian flying to Los Angeles every week to record the show.

First Internet Radio Fantasy Show

Starting in 1998, SportsLine had an internet radio fantasy show hosted by Carl Foster, with his sidekick John Zaleski from Ultimate Fantasy Sports. Called *Fantasy Fever*, it could be heard on www.sportsline.com for one hour, Monday through Thursday, with a two-hour show on Fridays. Zaleski remembers being paid $50 an hour, for a total of $300 per week, which was good additional part-time income back then. The show was year-round and lasted until 2000.

Foster also did a weekly fantasy TV show in 2003 and 2004 that was sponsored by Bud Light and broadcast from various Hooters restaurants in southern Florida. His co-host was Adam Bricker and it aired on south Florida regional sports networks.

MLB.com

When MLB.com radio launched in 2001, it began with programming during work hours. Typically, radio is huge during "drive time," such as 6-9 a.m., but this was internet-based and people couldn't use the internet in their cars. Most of the radio network's staff played fantasy baseball, so they knew they wanted to include a fantasy show. As mentioned, they hired Melnick and Zwilling to host, and *Fantasy 411* debuted soon after the network launched.

After about two years, Mike Siano and Cory Schwartz took over hosting from Melnick and Zwilling. Neither had prior radio experience, but they were avid fantasy players and were already working there—Schwartz as a stats guy and Siano in multimedia—so they added hosting to their duties. The show was a success, and they hosted it for more than a decade. Many well-known fantasy analysts—such as Jason Collette, Jeff Erickson, Jeffrey Ma, Joe Sheehan, and Nando Di Fino—were frequent guests. Some regular listeners who called in often also later became well-known analysts, such as "Paul from Detroit" and "Eno from California," who are Paul Sporer and Eno Sarris.

Siano and Schwartz took *Fantasy 411* to TV when the MLB Network launched in 2009, with Jeremy Brisiel joining them as co-host. The 30-minute show aired Monday through Friday, although it was sometimes bumped due to a live MLB game broadcast.

SiriusXM Radio

In 2004, Sirius satellite radio signed a deal with the NFL to launch an NFL channel. Steve Cohen, who had been at WFAN for 17 years and had experience as an NFL beat reporter traveling with the Jets, was offered the job to create the channel. Cohen loved the idea but wasn't sure if satellite radio would work. Robert Kraft, owner of the Patriots, had spearheaded the deal with Sirius. Cohen knew Kraft and asked for a meeting when they were both in Houston for the 2004 Super Bowl. Kraft told him, "You should absolutely do this. The NFL is all in on satellite radio."

Cohen took the job and, when launching NFL radio, included a Friday night fantasy football show hosted by John Hansen and Adam Caplan. Cohen personally co-hosted a daily NFL show with former NFL player Cris Carter, as well as co-hosting a Thursday night show with former NFL player Keyshawn Johnson.

The fantasy show was extremely popular, getting far more phone calls than any other Sirius channel, often thousands per hour. They also had many guests, including NFL players. This may have been the first time players had come on air to talk publicly about fantasy. One time, they had Adrian Peterson on the show, and after talking to him briefly realized they had booked the wrong Adrian Peterson. They weren't talking to the current Minnesota Vikings star running back, they were talking to the Adrian Peterson who had played for the Chicago Bears, was never a big star, and was retired.

After six months, Sirius had Cohen build more of their sports channels. With the additional work, he gave up hosting the daily show. In 2008 Sirius, merged with XM satellite radio and became SiriusXM satellite radio. Cohen's job was doubled as he was now also in charge of the sports platform XM already had, which included an MLB channel, PGA Tour channel, and College channel.

After the Hansen and Caplan show on the NFL channel launched, the next satellite radio fantasy show started in 2005, when Jeff Erickson hosted *Fantasy Focus*, sponsored by RotoWire, on XM radio's XM Home Plate channel (in later years the name was changed to MLB Network Radio). It aired weekdays for one hour during the baseball season through 2008.

With Erickson's show not going to be aired in 2009, Mike Siano and Cory Schwartz volunteered to do a show for free on the MLB channel on Friday nights. While their wives didn't like them not being available on Friday nights, Siano and Schwartz had fun doing the show.

When Cohen was at WFAN, he worked closely with Matt Deutsch, a show producer. Both avid fantasy players, they tried unsuccessfully to get WFAN to start a fantasy show. Deutsch left WFAN and joined Sirius in 2005 to take the job of executive producer for the *Mike and the Mad Dog* radio show. This was a great opportunity for him, and while he focused on that job, Cohen focused on building the sports programming. But by 2009, Cohen and Deutsch started talking about the possibility of having a 24/7 channel dedicated solely to fantasy.

"We both knew fantasy sports were enjoyed by millions of people," Deutsch said. "We were frustrated that traditional media wouldn't cover it. You couldn't call in and ask a fantasy question on WFAN or any other sports radio station."

Cohen asked Deutsch to put together a plan. Deutsch created a very thick pitch book outlining potential shows and guests, budget, events and sports covered, what updates would sound like, and other details. The huge success of Hansen and Caplan's fantasy show on the NFL channel helped support the idea.

Cohen pitched his boss, who didn't like the idea but brought it to CEO Mel Karmazin. Karmazin had been co-managing a fantasy football team with his son for many years, thus knew the appeal of fantasy, and gave Cohen the green light. In the summer of 2010, they launched the 24/7 fantasy sports channel, with Deutsch as the program director.

As Cohen explained it, "To get fantasy sports radio to work, we needed to bring in the best folks in the industry. You fish where the fish are. So, if you go to successful fantasy companies who have a following of fantasy enthusiasts who like their work, their followers are going to want more of it, and they'll listen to their radio show."

Hansen and Caplan's show was moved from the NFL channel to the new fantasy channel. RotoExperts had Scott Engel and Adam Ronis do a morning show. RotoWire did a show with Jeff Erickson and Chris Liss hosting. There have been many other notable hosts that began in 2010 or soon thereafter, with several lasting many years, some still there as of 2024. These include Bob Harris and Mike Dempsey (Fantasy Sports Publications), former New York Mets GM Steve Phillips, Rick Wolf and Glenn Colton (*Colton and the Wolfman*), Jeff Mans, Greg Ambrosius and Tom Kessenich (NFBC/NFFC), Lenny Melnick, Tony Cincotta and Paul Greco (Fantasy Pros), Ray Flowers and Kyle Elfrink (Kay Adams joined them later for a few years), and Anthony Perri with various hosts such as Lou Blasi, Drew Dinkmeyer, Dan Clasgens and James Adams (Fantistics).

One of the original 2010 shows was hosted by Maurice Jones Drew and Mike Dempsey, when Jones Drew was still playing for the Jaguars. According to Deutsch, "MJD was the first player to host a fantasy show. The Jaguars didn't want him to do it. It was on Friday night, and they were afraid he'd give away the game plan. But he convinced them to let him do it. And he opened the door for rest of the NFL to embrace fantasy."

After just two years, it was one of SiriusXM's most popular sports channels, averaging 28,000 calls per day. MJD was paid to do the show, as were some others—while some paid SiriusXM for airtime. But most shows were cross-promotional barter deals, where SiriusXM gave companies airtime in exchange for the companies promoting SiriusXM to their subscribers. Ever since the launch of the NFL channel, the hosts mostly do their shows from their own home. Technological advancements have made it even easier to do this now than it was in earlier years.

Other notable hosts through the years were actor and comedian Michael Rapaport, actor Jerry Ferrara, WWE star The Miz, former adult film star Lisa Ann, and musician Zakk Wylde. All share a love of fantasy sports. And former players who hosted shows include the NFL's Roddy White, Torry Holt, Fran Tarkenton and LaDainian Tomlinson, and MLB's Cliff Floyd.

In 2014, SiriusXM broadcast live from the NFL draft. Second round pick Jordan Matthews sat down at their table and talked about fantasy with them live on the radio. They once broadcast live from musician Jerry Cantrell's (Alice in Chains) house, as he and his friends held their fantasy football draft.

In 2015, FanDuel signed a contract with the channel—it was the largest advertising contract in the history of SiriusXM.

Deutsch, who was integral to the success of the fantasy channel, left in January 2022 to become an entrepreneur, founding Bettor Sports Network. Deutsch said, "Covering the NFL draft, the Super Bowl, FSTA drafts, LABR, Tout Wars, and everything else we did was exciting and an amazing experience to bring this channel to all these events."

In 2023, Cohen relinquished his job as SVP of Sports Programming to do other things, but worked full-time as an advisor for SiriusXM. He also got back on the air, hosting an NFL channel radio show on Sunday mornings. He was inducted into the FSTA Hall of Fame. Of his time with SiriusXM, Cohen said, "We've made everyone proud—we've made the leagues happy, we've made the listeners happy, and we've had programming at a very high level."

The Fantasy Guru

John Hansen was an on-air DJ for a rock station and part owner of a pizzeria in New Jersey when, in 1987, he was invited to play fantasy football for the first time—one hour before the draft. He won the league.

In 1994, a *Monday Night Football* preview cable TV show started broadcasting to two million homes in the same building as the radio station. Hansen told the host he should have him on to talk fantasy football because his league mates called him "The Guru." (In reality, only one guy called him that.) It went so well he was made co-host. Hansen said "Some of the old heads doing sports on this channel were perplexed. They said I was a 'star' out of nowhere, but it was really just the fantasy content that made so many people watch and call in to the show."

Hansen quickly gained a reputation for his predictions and evaluations. In 1995, the 27-year-old started writing a newsletter to make a little extra income for his young family and he launched the FantasyGuru website. In 1996, he started writing fantasy football for ESPN's new website and by 2000 was able to quit his day job and do fantasy full-time. After seven years writing for ESPN, he wrote for Yahoo Sports through 2015.

In addition to the previously mentioned radio shows on the Sirius NFL channel and SiriusXM fantasy channel, from 2003-2009 Hansen was the chief fantasy analyst on the *Fantasy Fix* show on Comcast Sportsnet. He has had many other radio and TV appearances, including, from 2014-2022, as the main fantasy analyst for DirectTV's "Fantasy Zone" channel.

FX (and later FXX) ran a sitcom from 2009 to 2015 called *The League*, about six friends who play in a fantasy football league. Hansen and Adam Caplan appeared in an episode playing themselves hosting their SiriusXM Radio show.

Hansen sold FantasyGuru.com in 2015. As of 2024, he was still on SiriusXM radio and was the majority owner of FantasyPoints.com, which he launched in 2020.

FNTSY Sports Network

Anthem Media Group (later changed to Anthem Sports and Entertainment) is a Canadian media company that was the parent company of Fight Network and My Combat Channel. Chad Midgley, their VP of programming, pitched the idea to launch a TV channel dedicated solely to fantasy sports. CEO Len Asper liked the idea, knowing it would access a highly sought-after demographic. The average fantasy player was just more than 41 years old and trending lower. Asper said, "We mentioned it to a few advertisers, and they leapt out of their chairs. Big advertisers who said whatever we give you for Fight Network, we'll give you 10 times that for fantasy sports."

Midgley put together a staff in three months. Anthem acquired fantasy websites RotoExperts and SportsGrid to support content for the upcoming network. In 2014, they launched FNTSY Sports Network, first in Canada and later in the US. Operating from their Toronto studio, they aired fantasy sports news and content 24/7 (including repeats), available in 400,000 homes in the US and 250,000 in Canada.

Their anchor show was *Fantasy Sports Today* at noon with Chris Meaney and Ashley Docking. And Adam Ronis and Scott Engel hosted a three-hour Sirius XM radio show called *RotoExperts in the Morning* that was simulcast on FNTSY. A couple years later, they added a second studio in Manhattan, in a restaurant at the Renaissance Midtown hotel. The TV broadcasts were the same for both the US and Canada, only the commercials differed. While they were successful, they couldn't get on cable TV everywhere, so they started a YouTube channel and eventually had 60,000 subscribers, getting millions of views. They were also on streaming services such as FUBO TV.

Nando Di Fino was an executive producer and later director of content. Some of the other hosts and frequent guests included Pat Mayo, Jake Ciely, Garion Thorne, Gabe Morency, Mike Florio, Frank Stampfl, Corey Parson, Dave Martinez, Chris Manzo, Cam Stewart, Benny Ricciardi, and Marcus Kuhn.

In 2019, Anthem rebranded FNTSY Sports Network as Game+ and added programming in addition to fantasy sports. Fantasy is now just a small portion of their content.

The Talented Matthew Berry

Matthew Berry was born in Denver—after his family moved several times, he ended up in College Station, Texas, when he was 12. At 14, he discovered the original *Rotisserie League Baseball* book, met some other guys who had read the book and formed a league.

After graduating from Syracuse University with a degree in writing for electronic media, Berry moved to Los Angeles with a dream of being a sitcom writer. After working a retail job, he was hired as a production assistant for *The George Carlin Show*. Helped by a recommendation letter from Carlin, he was accepted into the Warner Brothers Writer's Workshop. This led to Berry working with a college buddy, Eric Abrams, to write TV pilots and film scripts. Among other things, he wrote for the movie *Crocodile Dundee in Los Angeles*, and was one of the writers for the final year of the TV show *Married...with Children*.

All the while, he loved fantasy sports, flying back to Texas every year for his original league's draft, and having joined more baseball and football leagues, and even a basketball league. Although he was having success pursuing his dream of writing for Hollywood, he was miserable. He got tired of being in meetings with movie stars he didn't think were funny telling him what they thought was funny.

In 1999, RotoWorld advertised for writers and Berry applied. Matthew Pouliot said, "Berry had been a writer on *Married...with Children*, my favorite show, so I hired him instantly." He was paid $100 a week to write a column.

Berry noticed the RotoWorld columns all had generic names, like "Half-Court Shots" for basketball, "Red Zone" for football, and "Strike Zone" for baseball. Berry wanted to stand out and brand himself rather than the column. After seeing the Matt Damon movie *The Talented Mr. Ripley*, his then wife suggested he call his column "Talented Mr. Roto."

His column started for basketball, then he wrote for baseball, football and again basketball. All while he continued his career as a Hollywood comedy writer. Four years later, RotoWorld needed to cut expenses. Although his column was popular, they told Berry they were reducing his pay to $25 a week. Berry refused and they fired him. He didn't want to stop writing—and had a good following—so he launched his own website in 2004, TalentedMrRoto.com. Within just eight months he had gotten more than 500,000 unique visitors. He started hiring freelance writers and providing more content than just his personal writing. Simultaneously, he launched another website, RotoPass.com, that allowed people to sign up through RotoPass and access a bundle of six popular sites for just one low cost.

Steve Mason, a fantasy player who hosted a weekend national radio show for Fox Sports, was a fan of Berry's column. In 2004, he invited Berry to do a segment on his show. Berry could have called in for the five-minute segment, but lived close to the Fox Sports studio and went in person. He didn't want to just be a voice on the radio—he wanted to meet Mason and his staff to establish what might be a beneficial relationship. This worked, as he was invited back the next week, and his appearances became weekly—then he was asked to stick around for more than just one segment, then often for an hour.

In 2005, Berry stopped writing comedy scripts and went full-time in fantasy. That year, Mason left Fox to do a show on Los Angeles's ESPN 710 radio. He invited Berry to do segments on that show, which led to 710's program director offering Berry his own show, *Fantasy Football Friday Night*, with one other co-host. Berry did the two-hour show for a year, simultaneously still doing segments on Mason's show and being utilized for other appearances.

710 was the local Angels station, and on getaway days the Angels broadcast team would have to leave for the team flight right after the game. Berry was used on these days as a fill-in to host the Angels' post-game show. This wasn't for fantasy but got him more involved with ESPN.

Berry said, "In 2007, ESPN came to me and said, 'Fantasy football has become big enough that we think we need to find a guy like Mel Kiper is for the NFL, but for fantasy football.'" A meeting was held with John Kosner, the general manager of ESPN digital media.

"When I first met Matthew, he was a ball of fire," Kosner said. "I was mesmerized by his passion for fantasy." Kosner suggested Berry write out a plan. When they met again, Berry had a binder that Kosner likened to a Bill Walsh playbook—Berry referred to it as his "Jerry Maguire Manifesto." The plan included moving more fantasy content out from behind the pay wall. And more broadly, it was about making fantasy mainstream.

Kosner wanted to hire Berry, but John Walsh had to agree. As mentioned in Chapter 2, Walsh was the editor of *Inside Sport* magazine who published the famous Dan Okrent article in 1981. Walsh had subsequently gone on to work at ESPN starting in the late 1980s, and he oversaw all the content on ESPN. Berry said he's never been more nervous for a meeting in his life. He had been hoping to eventually be able to make a full-time living in the fantasy industry, and this was his chance. "If it went well, I was coming to ESPN," he said. "It's the stuff dreams are made of. If not, it's back to my little blog and an empty house."

The first 30 minutes of the meeting was standard "get-to-know-you type stuff" about his background, and his thoughts on fantasy and ESPN. But then it took an unexpected turn. As Berry explained, "I ask Walsh how he's doing in his fantasy baseball league. And he tells me he is getting killed in saves. I don't know what possessed me, but I said, 'Well, let's see if we can find you someone.' So I went around his desk, and we spent the next 30 minutes of the interview on his computer, scouring the waiver wire for setup men who might emerge as closers, as well as for potential trade partners who had a saves surplus. By the time I left, he had some potential closers on his bench and a couple of trade proposals out the door."

Not only did Berry get the job, but ESPN bought his website Talented Mr. Roto and made Berry their lead fantasy analyst. Berry said, "I've never asked Walsh about it, but I'm convinced that last 30 minutes of fantasy baseball cramming got me the gig."

Berry was able to retain some of his 25 or so TalentedMrRoto.com freelancers, which helped fortify ESPNs fantasy content. Ultimately, TalentedMrRoto.com was shut down, some of his writers landed jobs with ESPN, and many of his subscribers became *ESPN Insider* subscribers.

Berry started appearing on ESPN's *Cold Pizza* and ESPNews, and wrote a column in *ESPN The Magazine*. He went on to have an illustrious career at ESPN, becoming the face of fantasy sports across all its platforms. He has been called the biggest name in fantasy sports. He effectively uses his humor to entertain as he gives fantasy advice. As Ian Ritchie of FFToolbox put it, "He's able to take something that's very dry and make it funny."

Kosner said, "There are some people who never thought we'd have fantasy on *SportsCenter*, *NFL Countdown*, and so forth. But he was tireless making the point about how important fantasy is to so many of our fans."

In 2008, Berry played a guest role on the soap opera *One Life to Live*. In 2009, he filmed a segment for *Dancing with the Stars*. And he played himself in an episode of the FX fantasy sports sitcom *The League* in 2011.

He's met and given fantasy advice to many celebrities. In 2012, he got a phone call that went something like this:

Caller: "Hey, enjoy your stuff. We're having a fantasy draft in New York in late August, and we want you to come host it."

Berry: "Thanks, but I'm super busy in August and I don't really do that sort of–"

Caller: "It's for Jay-Z's league."

Berry: "What time do you want me there?"

While at ESPN, Berry spent Sundays watching football at ESPN's studios with Chris Berman, Tom Jackson, Chris Mortensen, and Bill Parcells. Each Sunday morning, during the *NFL Countdown* pregame show, Berman turned it over to Berry for his fantasy advice segment. Berry's dad once told him, "Every Sunday, it blows my mind—what's Boomer doing talking to my kid?"

Berry has said that a key to his success is relatability—in fact, ESPN once did an audience survey and Berry was voted the ESPN personality people would most like to have a beer with.

Berry wrote a 2013 *New York Times* bestseller, *Fantasy Life*, about his career and fantasy sports in general. He's a member of the FSTA and FSWA halls of fame. In 2022, Berry left ESPN and joined NBC—it was a return to where he began, since RotoWorld had been bought by NBC and was the basis for their fantasy platform. As of 2024, RotoPass was still going, and Berry had founded a new company called Fantasy Life.

Berry started playing roto as a 14-year-old, and his league was a member of the RLBA. He said one of the true thrills of his life was sitting at an auction table with Dan Okrent. As mentioned in Chapter 2, after taking a hiatus from playing, Okrent and some of the original members resumed playing in a less competitive format. One year, Rob Fleder couldn't make it, and Berry was asked to fill in for him.

Berry met his second wife at ESPN, and they have five kids. Berry explains, "Rotisserie baseball got me into fantasy sports. Fantasy sports got me to ESPN. ESPN got me to my wife. Which got me to my kids. Really, almost everything I am, and my life stands for, has, in some way, been because of Rotisserie League Baseball."

CHAPTER 12

News Services

Scott Newman, a Pittsburgh sportswriter, and Mitch Sheffler, a businessman, co-founded a rotisserie baseball advice and news service called The Sandlot Shrink in 1989. They offered a newsletter, a book, a fax service and two different 1-900 lines, one for recorded news and the other a live line for advice. Within a couple of years, they added football and basketball content. They were one of the first to offer daily news items about players. They originally got the news from sportswriters, newspapers, and wire services.

Dennis LePore, a freelance writer who had a weekly roto column in the *Cleveland Plain Dealer*, worked part-time for them writing and sometimes answering the live 1-900 line. After a few years, the founders wanted to move on to other projects, but LePore saw the potential they had and bought the company. LePore became the head writer and editor, and used some freelancers, including Rod Beaton of *USA Today*. Around 1995, Sandlot Shrink launched a website and posted news organized by teams, updating items once a day and a few times daily during spring training.

They started publishing *Rod Beaton's Fantasy Baseball Insider*, a yearly draft guide. John Hunt plugged this book in his *Baseball Weekly* column for several years, calling it the best book to take to the draft. As was the case with many other companies and services, Hunt's plug was extremely helpful. Hunt also gave the Shrink a spot in the 1994 inaugural LABR draft.

Steve Hubbard, who covered the NFL for the *Pittsburgh Press*, wrote the first Sandlot Shrink fantasy football guide in 1993. The subscription-based website also includes free content, such as depth charts and a list of sports movies which became popular instantly when it debuted in 1998.

With so many other news and advice websites joining the industry, Sandlot Shrink has lost market share over the years, but was still operating as of 2024. LePore has run the entire operation with the help of just a few part-timers.

In 1993, Rick Wilton and Jim Dressel launched the *Fantasy Baseball Journal* newsletter and a "Hot Sheet" that reported news sent to them from contributors in every MLB city. This was very popular for several years, albeit only reporting baseball news. (It is discussed in detail in Chapter 18.)

KFFL

Ryan Bonini lived in Keweenaw County, in the upper peninsula of Michigan. He was a member of the Keweenaw Fantasy Football League (KFFL). As a freshman at Michigan Tech, he took a class, "Introduction to the Web 101," in which a group project required students to build something that could be marketed on the internet. Along with six classmates, several of whom were also in the KFFL, they worked on a fantasy football site.

At the end of the project, Bonini wanted to keep going and make it a real business. One other classmate joined him, and naming the business after their league, they launched the KFFL website in May 1996. The first ISP they had been talking to thought they were gambling and wanted nothing to do with it. So Bonini needed to drive an hour further away to find one.

The other classmate was too busy and dropped out before long, leaving Bonini alone. KFFL started by offering online salary-cap leagues and in 1997 he added online live-draft leagues. He placed ads in magazines such as *Fantasy Football Pro Forecast*. His customers were also asking for information, so, along with Michael Nazarek, Bonini co-founded

Fantasy Football Mastermind (FFM) as their information wing just a few months after launching KFFL. Nazarek and Bonini decided to part ways after 1997, and FFM was moved to its own domain.

Bonini had been attending school full-time, had a part-time job, and was also running KFFL. He saw a lot of potential with KFFL and decided to go full-time with it, dropping out of college after two years.

For 1998, with FFM no longer part of it, KFFL underwent a reboot of sorts. Bonini brought in three partners, William Del Pilar, Bill Larlee, and Donald Blum. Bonini was working full-time 80-hour weeks. His three new co-owners worked full-time day jobs, and this was essentially a full-time night job. They often got very little sleep.

By the time they re-booted in 1998, they realized Keweenaw Fantasy Football League wasn't a very good name—nobody could pronounce it, let alone spell it—but they had established credibility and didn't want to change the name and appear to be a brand-new website.

Del Pilar grew up in Panama and loved watching American football. He moved to the United States and joined the Navy, where he started playing fantasy football in 1990. After the Navy he attended college, and in 1996 his wife told him, "You spend so much damn time doing that fantasy thing, why don't you figure out how to make some money from it?"

And he did. Although he lived in San Diego, he started writing a news column, "Hot off the Wire," for KFFL. Before long, they had NFL beat reporters in every locker room feeding them news and were generating huge traffic. Not only did fantasy players frequent the site but also NFL fans, gamblers, and even several NFL general managers and players' agents.

"We spent a ton of money on bandwidth; it was a double-edged sword," Bonini said. "We wanted traffic, but with traffic came higher hosting costs and a big spike in traffic could totally blow up our budget."

Sometimes their beat reporters would tell them to hold news until they could report it themselves in their local papers, such as in 2000 when Carolina running back Fred Lane was killed. They knew the news within a few minutes but had to wait for the beat reporter to break it first. However, many other times KFFL broke news even before the beat reporters did.

Their game offerings never topped more than about 100 leagues, but they really made their mark in the industry as one of the top sites for football news, covering even back-up long snappers. Bonini said their news posts were so good and timely that they were often copied by competitors. "Occasionally we would include a slight error to see how many of our competitors would publish the exact same thing," he said. "It was quite comical when you'd say a fictitious fullback was an exclusive-rights free agent and suddenly, this player that doesn't exist is being listed on other mainstream sites because they copied it from us."

Bonini moved to San Diego in 2000. The site grew to 12 million unique visitors per month and was ranked in the top 2,000 websites in the world. They had a staff of five in their office and a stable of 70 writers, 10 to 15 of which were used regularly and others as needed.

KFFL signed contracts to provide content and news for Yahoo, CBS SportsLine, NFL.com, NFL Network, RT Sports, FoxSports.com, MyFantasyLeague.com and others. They made money from business to business, business to consumer, and by selling ads. Besides news, they also built programs on who to start and bench, trade evaluations, custom cheat sheets, and rankings. And Bonini created one of the first chat functions on the internet, which drew a lot of people to the website. Their odd name ended up having a benefit, as when they called NFL teams for information, everyone assumed they were from a radio station, "KFFL," and were eager to talk.

Bonini and Del Pilar were fantasy analysts on the first year of NFL Network's *Total Access*. They commuted once a week from San Diego to the studio in LA. Time.com listed KFFL as one of the 10 essential sports sites for fans, athletes, and fantasy owners.

After Fantasy Sports Trade Association meetings, many attendees would go to the bar and bond over drinks. One night, a man from one of the major conglomerates told Del Pilar in a drunken stupor, "We love what you're doing. We're going to your site every day, and we're going to copy everything you're doing—and we're going to do it better because we've got millions of dollars. And we're going to drive you out of business."

They sold KFFL to Fantasy Sports Ventures (FSV) in 2006. Del Pilar stayed on as the GM until 2010. Bonini stayed on and quickly moved into management for FSV. In 2012, FSV was sold to Gannett, and KFFL was eventually merged into USA Today's fantasy coverage. As of 2024, Bonini had moved back to Michigan and continued to work in senior management for Gannett.

Del Pilar recalled, "Every year we'd lose a few writers because a rival company would see their work and grab them. It was heartbreaking to see them go, but at the same time I was happy for them. I came from a third-world country where my family had nothing, so to see somebody better themselves was great. And I was proud of them."

RotoWire

Peter Schoenke always liked baseball and stats. As a nine-year-old, he started recording all the stats for his neighborhood wiffle ball games and continued until he went to college and discovered roto baseball. He was a career .635 wiffle ball hitter.

Typically, roto auctions have a $260 budget, whether the money is real or imaginary—but Schoenke and his college friends couldn't afford that, so their budget was $15 in real money. The worst players would go for a penny at the end of the auction.

After college, Schoenke had been a reporter for Dow Jones, covering the futures markets in Chicago. One of his college friends and roto league mates, Herb Ilk, was a chemical engineer who hated his job. Ilk wanted to start a business with Schoenke. When Ilk's sister was getting married, he saw how excited everyone was, and Ilk thought that if they could make a website for weddings, they'd make a ton of money. They researched it and found a wedding website, TheKnot. com, had just launched, so they figured that idea was already taken and kept brainstorming.

While at Dow Jones, Schoenke was impressed by the Bloomberg terminal on the trading floor. It was like what the internet later became. You'd type in a stock symbol and get lots of news and data. He told Ilk, "Why don't we do that for fantasy baseball, so you can type in a player and get all kinds of information?"

They recruited Jeff Erickson, another college friend, to help, because he knew even more than them about roto and the players. The three all lived in Chicago near Wrigley Field after having graduated from Northwestern University. Schoenke bought a computer, learned how to program, and built a website after his day job. He typed in all the MLB player names, and RotoNews.com went live on February 16, 1997. Ilk and Erickson would go online every day looking for news, with Ilk writing the AL player notes and Erickson doing the same for the NL.

Erickson had graduated from Loyola Law School. But after passing the bar exam, he didn't interview much for law jobs, and finally realized he didn't want to be a lawyer. He had a job in the internet wing of an association management company. His boss said if he got his work done, he could stay at the office and work on RotoNews at night. He often stayed until midnight since he had no girlfriend and his office had fast internet.

Their player notes were brief, but covered transactions, injuries, hot streaks, etc., and they added the implications for fantasy. All the notes were searchable by player name. And it was free to access, funded by ads. They quickly also started writing articles, and that fall added notes for the NFL and NBA.

The site's traffic spiked quickly, thanks in part to John Hunt giving it a very favorable mention, in early 1997, in *Baseball Weekly*. And a Yahoo search showed them as one of the top listings for fantasy baseball. They also began working barter deals with other websites, along the lines of "You put up a link for us and we'll do the same for you."

They added customized player projections to the site, and in 1998 they built software to launch the industry's first free commissioner service. They very quickly hosted thousands of leagues. Schoenke posted an ad for help and started hiring people across the country who could access team news from local papers and media. By the summer of 1998, they were paying about 25 freelancers. Schoenke and Ilk quit their day jobs and went full-time, paying themselves each $15,000 a year. Schoenke explained, "I was 25, no debt, no kids, no responsibilities, I thought as long as I can pay rent and buy beer I might as well take a shot—and if it doesn't work out, I can always go back to the stock market jobs."

By late 1999, they were consistently one of the top 10 largest sports sites on the internet. RotoNews had so much traffic, they had trouble keeping the site going. Schoenke said, "I would have to get up at midnight every night, drive all the way downtown to where we had the server, manually reboot it, and drive back home. It was like putting my finger in a dam that was about to explode."

Schoenke noticed that more than 60% of their traffic was during business hours, confirming that lots of people were looking at fantasy when they should have been working. One man confessed, "Checking box scores is one of the first things I do when I get to work and then I print out stats for co-workers who don't have internet access."

In 1999, they were bought by Broadband Sports and moved to Los Angeles to operate under the new owners. Broadband gave them a little cash and lots of stock options. "We were chasing the dot-com dream like everyone else back then," Schoenke said. "We had a lot of traffic, but not a lot of revenue."

Erickson also moved to Los Angeles and went full-time. Now with Broadband, they were able to hire two of their freelancers for full-times jobs: Chris Liss, who already lived in LA, and Scott Pianowski, who moved from Michigan to take the job. Schoenke and Erickson shared an apartment, and Pianowski slept on their couch for a month until he got his own place.

When the dot-com bubble burst, Broadband was showing major signs of trouble. Erickson said, "We started getting half paychecks...quarter paychecks...skipped checks...we were scared to death." Broadband went bankrupt early in 2001. "It was a wild ride being paper millionaires and then bankrupt," Schoenke said.

The founders were still confident in their company, so they tried to buy back RotoNews. Schoenke offered $25,000 for the website address, but they wouldn't sell it to him. The attorney handling the bankruptcy tried to sell it to ESPN for $1 million and ESPN was interested until they learned all they would get was the URL—none of the employees were included. ESPN wouldn't have even known how to turn it on without Schoenke or Ilk. The bankruptcy attorney told ESPN they'd have to talk to the employees separately and that killed the deal. Even then, they weren't willing to sell to Schoenke.

Schoenke met with a lawyer who told him to back up all the company data, fire up the same exact website and call it something else. Schoenke said, "But they will sue me!" and the attorney said, "No, they won't. They will threaten to sue you, but they never will, because they're broke."

Schoenke backed up the data, and, working from Ilk's apartment, they built a new website. They launched RotoWire.com on March 31st. And they did get a lot of threatening letters from the prior owners, but nothing ever happened.

Tim Schuler had a job with Broadband as an editor, wrote on the side for RotoNews, and knew finance. The founders offered him a job as their finance and HR guy, and they also offered a job to Liss, and gave both equity in the new company.

In order to gain back customers, they kept RotoWire mostly free, but asked for voluntary contributions to keep the site going. The contributions didn't offset the depressed ad market, and they made the decision to switch to requiring a paid subscription, charging $59.99 per year. Schoenke said, "When we went pay, we probably lost 90% of our traffic. But it worked."

It also helped their biggest competitor, RotoWorld, who was still offering news for free. When RotoNews disappeared for a month and then when RotoWire went to a pay model, RotoWorld had a boost in traffic.

For 2002, RotoWire charged $70 for the year or $40 for just base-ball. They had opened an office in Culver City and played foosball on breaks. Seven full-time and 20 part-time employees turned out 150 player updates per day, plus articles and content. They covered the NFL, MLB, NBA, NHL, NASCAR, PGA, college basketball and football, and international soccer.

In prior years, some companies had asked to buy their news notes to post on their own websites, and Schoenke said no, thinking it best to drive as much traffic as possible to RotoWire. But when ESPN asked to buy their news in 2003, Schoenke agreed in order to make money and get their branding on ESPN. The same notes on RotoWire started appearing on ESPN.

By 2004, there was an average of 200,000 visitors and 1.5 million page views daily. RotoWire also started baseball and football annual magazines. Despite the success, there was still concern. Erickson said, "We still had to sweat out the legal battle with the players association. That episode was scary as hell."

Ilk moved to Madison, Wisconsin, in 2004 and worked remotely. Schoenke decided it would make sense to move as well, since LA was so expensive. In Madison, he could buy a house twice the size for half the money, and it would be a better environment for recruiting interns and freelancers. Students at UCLA or other local colleges weren't motivated to drive all the way to Culver City and then commute back for small pay. But in Madison they could put an office right near the college campus, plus kids there were more sports crazy. They moved in the spring of 2005, and it worked out just as Schoenke imagined, as they had no trouble recruiting and retaining interns and employees. Erickson and Liss stayed in LA and worked remotely.

When MLB was starting a channel on XM radio in 2005, they hired Erickson to be a host for a fantasy show. Erickson had done some local radio but never as a host. They flew him to Washington, DC for the launch party. He said, "I felt insignificant compared to the others there, such as Kevin Kennedy, and Rob Dibble." The show, *Fantasy Focus*, was co-hosted by Phil Wood, who had a lot of radio experience and knew baseball but didn't know fantasy. It aired through 2008, with Chris Liss and John Sickels also co-hosting at times. Liss also hosted a fantasy football show for a year on XM, and Erickson and Liss later co-hosted a

RotoWire fantasy show on SiriusXM for many years. Their contrasting styles—Erickson laid back, Liss more combative—helped make the show interesting.

In terms of employees and revenue, RotoWire was quite possibly the largest privately owned fantasy company until they sold it on January 1, 2022, to Gambling.com for $27.5 million. At the time of the sale, they had more than 40 employees (about 25 in the Madison office) and 180 freelancers. In 2021, they had more than 100,000 paid subscribers, more than 17 million unique web visitors, and revenue of approximately $7 million. After the sale, Ilk semi-retired and Liss left the industry (Erickson still hosts the SiriusXM radio show with new co-hosts). Schoenke, Erickson and Schuler have continued in their same roles as of 2024.

Moving to Madison worked out better than Schoenke could have imagined, as they still get 15-20 interns every year from University of Wisconsin-Madison. In 2024, two-thirds of their home-office staff had started as interns from the school.

After starting to sell their news to ESPN in 2003, Yahoo and then many others also wanted it. And by 2022, they had 70 clients for news, including most of the major companies in the industry such as FanDuel, DraftKings, Fox Sports, Underdog, still ESPN and Yahoo, and many others.

RotoWire has grown into a global endeavor with freelance writers working from countries as far away as Pakistan and Australia. They translate soccer coverage into Portuguese and Spanish to reach players in South America and provide real-time updates to people playing fantasy cricket in India.

27 Years Later

Erickson said, "We used to get excited when ESPN would even just mention the concept of fantasy—we were like the redheaded stepchild of the sports industry—but now it's so mainstream it's incredible. The fact that I've been doing this for over 25 years full-time is crazy. And I've made a hell of a career and a hell of a living doing what I love, writing and talking about fantasy sports. And I love being on the radio. When I first started on radio I felt like an imposter, but now I know what I am doing."

"RotoWire became so much bigger than I ever would have imagined," said Schoenke. "I remember around 2008 the FSTA did a survey and found 25 million people played fantasy and I thought we've maxed out—can't possibly get bigger than that—but now we're at almost 70 million. But at the same time, it doesn't feel that different, I'm still doing the same things I did back then. Today I wrote a player note about a Twins player. It's still as much fun as when we started."

TheKnot.com is still in business, offering a full range of help to plan your wedding. Had they launched just several months later, perhaps there would be no RotoWire and there would be a Peter and Herb's Wedding Planning.

RotoWorld

The other big early fantasy news company was RotoWorld, which launched one year after RotoNews launched. It is discussed in detail in Chapter 10. Another company, RotoTimes, launched in 2000, also getting significant traffic for several years.

CHAPTER 13

First Football Websites

David Dodds lived in southern California and had a job as an engineer. People sometimes like to say, "I'm not a rocket scientist," but Dodds couldn't say that because he *was* a rocket scientist. In 1987, the 23-year-old saw the *Fantasy Football* magazine (which in 1989 changed its name to *Fantasy Football Index*). He thought, "Are they really playing a game around watching football? I gotta buy this!" After reading the magazine, which included rules on how to play, he went back and bought five more copies to hand out to fellow engineers, and they immediately started an office league. There was a $20 entry fee, but Dodds typically had $400 in weekly side action.

There wasn't yet internet, but AOL and Prodigy had links to news groups, including some for fantasy football. Many people would discuss players, depth charts, links to articles, etc. And in 1989, people could make their own website on AOL, so Dodds started a personal website, MrFootball.com.

Dodds bought a book on how to code html. The website served mostly to collect his own thoughts, help him find links for information and organize the links by categories such as "news" and "depth charts." He started writing strategy articles, and on message boards would write, "Hey guys, check out this article I wrote." That brought the first traffic to his site.

He wrote articles about how to draft, trade, and other aspects of how to win, as he thought there wasn't much available anywhere for strategy. He wanted to be the site to analyze the news for fantasy impact, not report the news. He also started posting player projections, whereas most sites had rankings, because he thought rankings failed to adjust for various formats and scoring systems.

Dodds had no idea how many people were using his site until one day he received an e-mail from AOL saying his traffic—100,000 pages views on a weekend in August—had far exceeded their allowed limit for personal web pages and they gave him three weeks to get off the site. He had to find a host, which cost him $80 a month, and he wasn't even doing this as a business. But he thought perhaps he had enough traffic to get advertising. He posted an ad rate sheet, and he didn't have to try and contact advertisers, they found him. He got unsolicited calls from people wanting to advertise.

In the '90s, his visitors kept growing, aided by MrFootball.com being featured one year by Yahoo as one of the top three fantasy football sites on the internet. And the ad revenue kept growing. Dodds said, "People were just throwing money at me. I was making $70-or-$80,000 a year without even trying to contact advertisers." By the end of the '90s, the ad market was booming. He got calls like, "I'm the CEO of Pets.com. If I send you $6,000, can you put up a banner ad?"

Dodds had his full-time engineering job the entire time and was spending another eight or nine hours a day writing about football and managing his website. It was taking a toll on his marriage, which was in shambles, so when Fanball made an offer to buy his company in 1999, he sold it for $150,000.

But even when selling, he already had a plan to return to the business in the future. What he had learned is that most websites, including his, had static pages. He realized all websites were built wrong—the future of websites would be database driven. That would make them much more powerful and easier to create and maintain. Users would be able to link information, such as typing in a player and finding articles he appears in, depth charts he's listed on, etc.

When Fanball flew him to Minnesota to close the sale, they were coincidentally also holding a fantasy football convention that weekend. Two days before going to Minnesota, he bought the domain footballguys.com knowing he would probably want to be in the business again. Joe Bryant, a fantasy football writer, was also at this convention. Dodds told him his plan. He was going to go to night school and make himself an expert at all the new programming, so that he'd be able to create a database-driven website in the future. He had visions of building something big. He asked Bryant if he'd be interested in working on this with him, although Dodds would have to remain in the background until his two-year non-compete agreement with Fanball expired. So, the very weekend Dodds was in Minneapolis to sell Mrfootball to Fanball, he was planning to create something new with Joe Bryant.

Footballguys

Joe Bryant lived near Knoxville, Tennessee, and owned a successful boat manufacturing business. He started playing roto baseball and then fantasy football. Just like many others in this book who started a business, he looked for information to help play and found very little. He started writing about fantasy football in the mid-'90s.

When Dodds suggested at the Minnesota convention that they could collaborate on a website, Bryant liked the idea. Bryant could write but wasn't knowledgeable enough to start a website. He explained, "David had the expertise that I knew I needed. He could do all the things on the technology side that I didn't know how to do."

Dodds went to night school as planned, stayed under the radar during his non-compete period, and helped Bryant create a website. In 2000, Joe Bryant's cheatsheets.net launched, including news and analysis, cheat sheets, rankings, projections, and experts' polls. Bryant offered free content and a free e-mailed newsletter. He advertised in a handful of fantasy football magazines, but mostly people found the site by internet searches and word of mouth. However, word of mouth faced an obstacle, as Bryant explained: "Our industry has a unique problem in that nobody likes to tell anyone else about their secret weapon. If you have a source that is giving you an advantage, you don't want your competitors to know about it."

In 2002, when Dodds's no-compete expired, they renamed the site "Joe Bryant and David Dodds Footballguys." Bryant hadn't been making much money selling advertising and the ad market was drying up, so they knew they would have to try and switch to a paid subscription. They both had full-time jobs and couldn't do this essentially second full-time job for no money. But they decided to keep it free for a year to attract more users and prove their worth, with the plan to switch to a paid site the second year. They told writers their plan, and hired freelancers with the agreement they would initially pay them with "credits" instead of cash. If someone wrote an article worth $100, they'd get 100 credits, with the idea being that credits would be turned into cash when they went to a paid site in year two.

After the first year, they had 30,000 subscribers to their free newsletter. People were predicting they would convert 5% to 9% of them to a paid subscription. Dodds said, "Prior to the switch, Bryant was losing his mind because that wouldn't be nearly enough to pay people or maintain this." But remarkably they converted 50%—15,000 people—to the paid subscription. This was enough to guarantee Dodds a salary sufficient to finally quit his day job as an engineer. He was quite happy to finally be able to do fantasy full-time. They kept growing and by 2005 had a staff of about 60 freelance writers and content providers, many of whom worked full-time.

One low point was when they sent an e-mail with a link that inadvertently gave many on their free subscription list a virus. They had to manually re-enter all 30,000 e-mail addresses into a different format.

Bryant sold his boat business around 2015 and finally went full-time with Footballguys. He said, "I wasn't doing proper service to either company, so I needed to make a choice." While extremely successful overall, they did try some new things over the years that didn't go well. Bryant said, "I learned just take your lumps and don't be afraid to admit you made a mistake and cut your losses."

35 Years Later

As of 2024, Footballguys has about 700,000 subscribers to their free newsletter and 50,000 paid premium subscribers. Some of their popular tools are Draft Dominator, Lineup Dominator, Projections Dominator and Rate My Team. They have customized cheat sheets and host a series of podcasts, including their award-winning podcast *The Audible*. Many of their writers are still with them, and some have gone on to very successful careers elsewhere, such as Matt Harmon (Yahoo fantasy) and Heath Cummings (CBS Sports).

Both Dodds and Bryant were inducted into the FSWA Hall of Fame. Bryant was also inducted into the FSTA Hall of Fame. In 2020, Dodds sold his interest in Footballguys to Bryant and retired.

In 2023, Dodds said, "At the beginning, the internet was such a wild west, it's amazing to see how it's grown. I'm extremely happy with what we were able to do, the kind of people we brought in, many of them have become successful throughout the industry, on radio, even the NFL network. I think we did a good job for the people that worked for us, and the people that subscribed, and we had a lot of fun."

Fantasy Insights

James Serra was a programmer in Las Vegas who started putting projections in Excel and created software to help for his fantasy football drafts. He figured he could sell it to others, founded a company called First Place Sports Software and in 1993 advertised it in some magazines. To the 27-year-old's surprise, about 200 people bought it for $25 each. This was one of the first, or possibly the first, draft software to be sold, and included Serra's own player projections.

Many customers asked if he could make commissioner software, since what was available was not very good. So, in 1994 he wrote commissioner software, advertised it along with the draft software, and sold 100 copies at $80 each, with the draft software sales increasing to about 350. With his wife's help, he spent lots of time copying software onto floppy disks, printing labels, an instruction booklet, and mailing to customers. He made enough money that he decided to stop his consulting business for the next year, do this full time, and see what happened.

Back then there were companies like his that would send clients a floppy disk, and the clients would input stats and produce league results on their own—and there were companies such as All-Star Stats that charged more but did all the lineup changes, inputting of stats and producing league reports for you. With the advent of the internet, both types of companies evolved to the same format, where customers could do everything themselves on a website.

Pre-internet, Serra also advertised on forums on Prodigy, CompuServe, and AOL. Jim Lenz, who was selling a fantasy football newsletter on the forums, contacted Serra, and proposed they work together. Lenz said, "You have software and I want to do newsletters. I think that would be a good combination."

They kept their companies separate, but started working together, and, in 1994, launched one of the first fantasy football websites. It was originally NFLFantasy.com until they received a cease-and-desist letter from the NFL and changed to FantasyInsights.com. Lenz did most of the writing and Serra managed the software. By the late '90s, their website offered news, depth charts, player rankings, mock drafts, and more. And Serra had a few thousand customers using his draft software and commissioner service.

Serra remembers, "I went to Wells Fargo to set up a credit card account and they said, 'You have to get a storefront,' and I said, 'My business is on the internet,' and they said, 'What's the internet?'"

Serra also wrote weekly fantasy football columns for newspapers around the country and was a guest on many radio shows. He always kept going one year at a time, seeing if he would earn enough money to continue full-time for another year and not do his consulting work. He didn't get rich but was making a comfortable living. He also served as an FSTA board member.

A MLB All-Star pitcher was in a fantasy football league that used their service, and one September night Serra was watching him pitching on TV while monitoring the website. The pitcher was replaced by a relief pitcher and headed for the locker room. A few minutes later, Serra noticed the man who had just walked off the mound—and wouldn't have had time to take a shower—made a transaction for his football team.

We will never know, but perhaps the conversation went something like this:

Manager: "Can you give me another inning?"

Pitcher: "No, I gotta make a fantasy football move."

But the job included stress. Serra would get e-mails from customers arguing that he didn't score a play correctly. Someone might say, "I was watching the game, he ran for nine yards, not 10." They didn't understand the stats came from the NFL, not from him. Once, a guy called and told him, "The commissioner of our league has died, please give me his username and password so I can take over managing it." It turned out the guy was lying and deleted the entire league because he was mad at his league mates. (Serra was able to restore the league, but not without a lot of effort.)

These types of events caused stress and ate into his enjoyment of running the business. And it became worse, as the industry went from weekly scoring updates to daily updates, to hourly, and then every few seconds. It was very stressful needing to constantly monitor that everything was working properly. He had employees but they were never reliable or skilled enough, so he had to monitor everything himself. If he went to a ball game, he'd have to take his laptop with him to monitor the real-time scoring. If anything went wrong, he had to go to his car where there was better Wi-Fi reception to fix the problem. Then the NFL added Sunday night games, then Thursday night games, and some Saturday games, so that even more of Serra's time was needed to monitor stats.

Serra depended on STATS, Inc. to send data every few seconds. Around 2008, there was an NFL game with two players with the same name—Adrian Peterson—one the Bears running back and the other the Vikings running back—and this caused a glitch in the STATS delivery.

There was a 45-minute delay in the live scoring being updated. E-mails started coming from dozens and dozens of his clients. They started with, "Just to let you know, the stats haven't updated in a few minutes." Then they started getting angry: "The stats haven't updated, what's wrong with you people?" Eventually, they escalated from "I want a partial refund" to "I want a full refund" to "I'm going to sue you." After 30 minutes, it was "I'm going to start a class-action lawsuit" and then "I think you should fire everybody," "I hope you get cancer," and "I hope all your family gets cancer." Over 1,000 angry e-mails. Despite him telling them he was at the mercy of STATS, they didn't care. That's when Serra knew he couldn't do this anymore. He thought, "I'm getting mentally abused by people who can't deal with the fact that their stats are a little late."

Serra started talking to other companies about selling Fantasy Insights. The stress from this incident and continued monitoring of real-time scoring caused Serra to develop a twitch in his left eye. He finally sold to RT Sports in 2010. The same day he closed the sale, the twitch went away. Serra left the fantasy industry and finally went back to consulting. But as of 2023, he still plays in his original fantasy league, with six of the original owners still playing more than 30 years later.

Lenz worked in the insurance industry and never made enough money to quit his day job. In the '90s and early 2000s, running his fantasy business was so much fun he didn't mind working 18-to-20-hour days during the football season. But stress affected him as well. He also sold his business in 2010, to one of his writers. "Constant complaints were one of the things that drove me out of the industry," Lenz said. "I would get dozens of e-mails such as, 'You projected this guy would get 100 yards and a touchdown this week...he only got 60 yards and a touchdown...don't you know what you're doing?'"

TFL Report

Bob Harris began playing fantasy football in 1986. He started writing a newsletter for his league and his league mates loved it. In 1993 he thought, "If we love it this much, everyone must love it this much," and decided to turn his newsletter into a business. He placed a classified ad in USA Today, and his 1-800 number never stopped ringing. The Fantasy League Report was mailed to subscribers weekly from the pre-season through the last week of the regular NFL season.

Back then, NFL media relations departments were inundated non-stop with calls asking questions such as if an injured player was going to play. In 1991, Deana Patterson, a secretary in the Dallas Cowboys PR office said that some days she would get more than 100 calls. "I hate it," she said.

Harris built a relationship with these people and told them, "Give me the information and tell everyone else to call me." They were happy to do it. They couldn't wait to get rid of all these annoying calls. Harris got to where if someone called the switchboard for 25 of the NFL teams and said the word "fantasy," they would give out his 1-800 number. Before long, newspaper beat reporters also gave out the number because they had the same problem with people calling them.

In 1993, he had set up an office with one phone line, but by 1994 needed to expand to a phone system with 10 lines. After it was set up, he learned the trunk wasn't big enough to handle the phone system—he had to move the phones to the back of his dad's livestock supply store, which did have a big enough trunk, and some of his employees had to sit there and answer the phone day and night.

Fantasy players had to wait for USA Today to come out Monday mornings with stats, but the start of CompuServe allowed Harris to access the AP box scores. He set up a 1-900 for people to call. He would read the box scores into a recording and people would pay to call and get the stats. Harris wasn't aware of anyone else doing this yet and thinks he may have had the first 1-900 for football stats.

By 1995, they were able to accommodate the phone system at his office. As with other businesses at the time, Harris was able to start incorporating faxes replacing some of the mailings, and in 1996 he launched a website. Originally the website was just to make it easier and less expensive to get the newsletter to people, but Harris started adding more content as time went on.

Emil Kadlec had seen his classified ads and called Harris to sell him advertising in his magazines. Harris did buy ads, and the two developed a relationship that led to Harris doing some freelance writing for Kadlec's magazines. Harris loved what he was doing but wasn't making much money. He was living in a spare room at his grandma's house and by 1998 she told him it was time to do something else. Kadlec offered him a full-time job. Kadlec flew to Phoenix, rented a U-Haul, drove to Tucson, picked up Harris, drove him to Albuquerque and helped him rent an apartment. The Fantasy League Report website was incorporated into Kadlec's website, and Harris served as senior editor of the magazines through 2023. Since 2011, he's hosted the SiriusXM *Football Diehards* show, with co-host Mike Dempsey, and Harris has done hundreds of guest appearances on other radio shows.

As Harris sees it, "Fantasy Football is a way for fans who already love football to love it a little bit more. At drafts you are sitting in a room of people who are like-minded and there's this shared experience of 'Wow, this is great!'"

The Huddle

David Dorey grew up in Texas and was a huge Cowboys fan. In 1991, he was working as a computer programmer for a Silicon Valley company and was invited to join a company fantasy football league. Dorey loved football and stats and became the league's scorekeeper. He had to wait each week until he could buy the Tuesday *USA Today* to see the Monday night game box score and then get the league's stats done. "And," he said, "I wrote a weekly league newsletter, mainly just to trash everybody else's teams."

Several years later, Whitney Walters, a fellow programmer and league mate, suggested they start a website. The internet was new and, for the most part, there was hardly anything out there except sites where people could sign up for a newsletter and they would fax it to you. Dorey said, "They weren't taking advantage of what the internet would allow you to do."

Dorey agreed to the idea. He explained, "I lived in Silicon Valley and still somehow missed out on being involved in the evolution of the PC. People became millionaires overnight. So, when I saw the internet for the first time, I thought, 'If we don't take advantage of this right now, we'll never have this opportunity again in our lives.'"

Dorey and Walters had meetings at Roundtable Pizza, as it was halfway between their houses. They signed up with an ISP hosting company for $29.95 per month, and in 1997 launched TheHuddle. com. They were possibly the first to launch a website without already having an audience from an existing newsletter or magazine.

Dorey said, "We had two goals: make a community on the internet and give people a reason to come back to the site every day." They had content for fantasy football strategy, analysis on matchups and schedule strength, player rankings, and message boards. Their initial marketing plan was Dorey getting 100 e-mail addresses from a pre-internet news-group for fantasy football and e-mailing each one a personal invitation to visit The Huddle. That resulted in 30 visitors. Their traffic grew from word of mouth and trading links with other sites. Dorey said, "It was an amazing and thrilling thing to watch gather steam."

Dorey insisted on having a message board because it played into the theme of a huddle—bringing people together to talk about football. The board was intended to build a community, and make people want to come back each day. "If you went on our message board the first month it looked very active," Dorey said, "and that's because it was me asking questions under fake names—and me answering them. But after a month or two, it took off and I didn't need to do that anymore."

Dorey had two weeks per year of vacation from his day job. He took off every Monday during the football season so he could stay home and write. The first year, The Huddle didn't make a penny. They just paid for the ISP. Dorey worked his day job and the Huddle at night. He was working so hard and sleeping so little that one night he had to be hospitalized.

By 1998, the site was getting more than 5 million visitors a month. Walters had done some writing but stopped to concentrate fully on running the website and the financial aspects of the business. Walters started selling advertising and brought in about $50,000. In 1999, when FoxSports.com wanted to start fantasy football coverage, they asked The Huddle to provide their content.

Their traffic kept growing, but the online ad market crashed in 2000. They were killing themselves working two jobs and now only making $1,000 a month. By 2001, shutting down became a real possibility, and they scheduled a meeting at a restaurant to discuss. Since it was possibly going to be their last meeting, they went to a nice steakhouse rather than Roundtable Pizza. At the meeting, they decided that since they had so many visitors, they would give it one more year and charge a subscription fee. In July 2001, they started charging a fee of $12 per year. By the fall, they had more than 20,000 subscribers, worth $240,000. "Wow," they thought, "That was a great idea!"

They decided that Walters would quit his day job to work on the site full-time. They paid him a salary, but not Dorey who kept his day job. In 2002, Dorey also quit his day job and later that year moved back to Texas.

The Huddle has won many awards for best fantasy football website. Dorey and Walters sold to Fantasy Sports Ventures in 2007, who later sold to *USA Today* (the Gannett Corporation) and the site has remained extremely popular as of 2024. Dorey is still there. Walters left in 2020 and is no longer in the fantasy industry. Dorey also wrote a 2007 book, *Fantasy Football: The Next Level*. He estimates he has written over 10 million words about fantasy football. Selling his interest in the business satisfied his lifetime financial goals and allowed Dorey to feel secure about his future and retirement.

Other Success Stories

As mentioned, writing this book is like choosing players for an All-Star game—there's never room for all deserving players. There were other early popular websites, including Fantasy Football Mastermind (FFM), which was launched by Michael Nazarek and Ryan Bonini in 1996, originally as part of KFFL (Chapter 12). In 1998, Nazarek took FFM to its own domain, while Bonini continued with KFFL. Nazarek turned FFM into an extremely successful site still very popular as of 2024.

Sam Caplan started writing annual previews for fantasy football and fantasy baseball while still in high school in Philadelphia in the early '90s. He printed them on a home printer and mailed them. He was given a high school assignment to write a mock business plan, and proposed to his teacher that for extra credit he could scale his existing business and put it on the World Wide Web. He hired designers and launched FFInsider.com. In addition to putting the annual previews online, he added other content, including a fantasy football podcast he did with his uncle, Adam Caplan, that was perhaps one of the first. Adam was looking to get into sports broadcasting full-time and did achieve that goal, hosting on SiriusXM with John Hansen and later becoming an NFL Insider for ESPN. Sam sold his company to Fanball in 1997 and worked for them until 2000.

John Hansen, in addition to being a very successful fantasy analyst on radio and TV (Chapter 11) also launched a website called Fantasy Guru in 1995. He no longer owns the site, but it is still going strong as of 2024.

CHAPTER 14

High-Stakes Games

Lenny Pappano, owner of Draft Sharks, a fantasy football content site, became friends with Emil Kadlec from advertising in Kadlec's magazines. They talked about doing an event for fantasy players. There were industry trade shows where companies would pitch their product, but that wasn't particularly exciting for the average player. One day around Thanksgiving 2001, Kadlec called and asked Pappano what he was doing. He replied, "I'm answering e-mails and watching the *World Series of Poker*."

Kadlec exclaimed, "That's what we should do for fantasy football! Create a championship event in Las Vegas!"

For several days they discussed the idea. As Pappano explained, "We started with the phrase, 'If we could compete in this event, we would want to...' and then we filled in the blank. We would want to do it in Vegas. We would want to have a party at the ESPN Zone. We would want a chance to win NFL autographed memorabilia. We would want a grand prize of $200,000. Our business plan was like the movie *Field of Dreams*: 'Build it and they will come.'"

At first Pappano thought it was crazy. But the more they talked about it, he thought, "Man—who *wouldn't* want to do this?"

Kadlec said, "At the time, the only fantasy events were where "regular" people watched "experts" draft or speak. People won't go to Vegas to watch an event. They want to *be* the event."

They e-mailed some of their customers to gauge interest. There was a fantastic response, including comments such as "I've been waiting nine years for this contest" and "If you don't have this in Vegas, you're nuts."

Their World Championship of Fantasy Football (WCOFF) debuted in 2002 with an entry fee of $1,250, a grand prize of $200,000, and more than $500,000 in total prizes. The entries were slow, and many people were on the fence, as it was a new event and they were concerned they might pay for it, fly to Vegas, and find an empty room. Kadlec and Pappano determined it was essential to guarantee the prize money and earn the trust of the fantasy community. They decided to guarantee prizes, even though they would each lose about $100,000 if no one else signed up. "Lenny was petrified," according to Kadle. But after the guarantee, the entries started pouring in. They ended with 46 leagues of 12, for 552 total teams.

WCOFF marked the first time that the entire Las Vegas ESPN Zone had been rented out for an event. It cost $80,000 for the party, including an open bar and buffet. Approximately 900 people attended, as most participants brought a co-manager or significant other. The Saturday draft was in a 32,000-square-foot ballroom at the MGM Grand, the day before the NFL season kicked off. WCOFF gave away $15,000 in autographed memorabilia, drawing winners randomly. The event was a huge success.

The next spring, 2003, they launched the World Championship of Fantasy Baseball (WCOFB). It only drew 45 teams. The second WCOFF had 600 teams. In 2004, WCOFB again only had 45 teams and they never ran it again. Kadlec said they were football guys and just not really into baseball.

The WCOFF added additional leagues on Wednesdays, Thursdays, and Fridays, such as "best ball" and "auction" formats before the big Saturday draft. They also arranged informal golf outings and poker tournaments. And online leagues became available, as well as some live drafts in Atlantic City and Orlando, for those who didn't have the time or money to get to Vegas. They added a league with a $25,000 entry fee which was played by only the 12 people in the league with no overall competition. They peaked at 900 entries for the WCOFF main event.

Kadlec and Pappano had created a new industry, as many copycats quickly sprang up. They sold WCOFF in 2007 to an investment group,

GridIron Fantasy Sports. But after the 2010 NFL season, reportedly more than $300,000 in prize money went unpaid. GridIron was sued by at least one state Attorney General (Missouri) and went bankrupt.

WCOFF was the inaugural winner of the FSTA's Matthew Berry Game Changer Award in 2018. Kadlec was inducted into the FSTA Hall of Fame in 2021.

Around 2005, Scott Wapner did a feature about WCOFF for CNBC's *Squawk Box*. He attended the draft with 1,100 people in a 70,000-square-foot ballroom at the Las Vegas Hilton, interviewing Kadlec and many participants—including husbands and wives, fathers and sons, and mothers and daughters. Wapner also cited a recent survey of men aged 22 and over, where more than 40% said their number one thought during the day was about fantasy football, compared to 30% who answered sex.

NFBC/NFFC

Greg Ambrosius was the editor of *Fantasy Sports* and *Baseball Cards* magazines. In August 2002, *Baseball Cards* folded. The magazine industry was struggling. Ambrosius thought his career was ending. He had just had his third child and his wife quit her job, making his their only income. He was worried.

In September, the WCOFF placed an ad in his magazine. At a time when many fantasy games were free, they were asking people to pay $1,250 to enter, plus the costs of flying to Las Vegas and a hotel room. Ambrosius thought, "This has no chance in hell." He instructed his ad manager to get cash up front for their ad.

As part of the Friday night WCOFF party at the ESPN Zone, there was an experts league called Fanex that held their draft in a room so everyone could watch. Ambrosius' friend, Brady Tinker, was unable to attend the Fanex draft and asked Ambrosius to fill in. Ambrosius saw 900 people at the ESPN Zone drinking and having a great time. Saturday morning, he arrived at the convention room to see the same

900 people in a huge room filled with tables and draft boards as far as the eye could see. A man said, "This is the fucking Super Bowl of fantasy football!" Ambrosius was astounded, and the man who had thought this had no chance in hell knew right then that he wanted to run an event like this himself.

During a lunch break with a buffet, Ambrosius approached Emil Kadlec and said, "Emil, this is unbelievable. You know I have a good reputation in baseball. We can do this together in baseball. I would love to partner with you."

Kadlec replied, "Great, but can't talk about it right now."

Ambrosius later had discussions with Kadlec and Pappano. They were interested in working with Ambrosius because they knew nothing about fantasy baseball. Ambrosius, with his magazine, could promote it to a different audience than WCOFF had. Ambrosius wrote the rules. There would be 15 team leagues—which had never been done before—5x5 roto categories, a starting lineup of 14 hitters and nine pitchers, six bench spots, no disabled list. The entry fee would be $1,250 with a $100,000 grand prize.

Ambrosius needed to get approval from his boss at Krause Publications. He pitched him, and never got a reply. After much time passed, Kadlec and Pappano told him, "If you can't do it, we'll do it without you." In 2003, they used his rules and launched the World Championship of Fantasy Baseball (WCOFB). Just 45 teams signed up for a $25,000 grand prize and they lost money.

That summer, Ambrosius finally learned his boss had been stonewalling because Krause was sold. They couldn't take on any new ventures during that time. But the new owners, F & W Publications, okayed going forward with the idea. Rather than working with Kadlec and Pappano, Ambrosius was now going to launch a competitor, the National Fantasy Baseball Championship (NFBC) and the National Fantasy Football Championship (NFFC).

While he would be competing with WCOFB, he felt that he had a strong baseball following with his magazine, whereas the WCOFF didn't get much crossover from their football audience to their baseball game.

Ambrosius was also freelance writing for ESPN.com, he was president of the FSTA, and he had Krause backing the game, so he had a lot of credibility. And they guaranteed a $100,000 grand prize, which was the largest ever prize for fantasy baseball.

Ambrosius needed software. He asked STATS, Inc., which was already providing the stats needed for his magazine as well as running a game for Turner Sports. They agreed to build and manage a website for the NFBC and NFFC.

They offered drafts in New York and Chicago, as well as Las Vegas, to make it easier for people to attend. They put up a website and advertised it in *Fantasy Sports* magazine.

Ambrosius's goal was 300 entries. In early March 2004, he was flying to Phoenix, and they only had 148 signed up. He knew they were going to lose money—and he couldn't consider cancelling because he had contracts for convention space in three cities—and the prize money had to be guaranteed, including the $100,000 grand prize. He was so stressed out that when flying over the Rocky Mountains he literally was wishing his plane would crash.

They ended up with 195 teams. The NFBC draft was scheduled for the same time as the WCOFB draft. About 20 people, including Meat Loaf, wanted to do both. Ambrosius and Kadlec spoke, neither wanting to lose customers, so they agreed Kadlec would make his start time later, and Ambrosius would pay for a bus to bring people from his draft, at the Rio, to Kadlec's, at the Park MGM, at the conclusion of the NFBC draft. The NFFC drew 224 teams, also losing money. Ambrosius' two events combined to lose more than $100,000 and the new owners weren't happy. His boss said they would give him one more chance.

Ambrosius came through. In 2005, they sold out all 300 entries for baseball, and while football wasn't quite a sell out with 280 teams, it was profitable. They also had additional entries for auction leagues. They later added an online draft option, which made it easier and less expensive for people to play, since they didn't have to travel. And they added an entirely separate online competition with a $350 entry fee for those who couldn't afford the $1,250 leagues.

Anyone who has played one of their games is undoubtedly familiar with Tom Kessenich, their Manager of High Stakes Fantasy Games. Ambrosius hired him in 1999 to write for *Fantasy Sports*. Kessenich had been a Packers beat writer for nine years who had just lost his job when Gannett consolidated papers. After the second year of NFBC/NFFC, Ambrosius switched Kessenich to working with him on those.

On June 5, 2009, Ambrosius' 20th anniversary with the company, his boss said he needed to see him and Kessenich. He assumed he was getting a gift for the anniversary. But what he got was the president of F & W Publishing telling him, "We are selling your division and you."

Ambrosius asked, "You can sell people in the 21st century?"

The president looked him in the eye and replied, "Yes, we can."

NFBC/NFFC, *Fantasy Sports* magazine, and some of their other magazines, were all sold to Liberty Media. They were put in Liberty's division along with CDM, based in St. Louis. Ambrosius and Kessenich were allowed to stay in Wisconsin.

The next year, they started a $10,000-entry NFBC Diamond league. Ambrosius said the tension during the draft was palpable, unlike the usual jovial banter and trash talking during most drafts. He got an idea—and interrupted the draft to ask if anybody wanted a massage. Three hands went up. Ambrosius had masseuses from the poker room come to the draft and give these three a massage while drafting. One guy had his head down on the table, getting a massage, and announced his picks without lifting his head.

On January 5, 2011, Liberty announced they were shutting down CDM and the entire division. That same day, they contacted Ambrosius and asked if he wanted to buy the high-stakes games. His employment agreement stated if he was fired, he would be owed several months' salary. With that money, plus raiding his savings accounts and kids' savings accounts, Ambrosius bought it. But he immediately called Steve Byrd at STATS to see if they would buy it, because Ambrosius couldn't afford to run it and guarantee the prizes by himself. After owning the company for just a handful of days, Ambrosius sold it to STATS and became an employee. Kessenich also became a STATS employee.

Despite the various ownership changes, the entries kept growing and they kept adding new contests, some suggested by their customers. In 2016, NFBC/NFFC was sold to SportsHub. The main office is in Minneapolis, but as of 2024 Ambrosius and Kessenich still worked from a small office in Wisconsin, with a couple other employees working remotely and their two IT employees working from St. Louis. One of them was John Brison, formerly one of the CDM co-owners.

In 2023, they had a total of 41,000 entries for their contests, which then also included small participation in NBA and NHL games. And they paid more than $10 million in prizes. The average participant had five teams, so Ambrosius estimated they had about 4,000 unique owners for baseball and another 4,000 for football. With about half playing both sports, he estimated overall they had about 6,000 unique customers.

While many only play online, Ambrosius said, "Everyone always has a great time at the live drafts. Lawyers, doctors, working guys...we get everybody. Some bring their kids and let their nine-year-old announce their pick."

First $1 Million Prize

Several WCOFF copycats quickly appeared, with many advertising huge grand prizes. However, the prizes were based on what the fantasy company *hoped* participation would be, and they generally fell short. For example, one copycat called Payday Sports promised a $1 million grand prize based on its goal of 600 participants at $3,600 per entry. Only 39 signed up, forcing Payday to offer refunds to those who did not want to play for a reduced grand prize of $110,000.

But in 2008, a company called Poised to Stomp held a contest called Fantasy Football Open Championship, with just a $125 entry fee and a $1 million grand prize. All drafts were online. And this time they delivered. With 6,600 entrants, the top 15 advanced to the final week and gathered at the Bellagio Hotel in Las Vegas. The winner was Shane

Schroeder, a 31-year-old youth corrections officer from Fort Collins, Colorado.

Meanwhile, Chad Schroeder, from Omaha (no relation to Shane), suffered what is likely the most excruciating experience in the history of fantasy sports players. Everyone was watching the Sunday games in a Bellagio ballroom. At the end of the 4 p.m. EST games, Chad had a 27-point lead on Shane. There was just one game left: Chad had the New York Giants defense, at home against Carolina while Shane had running back DeAngelo Williams. With a 27-point lead and the Giants defense, it was virtually certain Chad would win. The owners of the contest told everyone they didn't need to stay and watch the night game in the ballroom if they didn't want to, except for Chad. They said, "We want you to stay, so we can film you winning the million dollars."

But DeAngelo Williams ran for three touchdowns in the first half, one more in the fourth quarter, and meanwhile not a single point by the Giants defense, giving Shane the win. Chad won $100,000 for second place. After being awarded the $1 million check and trophy by Jerry Rice on Monday night, Shane told the *Las Vegas Review-Journal*, "I'm going to get online, maybe tonight, and see if I can find a DeAngelo Williams jersey."

The contest produced another $1 million winner in 2009, but it lost money both years and there was never a third year.

Fantasy Football Players Championship

David Gerczak, Alex Kaganovsky and Lou Tranquilli had all played in the WCOFF since its inception, and they loved it. Kaganovsky said, "WCOFF was an important part of our lives, and for others who played as well...a lot of camaraderie, a lot of relationships formed from the event."

The three knew each other from the live events and the WCOFF message boards. Kaganovsky said, "Back then there was no social media, and the message boards were like what Twitter is now: non-stop banter about all sorts of things." But after WCOFF was sold in 2007 to GridIron, they saw changes in how the event was being run, such as spending lots of unnecessary money on catering with shrimp and crabs and bringing in retired NFL players as celebrities. They didn't like the direction it was going.

On a phone call in February 2008, the three decided to start their own contest. Within just a couple of months, they launched the Fantasy Football Players Championship (FFPC). Tranquilli, a financial advisor, became concerned there might be a conflict with him being involved, so he dropped out of the partnership before they ran their first draft in September.

Their first "main event" had a $1,250 entry fee, $75,000 grand prize, with a live draft at Caesars Palace in Las Vegas. They ran only one magazine ad and recruited participants primarily through word of mouth. They knew a lot of WCOFF players from being at the events and on their message boards for several years, and they e-mailed everyone, and they asked for referrals. Kaganovsky said it was like trying to recruit friends for a private fantasy league, only here they needed 200 people rather than the normal 10 or 12.

At a time when some companies had gone bankrupt and not paid prizes over the prior few years, they put their prize money in an attorney's escrow account. They put the attorney's name on their website and some people even called or e-mailed to confirm the money really was in escrow. This made people more comfortable entering the new game. "We felt it was an important thing to do," said Kaganovsky, "not just for marketing but also not to put ourselves in that position where we might not be able to pay prizes."

The draft was scheduled for the Friday night before the Saturday WCOFF, so people coming to Vegas for WCOFF could play their game Friday night. 180 entries were sold. The founders each invested $25,000 and used My Fantasy League commissioner service so they didn't need to invest money on technology. Kaganovsky was 40 when they launched and worked in his family's medical business in Brooklyn. Gerczak from Appleton, Wisconsin, was 37, and had a business selling watches in mall kiosks. Kaganovsky said, "We had no expectations that this would be a money maker that would support us. We thought best case scenario might be some nice additional extra income."

As owners of the FFPC, they couldn't play in their own game, so they continued playing WCOFF for another year and they played the NFFC for several years. Although the FFPC lost a little money that first year, Gerczak had a profitable year because he won the $100,000 grand prize in the NFFC online contest. The second year, they made a small profit. For the 2010 season, they partnered with David Dodds and Joe Bryant from Footballguys.com, and co-branded a $350 entry online tournament called the Footballguys Players Championship. This was very successful. In 2011, their concerns about the new owners of WCOFF became real when GridIron shut down WCOFF and went bankrupt.

Over the years, the FFPC used other strategic partnerships and kept growing at a steady pace. They became the largest high-stakes company, paying out more than $100 million in prizes by 2020. They added contests with entry fees as low as $35 and then even just $5, becoming an "all-stakes" company. They have a price point for everyone.

For 2022, their main event grand prize increased to $1 million, and the total prize pool was $6 million. This drew 4,000 entries at an average cost of about $1,700 (the entry fees vary depending on whether someone is going to Las Vegas or drafting online, and if they take advantage of discounts for multiple entries). 540 teams were drafted in Vegas, with the rest online. Even their $35 entry fee game had a grand prize of $50,000 ($268,000 total prizes), garnering 10,000 entries. For 2023, they increased the grand prize to $1 million for a second contest, their $350 entry fee game.

They did try baseball in the early 2010s, but it wasn't very successful, and they stopped after two years. "We aren't as passionate about baseball," Gerczak said, "and the market for baseball is much smaller than fantasy football."

FFPC has never had a corporate office. In addition to Gerczak and Kaganovsky, they have five full-time remote employees and additional seasonal staff. Gerczak still owns his watch company, which no longer has mall kiosks but sells them on his website WatchCo.com and on

Amazon. Kaganovsky left his family's business and went full-time with FFPC around 2013. Tranquilli has played in the FFPC every year and is a personal financial advisor for both Gerczak and Kaganovsky.

People from all over the world play the FFPC. Adrian Blincoe, a New Zealand distance runner in the 2008 and 2012 Olympics, was on vacation in the United States in 2013 and drafted a team on the flight back to New Zealand. He finished in the top 10.

Fantasy Football World Championship

At age 16, Ian Ritchie started playing fantasy football with his dad. Ian said, "As a teenager, you don't always have the easiest time finding things in common with your parents. Fantasy football drew us together. Planning drafts, looking at the waiver wire, watching games together—it became a bonding experience."

At age 30, Ritchie had been co-managing a team with his good friend Mark Deming for several years in their local Seattle friends league. Soon after the 2001 draft, Ritchie was married. He and his new wife, Viktoria, had a great honeymoon planned—first a trip to New York, then Miami, followed by a cruise.

They were staying at the Marriott inside the World Trade Center. On the fourth day of their honeymoon, September 11, planes struck, and they were lucky to get out of the building alive. They walked and walked—in shock—covered with soot, barefoot in their pajamas. They had no money and nowhere to go. Eventually a man saw them, took them into his business and let them call their parents to tell them they were alive. And this man—Joe Lorenzo—ran out and bought them shoes, then gave them the cash he had in his pocket.

His parents had friends who owned an apartment four miles away and they said, "If you can get there, we'll call the apartment manager and have him unlock it for you." They walked the four miles—fighter jets flying overhead—scared to death as there were rumors of nuclear weapons. The apartment manager not only let them in, but called his local bank manager, who went after hours to open the bank and the bank manager withdraw money from his personal account to give to Ritchie.

Ritchie's sister called the apartment the next morning. She happened to learn that the husband of one of her friends was in New York. He had a rental car and said, "If you can get to his hotel in Central Park by noon, you can have a ride back to Seattle." They walked to Central Park and made it home to Seattle three days later.

Ritchie said, "It was the most devastating, terrible, depressing, miserable experience of my life, and the following 18 months were the most depressing, dark days for me and my wife. Every time an airplane flew over our house whether I was in the shower or we were in bed, we'd have to run outside and find it; because in our mind now a reasonable expectation is that a plane could hit our house. We didn't leave our house a lot, we were very depressed."

Deming called one day to tell Ritchie he'd learned of the WCOFF and said, "Ian, this is gonna change your life. We'll do this every year. From now on, on September 11, you'll never be home again. Every year, you and Viktoria come down to Vegas, we'll draft, and it will be awesome."

And starting with the second year of WCOFF in 2003, they did. But for many years Ritchie was always afraid there'd be an anniversary attack. One year when the WCOFF draft fell on exactly the 11th, he had so much anxiety that while walking to the draft he was throwing up in every garbage can.

But the WCOFF was the first thing that started to get him out of his depression. "It became something I loved, and I wanted to share it with everybody," he said. He and Deming made a deal with Kadlec to have exclusive rights to film players at the events. They thought it was amazing and could be a documentary or a TV show. Ritchie explained, "One draft I'm sitting next to an auto body shop worker on one side and the CEO of a major company on my other side, and they're talking fantasy like they're best buddies."

The first several years, Ritchie and Deming filmed every contest and interviewed many participants. In 2005, they were close to a deal where

Hooters would sponsor a time buy on CBS for a show on high-stakes fantasy, but it fell apart.

When the 2010 NFL season ended and GridIron defaulted on prize payments, Ritchie was one of those affected, not being paid $20,000 he was owed. But much more than the money, he cared about the WCOFF disappearing. The contest that had been so helpful in bringing him out of his dark days, and had become so meaningful to him, was being lost.

Ritchie tried to save the WCOFF. He and Deming had talks with GridIron attempting to buy the WCOFF, pay everyone the money they were due, and keep it alive. But it didn't work out. He and Deming then had talks with the founders of the FFPC about partnering with them, but that didn't work out either.

Instead, Ritchie and Deming recruited Kadlec, and they co-founded the Fantasy Football World Championship (FFWC). They also bought the popular fantasy website FFToolbox. Later they brought in Scott Atkins, who hosted a weekly high-stakes fantasy podcast, and gave him equity.

Toolbox was started by Jeff Christiansen, a web developer from Fairfax, Virginia, who started posting a cheat sheet online in 1998. He listed it with several search engines, and the cheat sheet began getting steady traffic. While Jeff ran the website and did most of the writing himself, his wife Rebecca handled some of the business management.

By 2012, they were getting 12 million unique visitors and Ritchie thought this would be a great market to advertise the FFWC. But it didn't work out—FFToolbox was offering free information, so not many visitors were interested in paying $1,800 to get into a game. Their first year, in 2012, the FFWC lost money, but then grew and became profitable.

Ritchie and his partners now operate as Fulltime Fantasy Sports, which includes the FFWC and other fantasy companies they have bought. Ritchie has always regarded fantasy football as a fun side project. His main job has been real estate investment, and his biggest focus has been on his family—including his son, JR, who was drafted by the Atlanta Braves as the 35th overall pick of the 2022 MLB draft.

22 Years Later

After my initial zoom interview with Ritchie, I e-mailed him to request another zoom call, since I had more questions. He replied, "How about next Monday?"

I checked my calendar, and a chill went up my spine when I realized next Monday was September 11.

We had our call on September 11, 2023. I asked my follow-up questions and Ritchie also told me that he and Viktoria call Joe Lorenzo every year on this day. When *Sports Illustrated* bought his company, Ritchie had to travel often to Manhattan. One time, he brought Viktoria and their kids, and they had dinner with Lorenzo and his family. Ritchie told me, "The kindness we saw that day in 2001, I will never forget."

CHAPTER 15

Major Media Companies

Sooner or later, fantasy sports attracted most major media companies, including AOL, ESPN, Yahoo, CBS Sports, Fox Sports, NBC Sports, NFL.com, MLB.com, NBA.com, NHL.com and others. This chapter looks at some of these.

In the mid-'80s, Grandstand Sports Services offered online games for fantasy football and baseball on the AOL predecessor Q-Link. For a small charge, participants could enter a team. They also had access to chat rooms and fantasy content. Grandstand was on AOL when it launched, leading many to think it was an AOL-owned and -operated service, but it was a separate entity, until 1996 when it became an official part of AOL. They added basketball, hockey, and other sports. In 1997, 4,000 signed up for football. In 2000, they dropped the charge and offered games for free, as they were losing traffic to fantasy sites.

ESPN

Dan Okrent tried to get ESPN to add fantasy content. But in 1990, their editorial director told Okrent they did a survey of their viewers and only 1.5% played fantasy, so it didn't make sense to include it on shows like *SportsCenter* or *Baseball Tonight*. Over time, this changed, and some content started being added. In 1994, *Baseball Tonight* aired a two-hour roto pay-per-view special.

Geoff Reiss was a 33-year-old general manager of *Spy* magazine when, in what he calls an "incredible stroke of luck," he was hired in November 1993 by Starwave to lead their sports publishing. Starwave was a software and website company, founded earlier that year by Paul Allen, co-founder of Microsoft. A partnership between ESPN, Disney, and Starwave led to the creation of ESPN's first website, called ESPNET SportsZone, which launched April 1, 1995.

Reiss had played roto baseball since reading Okrent's 1981 article in *Inside Sport* magazine. And he was used to waiting for the Tuesday and Wednesday editions of *USA Today* to manually enter stats and get reports to league mates. He knew having games on the website would make playing easier for people. They could just sign up without needing to find 10 friends to form a league, and they'd have their stats done for them. Within a few months, SportsZone launched their first version of a fantasy football game, which was pay to play. They quickly had about 1,000 leagues and offered fantasy baseball the next spring. By 1997, their football game had 40,000 people in the overall competition.

Reiss said, "I was lucky to be in a corporate environment where I went to the CEO's office and diagrammed the business on a white board after we played half-court basketball during lunch, and he gave me approval on the spot to hire 15 people. That's not the way companies usually work."

In 1996, Rob Neyer was hired as the fantasy editor. Those first few years, freelancers such as John Hanson and Steve Cohen wrote about fantasy football, Peter Kreutzer about baseball, and Greg Ambrosius about both.

Technology was the biggest challenge in those early years. "We got a lot of stuff wrong, a lot of things failed," said Reiss. "We were trying to do things that hadn't been done before." It was a major technological issue to come up with thousands of alternate versions of sports leagues. It took as much effort to create a league standings page for someone's personal fantasy league as it took to create the page for the real NFL. It was the same exact process. So, there were thousands of different versions of NFL standings pages—it just happened that one of them was for the actual NFL and the rest were thousands of fantasy leagues, no two of them the same.

Reiss explained, "If the Cowboys are playing the Giants, and Troy Aikman throws a 20-yard touchdown pass to Michael Irvin that is a fact that gets stored in the database. And then how that fact gets played out across the site is different depending on thousands of different variations. Are we talking about the scoreboard against the Giants? Are we talking about your fantasy league? Are we talking about somebody else's fantasy league? It was an incredibly difficult problem to solve. Nitwits like me would draw this stuff up on a white board, and the engineers' heads would hurt for two years trying to figure out how to do it."

Reiss continued, "Everyone wants their fantasy draft within a short period of days before the start of the season. We had an incredibly difficult time managing capacity issues and keeping peoples' drafts working. It was nerve wracking."

By 2000 Sportscenter broadcasts started including detailed stats aimed at fantasy players for football, baseball, basketball, and hockey games. And ESPN2's *NFL2Night* nightly football show included a fantasy segment.

They continued to charge for their games until around 2002, when they went for a bigger market share by making their games free and supporting them with advertising. This was partly a reaction to Yahoo—which started fantasy a couple of years after ESPN—having made their games free.

In 2002, Reiss said he had expected hardcore players to embrace the chance to play fantasy online. What he didn't anticipate was people signing up who had never played fantasy before. Reiss said, "That's really been what's driven the whole phenomenon. The internet didn't convert a bunch of analog fantasy players. It opened the door to millions of people who never played these games before." That year, one in four visitors to ESPN.com went to the fantasy page, with over two billion page views.

Their fantasy games and writing staff grew as the years went on. Well-known fantasy analysts who started in the 2000s included Brandon Funston, Eric Karabell, Tristan Cockcroft, Nate Ravitz and Matthew Berry. Over time, they became more and more integrated with ESPN

TV and radio, where analysts would get on the air with fantasy segments. In 2006, ESPN TV started their first weekly fantasy football show.

From their launch through the 2000s, there were always many executives and producers at ESPN with varying views of how important fantasy should be—some embraced it while others thought it was ruining sports. Producers had a lot of power to run their own shows and add fantasy content or not. ESPN's fantasy games and content grew steadily over the years, as well as their presence on TV and radio. They also expanded globally. As early as 2001, they offered a cricket game, which had 500,000 participants—many from India—during the 2003 Cricket World Cup. In 2017, on match days, a fantasy rugby game often accounted for more than 60% of activity on ESPN's United Kingdom website.

In 2017, they introduced fantasy leagues for *The Bachelor* and *The Bachelorette* dating shows, developed with their sister company ABC. Participants try to predict who will advance each week. The first year drew 700,000 users, 75% of them women. Their 2023 fantasy football season had more than 12 million participants. On NFL Sundays, ESPN Fantasy accounts for more than half of all minutes consumed across ESPN digital platforms.

The revenue from fantasy was staggering. From 2009-2014, ESPN's revenue grew from $99 million to $180 million. They had started to factor fantasy into their bids when negotiating to acquire broadcasting rights. Around 2014, ESPN contracted to pay the NFL $1.8 billion per season for Monday night football. ESPN executive Jason Waram said, "A lot of fantasy games come down to Monday night, and even if you don't care about the teams, you'll stay up late to watch if one of your players is playing."

John Walsh, who had been the editor of *Inside Sport* magazine (Chapter 2) became the executive editor of ESPN in 1988. Reiss said that Walsh and Dick Glover, another ESPN executive, were the only senior people at ESPN in the early '90s who played fantasy and understood its potential. He said Walsh's support of fantasy can't be overstated. Matthew Berry, who joined ESPN in 2007, said Walsh was the biggest champion of making fantasy more prominent on their website, magazine, TV, radio, and digital video.

30 Years Later

Reiss said, "Back in those first years, I never would have believed how many people are now playing fantasy on ESPN and in general. It's been a dramatic evolution, over the course of the last 20 years, that fantasy grew from an utterly fringe activity to probably the single biggest driver of NFL consumption. I don't think any of us—even the most bullish on fantasy—could have envisioned that. It's hard to convey how far we've come, but it would be foolish to think we are at some kind of end state, as opposed to still being relatively early in how fantasy is likely to evolve."

Matthew Berry thinks the increased exposure of fantasy on ESPN helped fantasy sports gain acceptance with the professional leagues. "We got fantasy on TV and radio," he said, "and I think when the sports leagues saw that the worldwide leader in sports is talking about fantasy on *SportsCenter*, on *Baseball Tonight*, on *NFL Live*, and the world isn't falling—people aren't screaming "what the hell is this?", ratings aren't dropping—I think once they saw that, and there's a way to monetize it, they got on board. So, I think that time period at ESPN was a big catalyst for fantasy sports becoming mainstream."

CBS SportsLine

Mike Levy was a successful businessman who—in 1993, before commercially available internet—had the foresight to see that dial-up services AOL, CompuServe, and Prodigy were undoubtedly going to grow and be used by almost everyone. On New Year's Day of 1994, he watched the Orange Bowl between #1 Florida State and #2 Nebraska, and, afterwards, was dismayed to see the skimpy coverage of this game on the big three providers. He realized they were all lacking in sports coverage and had the idea of starting a dial-up online service for sports.

Starting with $200,000 of his own money, the 47-year-old founded SportsLine USA in February 1994, in Ft. Lauderdale, Florida. He created a business plan and a prototype and tried to raise capital. He needed $2 million. He was not having success recruiting investors and thought a celebrity spokesman would give him credibility. A friend of Levy's knew Joe Namath's agent, Jim Walsh, and put them in touch. He successfully got Namath—who lived in the area—to agree to take stock in the new company in exchange for his endorsement. Walsh was also given stock for his help. Walsh helped Levy meet potential investors and in August 1994 one agreed to put up the $2 million. Over the next two years, they raised $40 million in venture capital.

In August 1995, SportsLine launched its online sports news and information service. Meanwhile ESPN was doing the same thing and had launched their own website, SportsZone, four months earlier. Levy was competing against a heavyweight who massively advertised their services on the ESPN TV network. SportsLine desperately needed publicity and in 1996 signed Shaquille O'Neal as a spokesperson. During 1996, they also approached Fox, NBC, and CBS and, in 1997, struck a deal where CBS would become a minority partner, promote SportsLine on all their televised sports, and they renamed the website CBSSportsline.com. That gave them the credibility to sign Michael Jordan, Tiger Woods, and Wayne Gretzky as spokespersons.

In the mid-'90s there were very few web developers, so when Levy started recruiting talent, he wanted to get the people who had put ESPN on Prodigy. There were three guys—Harold Topper, Bill Fiorentino, and Rick Wolf. Topper, then Fiorentino went to SportsLine. Wolf initially wasn't interested in risking the security of IBM for a start-up. But everything changed when his wife—becoming a doctor—decided to do her residency at a hospital in Miami. In 1995, Wolf was on his way from White Plains, New York to southern Florida to become the 13th employee of SportsLine.

Wolf was hired as the Director of Product Development, which included creating fantasy sports content. He wrote some code himself but mostly directed the people who wrote the code. Among other things, they created a salary cap game, an in-season advice product called the Advance Scout, and a commissioner product. First was MLB, then the NFL. They also made the first online draft guides. And there was a Shaq-endorsed fantasy basketball game where participants chose eight NBA players but only one could be a center and it had to be Shaq.

In 1996, SportsLine launched the first all-sports audio programming on the internet. If someone had a modem, a sound card, and speakers on their computer—which not everyone had yet—they could listen to 70 hours of programs a week, including a show called *Fantasy Sports Tonight* with Carl Foster and John Zaleski.

"It was a lot of fun," Wolf said. "After work we would often go out to have a beer. And we would come up with an idea and go back into the building and build it that night. The three developers and I would go back in and just start coding away until dawn." On Friday afternoons, SportsLine bought a keg of Heineken and they would drink at the office. Joe Namath and his agent would occasionally visit. One time Wolf wanted to reward his team, so he bought 25 NFL footballs and Namath signed them all.

SportsLine also built a strong staff for fantasy content, including many who went on to have great careers in the industry. Scott Engel was hired in 1996 and became the managing editor. He left for ESPN in 2004, and his career has included stints at RotoExperts, RotoBaller and hosting on SiriusXM starting in 2010 and continuing to this day. Michael Fabiano and Tristan Cockcroft joined SportsLine in 2000. Cockcroft also went to ESPN in 2004 and has been there ever since as a senior fantasy writer. Fabiano was the first fantasy analyst to appear on one of the major television networks when he was on CBS Sports in 2005, and was the first fantasy contributor on The NFL Today on CBS. He went on to become the NFL's first fantasy-only analyst and was the lead fantasy analyst for NFL Network for over 15 years. As of

2024 he was a senior fantasy analyst for *Sports Illustrated*. All three are in the FSWA Hall of Fame.

In 1996, Levy recruited Mark Mariani to be SportsLine's President of Sales and Marketing. Mariani had been the Executive VP of Sales for Turner Sports for several years. He was also an avid fantasy player. In 1982, while working at a CBS affiliate in Chicago, his boss asked if he'd like to play fantasy football. Mariani had never heard of it. But when Mariani realized that his boss's, boss's, boss in the fancy Manhattan headquarters was playing—and he would be able to pick up a phone and talk trade or whatever with someone who would ordinarily never answer his call—he jumped at the chance.

While at Turner, they were broadcasting the NFL Sunday night games for the first nine weeks of the season (ESPN then carried weeks 10-16). For two years, Mariani kept bugging Don McGuire, the executive producer of TNT sports, to put up fantasy information during their telecasts. He told McGuire, "There are lots of people playing fantasy, we've got to give a recap of the top performances by quarterbacks, running backs and receivers during the broadcast." On Sunday, October 29, 1995, McGuire invited Mariani to join him on the production truck outside RFK Stadium in Washington. During the telecast, McGuire said, "Congratulations, you're now seeing fantasy on NFL football." This was the first time an NFL broadcast showed fantasy relevant statistics. ESPN then followed, starting with week 10. (Mariani was with SportsLine until 2006 and was instrumental in their success for fantasy and everything else.)

But the battle to get fantasy information on TV continued for years. Jim Bernard of Fox Sports Interactive had debates as late as the mid-2000s with his graphics people telling them the fantasy players needed to see who scored, not just the game score. By 2003, SportsLine had more than 800,000 people playing in more than 80,000 paid football leagues. Fantasy accounted for 30% of SportsLine's total revenue, compared to just 10% in 2000.

David Hersh, who had become SportsLine's Vice President of Fantasy Sports, mentioned how fantasy football overtook fantasy baseball in popularity in the '90s. Hersh said, "The gap has become wider each season. In 2002, football was five or six times the size of baseball for SportsLine." Hersh credited this to the shorter NFL season, weekend matchups and that fantasy football is "less stat-heavy compared to baseball."

Their league had instant scoring and messenger capabilities. In 2003 Larry Wahl, a spokesperson for SportsLine, said, "You can see what you're scoring, what your opponent's scoring, send them an instant message and trash talk all at once as it's happening."

In 2004, Viacom, the owner of CBS Sports, which already owned 38% of SportsLine, bought the remaining 62% for $46 million. They changed the name to CBSSports.com. That year, SportsLine reported $14.7 million in fantasy football billings and $3 million in fantasy baseball billings, with each increasing about 20 percent from 2003.

CBSSports.com continued to grow and remains among the top handful of sites for sports news and fantasy games, news, and analysis as of 2024.

Rick Wolf

Wolf has had an illustrious career in the fantasy industry. Beginning with Prodigy, where he worked on Baseball Manager (Chapter 4), he then went to SportsLine, followed by All-Star Stats and RotoWorld (Chapter 10), then NBC Sports. He was then president of Alarm Sports Network and then SVP of Spotlight Sports Group. Wolf has been an FSTA board member since its inception, was chairman for four years, and is a member of their Hall of Fame. He has mentored dozens of successful people in the fantasy industry, including the likes of Matthew Berry, Gregg Rosenthal, Tristan Cockcroft, Michael Fabiano, Scott Engel, Howard Bender, Kay Adams, Maria Marino, and Stacie Stern.

Since 2012 (and continuing as of 2024) Wolf has co-hosted a weekly fantasy sports radio show on SiriusXM with Glenn Colton, *Colton and the Wolfman.* The two have been close friends ever since meeting as college dorm mates. Colton, also a member of the FSGA Hall of Fame, has been a fantasy writer since he started writing for RotoWorld in 2002. They also co-manage teams in experts leagues such as LABR and Tout Wars. Wolf says they are a little like the Odd Couple, Oscar and Felix: "Glenn is a high-powered lawyer, passed the bar—and I don't like to pass a bar."

Wolf has played almost all fantasy sports, including bass fishing and wakeboarding. His advice for new fantasy players is "Have fun. Choose players you like to root for. And above all, trash talk—even if you are losing." He never gets tired of telling people that, in 1999, he bought Jermaine Dye for $1, and he hit 27 homers and 119 RBIs.

Wolf also works with Break the Hold, a non-profit for teenage suicide prevention. As of 2019, 3,200 kids between ages 14-18 would try to commit suicide per day. 13% were successful.

Scott Engel said, "Wolf is one of the greatest visionaries and most impactful people in the history of fantasy sports."

Yahoo

When Shawn Robinson was a computer engineering student at Cal Poly in 1996, he was required to do a senior project. His brother was commissioner of a fantasy football league and had been doing the stats by hand for many years. As his senior project, Robinson offered to build a website for his brother that could calculate the stats and standings. Robinson recruited friends Brian Webb and Scott Ware—also computer science students—to help. They were eager to help, since they also computed stats by hand for their own fantasy leagues.

As with many others mentioned in this book, what started as a college project turned into a real business. The three friends launched a stat service called Sportasy. They only got business by word of mouth and internet searches. They never advertised. As a result, by mid-1998 they only had about 100 customers.

Yahoo wanted to start offering fantasy sports, and went looking for good programmers, ideally with fantasy experience. They found Sportasy, interviewed the three partners, and offered to buy Sportasy for $150,000 and have the three become employees of Yahoo. Yahoo didn't care if they had 20,000 customers or only 100, they wanted people who could build their fantasy platform. The purchase occurred in September 1998. Robinson bought a new car with some of his share of the purchase price, and the three moved to Silicon Valley to work at Yahoo's offices.

In 1999, Yahoo started offering free fantasy baseball and then football. This was a big event, as Yahoo was the web's primary search engine, a major e-mail provider and the web's second most visited site (behind only AOL). The free games drove traffic to the website and created ad revenue. That first year, Yahoo had about 500,000 fantasy football players and grew from there in football and other sports. They also monetized by creating a "stat tracker," which allowed competitors to see their H2H game score in real time. It was offered free for the first week of the NFL season, and then it cost something like $10-$15 to keep it for the rest of the season. Most players paid for this. Starting in 2001, there was an option to pay $24.95 per team and win prizes and have access to extra features. Not many chose this option.

Dan Berger, the general manager of Yahoo Sports at the time, said, "While we try to get players of the free game to purchase stat tracker and weekly forecasts, or join our pay version of the game, a primary goal is to integrate fantasy football players to other parts of the Yahoo website." Berger said most fantasy football players join a league primarily so they can have bragging rights over their friends, and not for prizes. Yahoo's free game had no prizes, and the pay version gave a trophy. (Although undoubtedly some leagues had their own prizes or cash involved that didn't go through Yahoo's service.)

Robinson, Webb, and Ware stayed with Yahoo for several years and more engineers were added to the team. Ware moved to London in 2001 and spent a couple years there building international games, including soccer and tennis.

David Geller, who was head of Yahoo fantasy sports from 2006-2012, explained that Yahoo was a tech rather than a sports company, so they wanted to improve their product on the tech side. One thing they did was look at their top page views, and discovered one of the biggest was an "error" message given when people tried to change their weekly lineups. They improved the way these changes were made and instantly cut millions of page views, which made for a better user experience. They revamped the live draft experience to include player photos and stats along with player names. And they integrated live highlights, so when your player scored you could see a 15-second video highlight of it. This started with the NHL and went to other sports.

Geller said, "Other than Yahoo mail, there was no more valuable user for us than the fantasy player, because of the enormous time spent on the site and billions of page views." This allowed them to sell sponsorship ads for major companies such as Budweiser, Southwest Airlines, and Coke. To advertise its pickup trucks, Toyota sponsored the "Toyota Pickup of the Week," a weekly mention of the most acquired free agent from the waiver wire.

Yahoo developed a robust team of fantasy writers and analysts, including Brandon Funston (previously with ESPN), Brad Evans, Andy Behrens, and Scott Pianowski. Evans said they had to fight to get fantasy content on Yahoo's main home page. But as time went on, and fantasy became mainstream, editors became open to doing it. Behrens said, "It helped that advertisers were interested in fantasy, because our audience is sticky—they consume content like crazy, spend tons of time on the pages, and view all the video."

Yahoo started a live internet show, *Fantasy Football Live*, that aired on Sunday mornings and became one of the most watched shows on the internet. About 2009, they offered stat tracker for free, taking a big hit to their revenue, but increasing overall engagement.

Yahoo made a deal with Automated Insights, an artificial intelligence company, to produce personalized write-ups for people's fantasy leagues and their teams. On Tuesday morning, participants received a summary of their league's results written as though an NFL beat reporter was covering their league. With millions of reports generated, this became another chance for Yahoo to sell an advertising sponsorship to a major company.

Yahoo made it easy for people to roll over their leagues to the next year, keep historical data for their league and have a dynasty league if they wanted. All of this helped retention. Leagues rarely switched to a different provider.

Geller estimated about 8% of their fantasy players are international, which includes a lot of US military stationed abroad. By 2019, Yahoo was reported to have seven million users just for football.

17 Years Later

Behrens, who's been a Yahoo writer and analyst since 2007, said, "I feel fortunate to work for a media company that's consistently viewed fantasy as a huge priority—now more than ever—and respected the fantasy audience. There's always been incredible camaraderie on our team, and I think it comes across on camera and on our pages."

Pro Leagues

Unlike Clay Walker and the NFLPA, the NFL wanted nothing to do with fantasy for many years. In 2002, the NFL conducted a study, and found that while the average male surveyed on its website spent 6.6 hours a week watching the league on television, fantasy players surveyed said they watched 8.4 hours of NFL football per week. "This is the first time we've been able to demonstrate specifically that fantasy play drives TV viewing," said Chris Russo, the NFL's senior vice president at the time.

With this, the league made fantasy more prominent on its website, NFL.com, and started airing commercials with current star players—such as Kurt Warner, Priest Holmes, and Michael Strahan—promoting fantasy. This was a big moment in fantasy sports history.

By this time, MLB, NBA, and the NHL were also offering their own games on their websites.

In 2006, the NFL and Sprint Mobile made a five-year, $600 million deal directly aimed at fantasy players. Sprint's phones would allow their customers to download apps to run their fantasy football teams.

CHAPTER 16

Fantasy Sports Trade Association

In August 1996, Paul Charchian and Rob Pythian, from *Fantasy Football Weekly*, hosted what was probably the largest gathering of fantasy players at the time. Roughly 600 people paid a small fee to attend the Fantasy Football Expo, at the Mystic Lake Casino, near Minneapolis. The featured speaker was Chris Mortenson, from ESPN, and representatives of many fantasy companies—including Charlie Wiegert, Jeff Thomas, Rick Wolf, and several others—bought booths to advertise their services. Charchian's parents worked the pay line, and friends helped with other jobs.

After another year at the casino, the 1998 expo was held at the Metrodome, with about 3,000 people attending. Vikings coach Brian Billick and rookie Randy Moss were featured. The 1999 expo was at the Mall of America. After that, they stopped the expos as it was a lot of work, they didn't make money from them, and August was always their busiest time of the year.

In August 1998, James Serra and Jim Lenz of Fantasy Insights held the Fantasy Sports Convention at the Tropicana in Las Vegas. The weekend event drew about 400 attendees, with 22 industry vendors who had booths to pitch their products. Serra said the "booths" were mostly card tables except for ESPN which had a nice booth.

Industry attendees included Greg Ambrosius from *Fantasy Sports* magazine, Emil Kadlec from *Fantasy Football Pro Forecast*, and Christina Shellhart of *The Sporting News*, who were all looking for more advertisers and subscribers; Steve Byrd of STATS, Inc., who wanted to find companies to buy his data services; Charlie Wiegert, looking for more people to play CDM games; and many others. Ex-NFL players Tim Green and Randy Cross were the headliners, and the industry people participated in panel discussions on various topics. Serra and Lenz only held this event once, as it turned out to be a lot of work, very expensive, and they had been hoping to draw a few thousand attendees. Ryan Bonini, of KFFL, had spent days making CD-ROMs with his draft guide to sell, expecting those few thousand attendees. He left town with most of them and said, "They made good coasters later."

But it was at this event that several of the industry members held an impromptu meeting to discuss issues that affected them all. And the idea of forming a trade association was born. Although some were competitors, they saw that they could work together to grow the industry and protect fantasy from issues such as being considered gambling. By increasing the size of fantasy sports participants, they would all benefit.

After the event, phone calls and e-mails followed between those who had been at the informal meeting and others who hadn't been. Most everyone agreed it was a good idea. The non-profit organization was established and called the Fantasy Sports Players Association (FSPA), as their initial emphasis was to protect fantasy participants. Carl Foster, the first FSPA president, said at the time, "A primary mission of the FSPA is to make sure leagues are not ripping people off."

Their first meeting was in Tampa, March 1999, held in conjunction with the LABR auctions. The FSPA sponsored LABR, paying for hotel meeting rooms. The weekend event was billed as the "Fantasy Baseball Experience" with seminars, cocktail parties, and LABR auctions.

Companies each contributed $500 and became the first FSPA board members. They were Foster, Wiegert, Ambrosius, Wolf, Shellhart, Byrd, Serra, Jeff Thomas, John Zaleski, Brandon Funston of ESPN, and Scott Higgins and Barry Dorf of EA Sports (11 companies and 12 board members). EA Sports, while not a fantasy company, saw a crossover between fantasy players and those who liked their games. The tab for the weekend was $9,500. Wolf and Schelhart got their companies, SportsLine and *The Sporting News*, to cover the shortfall.

Zaleski remembers that first board meeting. "We were in a conference room with one of those very long, lawyer-like, nice tables. I was sitting at the head at one end of the table, and Scott Higgins was at the other end, about 20 feet away. Right before the start of the meeting, we looked at each other and started laughing out loud. Someone asked why we were laughing, and at the same time, we both said, "We're at a fucking board meeting for fantasy sports!"

Ambrosius suggested they could meet again at his company's Sports-Fest card show that summer in Chicago. He said he'd include a Fantasy Pavilion area. In addition to holding the second board meeting, they had 30 booths of vendors. Chicago Bears NFL Hall of Famer Dick Butkus was there, working with one of the card companies, and they let him draft for a few rounds of their live FSPA experts league draft.

The FSPA didn't have enough money to hold any events, but in 2000, Ambrosius' company, Krause Publications, hosted the first Fantasy Sports Trade Conference in Orlando. Ambrosius said, "It was so successful that we hosted a summer trade conference in Chicago and that was even more successful."

Krause continued to hold two conferences a year, one in the winter and one in summer, through 2007, at which point the FSTA took over running the conferences. They became opportunities for industry members to share ideas, learn about new technology, and react to potential industry threats. The conferences featured speakers including industry experts, legal specialists, researchers, and technology innovators. There were always guest speakers such as Tug McGraw, Vida Blue, Rollie Fingers, and Harmon Killebrew. Association members ranged from small start-ups to large media corporations. And FSTA board meetings were held during the conferences.

Although paying licensing fees was a concern for the industry and CDM sued MLBAM in 2005, the NFLPA and MLBPA became members of the FSTA and sponsored the trade conferences from 2000-2007. They spoke about licensing and encouraged all companies to get licensed.

In 2003, Ambrosius became FSTA president. "That year we realized we were really a trade association—not a player's association," he said. "We needed to focus on helping fantasy businesses rather than consumers. We realized if we are going to be a real trade association, we must change the name to Fantasy Sports Trade Association. And we realized we had no money—we had no real benefits for members. We needed to get surveys, some data that people are willing to pay a membership for."

They hired Dr. Kim Beason of the University of Mississippi to do a survey to find out how many people played, what types of fantasy games they played, what sports, how many leagues they were in, etc. Among other things, they learned more than 15 million people played fantasy sports and spent an average of $150 per year.

"This survey got a lot of publicity," Ambrosius said. "That was the first time anyone really knew how big the market was, and knowing it was this big brought the fantasy industry into the mainstream." Board member Peter Schoenke said, "Before this, nobody knew how big the market was—was it 500,000? Was it 20 million? Nobody knew. But with this, every business plan could have numbers and demographics. You could now tell potential advertisers they can reach 15 million people."

The surveys did help increase FSTA membership, growing to almost 100 members by 2006. The FSTA has continued commissioning surveys ever since, mostly using IPSOS-Reid.

Jeff Thomas took over as president from 2006-2008, then Paul Charchian from 2009-2020, Stacie Stern from 2020-2022 (with her title changed to Chairperson) and Brandon Loeschner in 2023.

Elevator Pitch

For many years, FSTA conferences have included an opportunity for fantasy entrepreneurs to give a quick presentation for a new company, product, or idea. They are given three minutes each to make a presentation in front of dozens of the most influential people in the industry. The audience votes on the most promising idea and the winner gets a prize such as a trophy and free FSTA membership. But even those who don't win have a chance to garner interest from attendees. Without this, very few of these new entrepreneurs would ever get a chance to pitch industry heavyweights such as ESPN and Yahoo.

The FSTA has annual awards recognizing the best companies and products for various categories. In 2018 they started the Matthew Berry Game Changer Award, honoring events that helped fantasy sports get to where it is. They also have a hall of fame and have given a handful of people a lifetime achievement award. There are also FSTA experts fantasy leagues for football and baseball, with drafts occurring at two annual conferences. In recent years, these have been broadcast live on SiriusXM.

Issues FSTA Has Dealt With

When the FSPA formed, most people didn't know what fantasy sports were, and many assumed all players were nerds. The FSPA set out to help gain credibility. It was easy for someone like Charlie Weigert or Greg Ambrosius to know how popular fantasy could become, and how passionate the participants were—they knew from personal experience. But it's different when you have a senior management person at a huge company like ESPN or Yahoo who doesn't play fantasy and doesn't know much about it, and the lower-level people at their company need to try to convince them the company should devote resources to growing their fantasy platform. This changed over the years, but back in 1998 and several years thereafter, upper management needed convincing. The surveys sponsored by the FSTA gathered demographic information and disproved the misconception that fantasy games were played by lonely, anti-social males in their parents' basement. These demographics helped convince executives to do more with fantasy sports.

Some companies saw the opportunity and took advantage of it while others missed the boat. Howard Kamen, from *USA Today*, said, "I think we collectively didn't realize the potential for fantasy—and quite frankly we got passed there. Management didn't understand this could be a moneymaker. It was seen as 'it's a little niche thing that a few geeky guys are playing.'" In 1997, he wrote memos to management suggesting they do more for fantasy, but they didn't.

One major issue the association had to deal with was the players associations demanding licensing fees (prior to the issue being resolved in 2008 with the CBC vs MLBAM lawsuit). At that summer 1999 card show where Ambrosius added a Fantasy Sports Pavilion, the NFLPA agreed to send a representative. The FSTA members thought it would be a good opportunity to show how fantasy benefits the NFL. But their representative, LaShun Lawson, went to every booth picking up business cards. At the KFFL booth, she told owner William Del Pilar he needed to be licensed and he became very angry. Ambrosius and James Serra then realized why she had been gathering business cards and told her to leave. Sure enough, a week later, everyone whose card she had picked up received a cease-and-desist letter from the NFLPA claiming that not just commissioner services, but newsletters and everything, needed to be licensed.

When everyone received these letters, they called each other, started doing research, and talked to their attorneys. Ultimately everyone pretty much agreed they didn't need to be licensed to use stats, so they ignored the cease and desist, and the NFLPA never sued anyone.

Serra recalls, "One year, Greg Ambrosius and I were having lunch with Pat Allen, the executive vice president for the NFLPA, and she was going off on us, and yelling at us in the middle of this restaurant that what we were doing was illegal and we had to be licensed. And we were explaining to her how stats were used in the software, and she asked us questions, and Greg and I looked at each other, realizing she has no idea what fantasy football is."

Serra continued, "She was mean. There was no negotiating with her. She wanted something like 10% of our gross. We tried to explain most of us were small businesses and couldn't afford that, could she accept 3 or 4%? She said, 'No, either you do 10% or we shut you down.'"

Ambrosius said, "When I hosted the 2000 trade conference, MLBPA was the sponsor and in the August Chicago trade conference, NFLPA was the sponsor. I wanted to work with them and find a solution, whereas a lot of industry guys wanted no part of them. It created a tough dynamic until the CDM lawsuit cleared the air on licensing."

The other big issue facing the association since its inception has been the question of fantasy sports being considered gambling. The FSTA has helped make the case to state and federal courts, as well as legislators, that fantasy is a game primarily of skill rather than luck, and thus it is not gambling. Also, since 90% play in leagues for $50 or less, the vast majority aren't motivated by money. Ultimately the federal courts and most states have ruled it is not gambling, with a large part of that due to agreeing it is more skill than luck. This is discussed in detail in Chapter 17.

The FSTA has also helped with issues such as banks and credit card companies refusing to work with companies because they misunderstood the word "fantasy." Additionally, some sites were being blocked due to the misconception they were gambling websites.

Association members range from small startups to large media companies. In 2019, the FSTA became the Fantasy Sports & Gaming Association (FSGA), expanding its scope to include new markets emerging after the legalization of sports betting. The board of directors was expanded to include executives from sports betting companies. Prior FSTA research had found a strong correlation between fantasy activity and sports wagering. "And with that strong crossover, we believe there is a lot we can do together and that this is a natural evolution for us," said Paul Charchian, FSTA president at the time.

26 Years Later

William Del Pilar, of KFFL, said, "I remember the weekend at the Tropicana. We all bonded so well at that event, I think that's why the association was able to successfully launch."

James Serra said in 2023, "I was at an FSGA meeting in Times Square a few years ago and it was amazing to see how far we had come since the beginning, with all the major companies there with large professional signs, and hundreds of people."

Jeff Thomas said, "One of the keys to the FSTA success was entrepreneurs helping each other, giving their time freely, working multiple hours and expecting nothing... to build the industry."

Steve Cohen, who had been at the 1998 Tropicana event and was involved very early on with the FSPA and FSTA, was inducted into their hall of fame in 2017. About his induction night, he said, "Hanging out and partying with so many friends that night, that was what made it so special. To raise a glass with so many people that have been there for me. Back in the day, we'd help each other; we weren't competitors, we couldn't be, because we needed each other so badly."

Fantasy Sports Writers Association

By the early 2000s, more and more newspapers, magazines, and websites were hiring writers to cover fantasy sports. The Fantasy Sports Writers Association (FSWA) was established in 2004 by Emil Kadlec, Bob Harris, Ryan Houston, and Kirk Bouyelas, to be a voice for writers in the industry—and to promote and acknowledge their work.

Several FSGA members are also members of the FSWA. Awards are given annually for categories such as Fantasy Football Writer of the Year, Fantasy Football Article of the Year, best publication, best podcast, best radio show, etc. There are similar categories for baseball and other sports. In 2010, a Hall of Fame was launched to recognize those who have a distinguished body of work for at least 10 years. As of 2024, the FSWA had 1,100 members.

Fantasy Sports Association

In 2006, Clay Walker of the NFLPA created Fantasy Sports Association (FSA), the purpose of which was to get the professional leagues and large media companies together to raise support for fantasy sports. Walker flew all over the country—on NFLPA money—to try and get the leagues and teams on the same page, realizing fantasy was something that would benefit both the leagues and the players. He recruited about 25 members, including the NFL, MLB, NBA, PGA tour, NASCAR, Yahoo, Fox, ESPN, CBS, NBC, America Online, EA Sports, Fanball, Pro Trade, *Sporting News*, STATS, Head2Head, Krause, and others.

Walker was the initial FSA Chairman, followed by Rick Wolf from 2007-2010. The annual dues were based on companies' revenues, and generally were $5,000-$10,000. This gave the FSA a good budget to work with, and they sponsored events such as the *Sports Business Journal's* annual Media and Technology conference. Wolf for two years, and then Stacie Stern the third year, gave the sponsor's remarks in front of 600 company executives where they could share research and data about the fantasy industry.

They also held events around the NFL draft. As an FSA member, the NFL allowed other members to attend private events, where they would have "meet and greets" with ex-NFL players, as well as the rookies who had just been drafted the night before. These efforts paid off handsomely, getting the likes of Visa, Hilton, McDonald's, Holiday Inn, Mercedes, Coca-Cola, and many others to advertise and getting millions of dollars flowing into fantasy sports.

The FSA closed at the end of 2010, having completed their mission to raise awareness and get fantasy sports into the advertising budgets of major companies. Many of their members then joined the FSTA if they weren't already members.

Growth and Demographic Statistics

It's estimated that just in the US, the fantasy industry generated $9.5 billion revenue in 2022.

Estimates for the global fantasy sports industry for 2022 are approximately $25 billion and expected to increase to $40-50 billion by the late 2020s.

Per the FSGA, the estimated number of people who play fantasy sports in the USA and Canada age 18 or older, by year:

Year	Players
1988	500,000
1989	1 million
1994	1-3 million
2003	15 million
2006	18 million
2010	32 million
2015	57 million
2022	62 million

Of the 62 million in 2022, 50 million were in the US, meaning approximately 20% of American adults play fantasy.

The 2022 FSGA survey found season-long fantasy sports players in the US and Canada played the following:

- 79% football (NFL)
- 32% basketball (NBA)
- 22% baseball (MLB)
- 12% hockey (NHL)
- 11% soccer
- 11% NCAA football
- 9% NASCAR
- 9% golf
- 8% Esports
- 7% NCAA basketball
- 4% *The Bachelor* and *Bachelorette*
- 4% CFL

In surveys from 2014-2023, the breakdown of male/female participants have fluctuated from 80/20% to 65/35%. A 2013 study reported that men spend an average of 3.1 hours per week on fantasy as opposed to only 1.5 for women. It also found that fantasy players watch sports about eight hours more per week than non-fantasy players, and people who go to the ESPN website spend three times more time on it if they are a fantasy player.

The 2017 FSTA survey found that 73% of players paid for non-cash prizes such as a trophy or belt; 68% paid for a league punishment, such as the worst team must get a tattoo or is given a toilet bowl trophy; and 84% had a draft party at an average cost of $650.

A 2019 FSTA survey found 67% of fantasy players are employed full-time, and 47% made more than $75,000 per year. 50% of players were between the ages of 18 and 34, with the average age being 38. A 2023 study found 84% have a college degree.

As of 2019, there were an estimated 646 fantasy-sports-related businesses in the US alone, employing approximately 50,000 people.

A 2014 study reported that 80% of those surveyed expected to still be playing fantasy in 10 years and 40% until they die.

A 2008 FSTA survey found 60% of participants knew the other people in their leagues. 40% said that participation increased the camaraderie amongst employees in their workplace, and 30% said they had sparked new friendships at work due to playing fantasy sports. 16% said that playing fantasy football allowed them to make valuable business contacts.

All surveys that have been done only include people aged 18 and over. It is unknown how many under the age of 18 play, but it is undoubtedly a very large number. Many parents manage teams with their kids. Many kids have their own teams. In 2023, Paul Charchian was a featured guest at a fantasy football after-school class at Greenwood Elementary School (Plymouth, Minnesota) where fifth-graders applied mathematics to constructing fantasy teams.

Mike Stein, of Fantasy Judgment, has been playing since he was 6 years old and was in a junior division of his dad's fantasy football league back in 1985. There were seven others in the league aged 7–9.

At age 9, Jay Zuckerman started playing fantasy football and fantasy baseball through his local newspaper in Chattanooga, Tennessee. He thought these games were more beneficial for his math skills than what he was learning in elementary school.

When Izac Valenti was two months shy of his 10th birthday, his parents lied and told a newspaper company he was already 10 (the minimum age) so he could start a paper route to earn the money needed to join his dad's fantasy football league. He played against 27 adults (two divisions of 14 teams) and won the league.

In writing this book, I have compiled a list of fantasy sports people play, which undoubtedly is not all inclusive. It includes baseball, football, basketball, hockey, NCAA football, NCAA basketball, soccer, XFL, USFL, MMA, Arena Football League, Canadian Football League, WNBA, golf, NASCAR, Formula 1 racing, cricket, alpine skiing, Iditarod, ski jumping, ski racing, bull riding, rodeo, biathlon, bass fishing, wakeboarding, wrestling, kabaddi, futsal, volleyball, handball, lacrosse, NCAA lacrosse, Esports, *The Bachelor*, bowling, pickleball, Olympics, rugby, horse racing, tennis, boxing, sumo wrestling, badminton, major league table tennis, EuroLeague, KBO, curling, and UFC.

And there's Fantasy Congress (FantasyCongress.com), where contestants pick legislators in the US House or Senate and get points for sponsoring a bill, passing a bill, speaking on the floor, and other activities, including bonus points if the member votes against the majority of votes in their own party. As of 2024, there are about 300 players, mostly students in high school civics classes.

Peter Schoenke, of RotoWire, explained, "If there's anything you can keep track of, you can make a fantasy sport out of it."

CHAPTER 17

Legal Battles and Legislation

The fantasy sports industry has faced two major legal issues. One was whether companies were required to pay licensing fees to the professional leagues. This was covered in Chapter 6 where CDM successfully sued MLBAM and settled the issue. The other major issue has been the question "is fantasy sports illegal gambling?"

This has been a concern ever since Andy Mousalimas called his scoring system "points" rather than "cents" out of a concern the vice squad might notice. As of 2024, the question has been answered by the US federal government and most states, but the question is still outstanding in some states and foreign countries.

Austin, Texas

Eight men, all in their mid-20s, were playing in a fantasy football league at a local bar called Scholz Garten, in Austin, Texas, when, during a *Monday Night Football* game in September 1989, police arrived and arrested them. They were later charged with engaging in organized criminal activity, a second-degree felony punishable by up to 20 years in prison. There was a public outcry, as many said they should have been charged with a class C misdemeanor gambling charge punishable by a $200 fine, or even just given a warning.

This came at a time when many other Austin sports bars had similar leagues. The police sergeant in charge of the vice squad, Sgt. Byron Cates, said that they hadn't actively been going after gambling activity—rather, the investigation had resulted from a woman having filed a complaint after her husband had gotten drunk at Scholz and wagered there. But at the same time, Cates also said they were aiming to shut down similar leagues. Many local bar leagues stopped immediately after the arrests.

It took almost two years—and Cates having been replaced as head of the vice squad—before prosecutors decided in May 1991 that the charges should be lowered for all but one of the defendants to a class C misdemeanor. But David Bales, the son of the bar owner who created the league, still faced a third-degree felony charge punishable by up to 10 years in prison.

It is often said a prosecutor can get a grand jury to indict a ham sandwich, but this grand jury refused to indict, and the case was dropped.

At the time, an attorney who represented three of the defendants said, "I'm not sure that fantasy football is legal, but the punishment must fit the crime. I wouldn't suggest that people start fantasy football leagues."

Fort Lauderdale, Florida

Randy Bramos was a 13-year veteran of the North Fort Lauderdale, Florida, fire department who started a fantasy baseball league in 1988. The league's 12 members paid $40 per month to play, plus additional transaction fees. At the end of the season, the top finishers split a pot of about $5,000. Bramos made notations in his journal at work and received and returned league phone calls while at work.

In August 1990, their third year, a fire department employee tipped off police that Bramos was receiving a high number of pages on his personal beeper and then making phone calls from various rooms in the firehouse. In September, police raided the firehouse and took Bramos's records, and in November, the 36-year-old was charged with misdemeanor illegal gambling. Prosecutors said he was charged because he was the "central figure in the operation."

He was subsequently demoted from his lieutenant's rank, suspended without pay and eventually fired. City officials said they weren't determining his guilt or innocence related to the gambling charges, but it's not something he should have been doing while on the job—plus he had two previous suspensions. A league member, Charles Pendergast—chairman of the city's planning and zoning board—said at the time, "It's harmless. It's a hobby."

In January 1991, an Orlando-area police chief requested an opinion on whether fantasy football leagues were considered illegal gambling. The request went to Florida Attorney General Bob Butterworth, who issued a non-binding advisory opinion that fantasy leagues charging entry fees and offering cash prizes was a misdemeanor form of gambling. The linchpin to his finding was determining that while winning a fantasy league did involve skill, it was based more on luck. This strengthened the case against Bramos. Since this was probably the first time ever that a state AG offered an opinion on fantasy possibly being gambling, it made national news and sent concern throughout the industry and fantasy leagues.

In the summer of 1991, as they were getting ready for a trial, Bramos's attorneys flew Greg Ambrosius in to do a deposition as an expert witness. Ambrosius never had to return to testify at a trial, because in August the case against Bramos fell apart when the judge wouldn't allow copies of a fantasy league ledger to be introduced as evidence. The judge said it had been seized illegally.

If convicted, he could have faced a year in jail, but prosecutors said they hadn't intended to seek jail time. Bramos said at the time, "Physically, emotionally, financially, this has taken a toll." The case cost him $30,000. He had gotten jobs painting and wallpapering and borrowed money from his parents and in-laws. His central air-conditioning was broken, his van headlights burned out, and he couldn't afford to fix anything. And this was even with his two lawyers having agreed to represent him at no charge—since they also played fantasy baseball.

A year after being fired, he got his job back, plus $55,000 in back pay and legal expenses. But instead of getting his lieutenant position back, he returned to the lower level of driver-engineer. It was a settlement with the city to forestall Bramos's legal action to get his job back.

Fantasy players and companies throughout the US followed the Bramos case, expecting a possible resolution of the question of whether prize money could be considered illegal gambling. But with the case being thrown out, a precedent wasn't set. The question of fantasy's legality remained unanswered.

Senator Kyl

In 1997, Senator Jon Kyl, of Arizona, was proposing legislation that would have banned internet gambling. While the major impetus for this was online offshore sports betting, online poker and "cyber casinos," fantasy sports that collected money to later pay cash prizes would have also been deemed "gambling" and outlawed from any online activity. Obviously, this would have had a devastating effect on the fantasy industry.

Concerned about this legislation, CDM invited some competitors to a meeting at their St. Louis offices in 1997. The four CDM co-owners hosted Jeff Thomas from Sports Buff and Steve Byrd from STATS. They also consulted Brad Mumm from Prime Sports Interactive. This was an example of some of the pre-FSTA informal cooperation happening between fantasy industry members.

After the meeting, CDM hired John Podesta as a lobbyist, to work on getting an exemption for fantasy sports in any potential legislation. They were not successful at getting the exemption, and in 1998 the bill passed the Senate 90-10. But it got bogged down in the House Judiciary Committee after it launched its impeachment of President Clinton and the legislation died on adjournment. Since the Senate had such great bi-partisan support, it seems likely that had Clinton not been impeached, it would have passed the House. So perhaps Monica Lewinsky saved fantasy sports?

UIGEA

From 2000-2005, Congress held hearings on a few internet gambling bills, with nothing being passed into law. Finally, in 2006, Congress passed the Unlawful Internet Gambling Enforcement Act (UIGEA). It was passed to stop people in the US from illegally gambling online. It was still primarily aimed at activities such as online poker, and when being debated it was again unclear if fantasy sports would be included.

Finally realizing fantasy sports were good for them, sports leagues lobbied for the exemption. In a February 2006 letter, the top lawyers from the NFL, MLB, NBA, NHL, and NCAA asked members of Congress to co-sponsor UIGEA, which included a carve-out exempting fantasy.

One big concern legislators and the pro leagues always had about gambling was that it could potentially lead to players being bribed. Clay Walker of the NFLPA testified before Congress and when a senator asked if the prize money for fantasy could lead to bribery, Walker explained that you can't bribe Dallas Cowboys running back Emmitt Smith to score more touchdowns.

The fantasy industry was given the exemption, with specific language that fantasy sports was not the same as gambling. But the bill outlined requirements to meet the legal criteria for the exemption, e.g. payouts must be established up front before the season begins; the scoring system must be based on a collection of individual players' statistics in actual games played, not just one individual player in one game; and the scoring system must not be based on team results. Therefore, fantasy sports contests must require contestants to assemble a roster consisting of several athletes from more than one team and participating in more than one game. Fantasy contests that meet these requirements are deemed not a form of gambling because they require a sufficient level of skill, as opposed to just luck.

The importance of this exemption for the fantasy industry can't be overstated, as much of fantasy would have been deemed illegal. However, this didn't affect state laws. States still had the ability to declare fantasy legal or illegal.

The UIGEA blocked financial institutions from processing payments to gaming companies. The FSTA had to explain the carve-out to banks and credit card processors to ensure they would keep fantasy companies as clients.

Daily Fantasy Sports Scandal

In the fall, 2015, a DraftKings midlevel content manager, Ethan Haskell, tweeted a list showing which NFL players were most used in all DraftKings lineups prior to the deadline for entering teams for the third week of the NFL season. This information is not supposed to be released until after the deadline for submitting lineups. Having this information when others don't is a huge advantage for participants. Haskell said it was done by mistake.

But later that same week, Haskell bragged on social media that he had won $350,000 in a FanDuel event. Haskell was already known to be a frequent winner of FanDuel contests. People who played in these contests and noticed all of this became suspicious about the use of insider knowledge. This created a public outcry and allegations that it was akin to insider trading in the stock market. DraftKings and FanDuel employees were prohibited from playing games on their own site, but not the other. Because this data was always going to be similar for both companies, anyone using it—even for a game with their rival company—would have an unfair advantage. There were allegations that employees from each company were using this information to win contests on the other's site.

The New York Times first broke the story on October 5, and it was immediately picked up nationally by news outlets and TV networks. Jason Robins, CEO of DraftKings, landed at Logan airport after a flight from London that day to see airport TV screens tuned to CNN with a ticker "Daily Fantasy Sites embroiled in an insider trading scandal." On NBC's evening news, Lester Holt called DFS a billion-dollar con. The scores and news scroll at the bottom of ESPN had a category for DFS news headlines.

October 6, New York State Attorney General Eric Schneiderman announced that he had opened an investigation into the two companies. He threatened to look to classify their games as gambling and shut them down. A week later, the FBI launched its own investigation. Subsequently several class-action lawsuits were filed against both DraftKings and FanDuel, alleging charges such as fraud, racketeering, negligence, and false advertising, and arguing that the employees' use of inside information had made the games unfair.

In the wake of the scandal, it was further alleged that employees of these companies had the ability to access the accounts of users they knew to be "professional" daily sports gamers. They then used those picks for themselves on the other website. It was reported that employees from DraftKings and FanDuel had won more than $6 million. Both companies immediately changed their policies and no longer allowed employees to play on any other competing site. An independent investigation concluded that Haskell did not receive the ownership percentages until 40 minutes after his winning lineup had locked.

In November, Schneiderman decided that the two sites were in violation of New York's gambling laws. He sent them cease-and-desist letters ordering that they stop accepting "wagers" in the state. DraftKings alone had more than 500,000 customers in New York. After a brief shutdown, an appeals court judge ruled the sites could keep operating pending their legal status being settled.

In March 2016, Schneiderman and the companies agreed that the DFS sites would stop taking bets in New York State until either a judge ruled in their favor in their pending court case, or the state legislature made them legal. Yahoo, which also had a paid daily game, albeit with a much smaller share of the industry, also agreed to stop. DraftKings and FanDuel advocated heavily for a law that would make DFS legal, which had just recently happened in Virginia.

The state legislature did take up the issue, with backers of the businesses arguing that fantasy sports is not gambling but rather is "based upon the skill and knowledge of the participants." The legislature spent two days debating the issue in Albany. Robins and Nigel Eccles, the

FanDuel CEO, had dinner together while in Albany. The once bitter rivals were now on the same side, their companies potentially facing the end. DraftKings and FanDuel were already on life support with all the lost business and legal fees.

Their supporters in the legislature told them it wasn't looking promising, but during those two days they were debating, there was a flood of about 250,000 e-mails to various state legislators, almost entirely for the bill. Every senate district had 7,500-15,000 people playing DFS. This helped sway the vote and the law passed in June 2016 declaring fantasy games legal. It came with rules to regulate and tax the operators of games. Companies would be required to pay the state the equivalent of 15.5% of their revenue, which was estimated to be nearly $6 million a year at the time.

The FBI investigation and class-action lawsuits went away quietly. But Schneiderman had opened a separate investigation alleging DraftKings engaged in false and deceptive advertising— that was settled in October 2016, with DraftKings agreeing to pay a fine of $6 million.

"This was the second time the industry faced possible extinction," said Paul Charchian. All paid fantasy would have been labeled as gambling, since legislatures wouldn't make a distinction between DFS and season-long games.

One State at a Time

Every state has different laws and interpretations of what constitutes "gambling." As of 2024, in 45 states the litmus test is that if there's more skill than luck, it's not considered gambling. In the other five states, it's considered gambling if there's any luck involved at all. These are Arizona, Washington, Montana, Louisiana, and Iowa.

In 2011, a man won a fantasy contest in Maryland but wasn't being allowed to collect his prize money as it was thought to violate state gambling laws. Understandably upset about this, he contacted his local legislator. The legislator put in a bill to make fantasy legal and contacted the FSTA for help. Peter Schoenke had been the FSTA chairman since 2009 (unlike most organizations, the FSTA considered its "president," then Paul Charchian, #1 and the chairman #2). Schoenke agreed to help, and arranged for an FSTA board member, Howard Kamen, who lived near Maryland, to testify at a hearing about the bill. Facing almost no opposition, the bill passed easily.

After this, Schoenke thought, "We should keep doing this. Let's try and get more state laws passed." A couple of years later, when a bill proposing to make fantasy legal in Iowa was being discussed, the FSTA hired a lobbyist in Iowa and Schoenke went and testified. It took several years, but Iowa finally passed a law legalizing fantasy.

Schoenke became the FSTA's go-to person for flying to various state capitals and helping get laws passed. He essentially became the "government affairs" person for the FSTA, and the only one in the entire industry. Unless someone specifically asked, he was fine letting people think that as "chairman" he was the #1 guy.

The FSTA hired lobbyists in other states. Schoenke cold called legislators in various states to find some to sponsor bills. Many were not interested, since they didn't see a need for it. But some agreed, and when hearings were scheduled, in addition to testifying himself, Schoenke tried to find local fantasy business owners and/or fantasy players to also testify.

Schoenke said that, in 2014, when FanDuel and DraftKings launched massive advertising campaigns promising to give away millions of dollars of prizes, "everyone in America saw those ads and was sick of them. It put a huge spotlight on us." Florida sports and gaming attorney Daniel Wallach said the multi-million-dollar media blitz was "almost like kicking sand in the face of regulators, lawmakers and the public."

Schoenke was concerned some state might pass a bill declaring fantasy illegal and tried to encourage FanDuel and DraftKings to hire lobbyists or donate money to the FSTA to hire lobbyists. At the time, these companies didn't have any lobbyists or even full-time lawyers. He spoke with Nigel Eccles and Jason Robins on a regular basis.

In the spring of 2015, Eccles hired Christian Genetski as FanDuel's chief legal officer. Around the same time, Jeremy Kudon, an attorney who worked for a lobbying firm, heard the massive advertising blitz, foresaw that these companies' legality would be questioned, and contacted Eccles to offer his lobbying to FanDuel. Kudon saw the need to get ahead of inevitable legality questions and try to pre-emptively get laws passed that declared DFS legal. Eccles hired Kudon, and, shortly after, DraftKings hired him as well.

This was a godsend for Schoenke, who knew he badly needed the help of someone with Kudon's experience and ability. Kudon helped defeat a proposed bill in Washington State that would have been negative for fantasy and then helped get a law passed in Kansas confirming fantasy was legal. When the scandal happened, having Genetski and Kudon in place made the companies better prepared to deal with it. After the scandal broke, the first big hearing, in Albany, New York, drew a massive media presence. Schoenke and Kudon took questions for more than three hours of the six-hour hearing. The following week, they testified at a hearing in California. Schoenke later represented FanDuel and DraftKings at a Congressional hearing in Washington.

Seeing how crazy it was getting, Schoenke went to his RotoWire partners and said, "Guys, for a couple of months or more I'm not going to be working for RotoWire much. This will be my full-time job, because I'm the only person that can do it, and it's very important for our company." At the time, about one-third of RotoWire's business was from DFS. From December 2015 to June 2016, Schoenke spent about 60 hours a week on the FSTA and 10 hours on RotoWire. And he was on the road testifying three out of every four weeks.

Kudon and Schoenke had been working on their strategy of trying to get state bills passed, but when the scandal erupted, they accelerated the plan. In 2016, they had bills up for consideration in more than 30 states. DraftKings and FanDuel had a massive nationwide lobbying campaign, with approximately 80-100 lobbyists in 45 states.

There were many hearings in many states. In Springfield, Illinois, a legislator compared DFS to heroin. In St. Paul, a state senator said DFS was as despicable as prostitution. One day in January, there were hearings in four different states on the legality of DFS. There were so many hearings, they needed more help testifying. Schoenke recommended they get Stacie Stern involved. She was the general manager of Head2Head Sports and an FSTA board member. While Schoenke was testifying in a different state, she went with Kudon to testify in Colorado, and she was brilliant. She became part of the traveling team along with Kudon and Schoenke. Genetski helped mostly from his office in DC.

This episode caused problems within the FSTA membership, as many of the season-long companies hated the DFS companies. DFS had pushed the envelope with regard to the legality of paid fantasy sports, and the massive advertising and prizes paid had put the entire industry under scrutiny. At the height of the uncertainty, the January 2016 FSTA conference was held in Dallas with 440 attendees. Dallas Mavericks owner Mark Cuban gave a speech that assured everyone that people loved fantasy, they were going to keep playing, companies would weather the storm, and those still there in two years were going to do great.

By the end of 2017, 19 states had passed bills legalizing fantasy sports. Most were written with help from Kudon's team. As of 2024, 26 states, plus Puerto Rico, had passed laws that say fantasy sports are legal.

Stern was hired by FanDuel in 2017 to manage their government affairs and then took a similar position in 2022 with another DFS company, Underdog Fantasy. She took over from Schoenke as the go-to person in the industry for government affairs. Stern, who also served as the chairperson of the FSGA from 2020-2022, is one of the most prominent women in the fantasy industry. She got her start with Head2Head in 2001 when Bill Reinking was looking for a marketing director. He hired her even though she knew nothing about fantasy sports—she had previously worked as a store manager for a golf shop and had sold advertising for Comcast. She was Head2Head's marketing director for eight years and then their general manager for another eight years before taking the job with FanDuel.

It's Complicated

As of 2024, the state-by-state fight continues, as not all states allow fantasy sports—or in some cases, they allow season-long fantasy but not daily. But while many states have declared fantasy legal, they all come with different rules and regulations, as well as some that have exorbitant licensing fees. DraftKings and FanDuel helped create this problem by spending millions and millions of dollars on advertising. Politicians saw this and assumed they were making millions of dollars. They didn't know these companies were operating in the red, spending hundreds of millions of dollars in venture capital trying to corner the market. And many state legislators didn't comprehend that not all fantasy companies are as big as DraftKings and FanDuel. Thus, there are states like Delaware with a $50,000 annual licensing fee per company and Indiana with a $50,000 initial fee and then $5,000 annually.

When Virginia voted to legalize DFS in 2016, they did so with a $50,000 yearly licensing fee. DraftKings and FanDuel could live with that, but it was a death blow to any other companies doing business in Virginia—it wasn't even close to affordable for them. Since then, the FSTA and their lobbyists successfully convinced Virginia to lower the fee, and it's down to $8,300 per year as of 2024. They've also successfully gotten some states to replace a set fee with a sliding scale, based on a company's size.

Stern said that when Virginia passed the law in 2016, lawmakers "kept harkening back to those commercials, thinking, 'This a billion-dollar industry. We're going to get our share.' I can't tell you how many times I've heard, 'We're going to save education in this state, thanks to fantasy sports.'"

One of those times was the 2016 "state of the state" address by Missouri's governor, who said he would pay for education by licensing and taxing DFS. "This was crazy, that would never happen in a million years," Schoenke said.

Greg Ambrosius of the NFBC/NFFC said that, as of 2024, "we are now exempting 10 states, plus the province of Ontario, because those states have passed legalized sports betting bills—that includes fantasy companies. They're too dumb—or not taking the time—to look at the difference between legalized sports betting and fantasy game operators, they just lump them all together. We are now legally licensed in 21 states and pay over six figures a year." This is a big barrier to entry for any new start-up businesses. Ambrosius continued, "The states have done nothing positive for us...are they protecting our license? No. Are they helping us promote our contests? No. It's just a money grab."

The NFBC/NFFC has identity software, so that when a person is in a state that is exempted, they are not allowed to sign up for their games. However, if someone is already registered in a game, they are allowed to manage their team during the season regardless of where they are. Therefore, it's not difficult for someone in an exempted state to drive across the border to another state and sign up—or have a friend in a different state register them. Not all companies have identity software or even try to police it.

When states started all their licensing, it made it too difficult and expensive for many smaller companies. As Geoffrey Stein explains about his company, "We had to sell MFL10's because of the regulations. Each state started doing their own thing and it was impossible for our group of only five people to follow 50 sets of different rules and regulations, and some states wanted as much as $50,000 per year for license fees." They sold it to SportsHub Tech, who bought several smaller companies for this very reason. By putting them all under one umbrella, SportsHub only needs to pay one license for the company.

As this has unfolded, a growing number of attorneys started specializing in fantasy sports law. Law schools started offering courses on it, and there are blogs sharing the latest legal developments. Almost none of this existed in 2000.

Mark Hanna from RT Sports said, "I went from software engineer to CEO to regulator. All I do now is look at law."

CHAPTER 18

Injury Experts

Players getting hurt is a big part of fantasy sports. Sometimes the prognosis is clear—such as a player has a torn ACL and is out for the year—but often there is uncertainty as to how long a player will be out and how effective he will be when he returns. With the growth of fantasy sports, it was only a matter of time before specialists would offer advice about this.

Rick Wilton

Rick Wilton's early baseball career showed promise. He was known as a good defensive first baseman with gap power. But then Babe Ruth League pitchers discovered he couldn't hit a curveball and that was the end of it.

As a student athletic trainer in high school, Wilton started getting sports medicine training. After graduation, he was the athletic trainer for a semi-pro football team for one year before enlisting in the US Navy. With the Navy, he served at various hospitals, gaining experience in physical therapy, pharmacology, and radiology. After the Navy, he attended the University of Utah as an athletic training major. He was also a cohost of the university's pregame football and basketball radio shows from 1981-1984, as well as a regular on *Sports KALL*, the weekly sports call-in show in Salt Lake City. In addition to general discussions, Wilton would provide information about players that were hurt and how their injury would impact their performance.

In early 1984, Wilton found the Bantam Books roto book and recruited friends to start a league. He moved to Chicago the next year and joined a local league there. One day he stumbled upon a newsstand in Evanston full of dozens of out-of-town newspapers—a goldmine of roto information. Although it was an hour from his home, he made a point of going there before all his drafts and other important deadlines, buying every Sunday paper he could get. He would bring his 10-year-old daughter along for the ride to spend time together, wheel his collapsible shopping cart to the newsstand, and fill it with papers. On the drive home, he'd separate the sports pages from the rest of the papers while at stop lights.

Wilton fought for the league title every year with a chief rival, Jim Dressel. Then one day in 1991, Wilton and Dressel came up with an idea to start a fantasy content company, using their combined strengths—Wilton had a medical background, while Dressel was an award-winning writer and editor for *Bowlers Journal*.

Before launching their products, they started building a scouting network in 1992 and got every MLB city covered. In January 1993, they debuted a newsletter called *Fantasy Baseball Journal* (FBJ) as well as a "Hot Sheet" with fantasy relevant baseball news and a MASH report with injury news. This may have been the first time anyone could get fantasy baseball relevant injury analysis.

The scouting network was comprised of baseball fans who provided information from reading their local papers and watching games. Wilton gave them a 1-800 number to call in news about injuries, playing time changes, etc. In exchange for this help, they were given free products. This may have been the first nationwide network of reporters established to gather baseball news.

They had a stroke of luck when they were allowed to use a mailing list from *The Sporting News*. They mailed thousands of free sample newsletters, getting a fantastic response. FBJ and the Hot Sheet became very popular, and Wilton was probably the first true injury expert for fantasy baseball. The Hot Sheet was faxed two or three times weekly, and because phone charges were so costly, they used extremely tiny print to get it all on one page and started faxing at 11:01 p.m. (when rates were lower). Wilton and Dressel had five phone lines dedicated to faxing and some nights weren't done faxing until 3 or 4 a.m.

After the 1994 player strike, they ran into problems and folded. Ron Shandler brought Wilton and his Hot Sheet and Mash Report to BaseballHQ. Dressel was no longer involved. Wilton wrote the MASH report for 20 years. It was the longest-running column dedicated to baseball injuries. As of 2024, Wilton still supplied Baseball HQ with the information that appears in the *Baseball Forecaster*'s 5-Year Injury Log.

Injury Guru

Steve Cohen attended the University of Arizona for broadcasting and then moved to New York in 1987, getting a job at the nation's first sports talk radio station, WFAN, as a board operator and tape editor. While there, he also obtained his first writing job in 1989, writing for free for Bob Harris' TFL Report. Cohen worked his way up to become the WFAN NFL beat reporter and traveled with the Jets starting in 1991. At the same time, as chief researcher for the nationally syndicated TV show *Around the NFL*, with Mike Francesa and Bill Parcells, he would gather information about NFL player injuries.

Cohen became friendly with Dr. Steven Nicholas, the Jets orthopedic surgeon. On road trips, Nicholas taught him all about injuries. Cohen learned the difference between a grade 1, grade 2, or grade 3 sprain; what a PCL meant to the cartilage in the knee; recovery times for various injuries, and more.

Cohen started a 1-900 phone line for recorded injury reports. He partnered with *New York Post* columnist Jay Glazer because covering all the NFL teams by himself was too much as he still had his full-time job. The 1-900 number evolved into a newsletter, called the *Pro Football News and Injury Report*. He offered it as a fax service, for 10 cents a page, and they added Adam Caplan as a partner to help with the information gathering. Cohen became known as the "injury guru."

In 1993, while still working full-time for WFAN, traveling with the

Jets, and putting out his newsletter, Cohen began writing a column and sold it to the *New York Daily News, Seattle Post Intelligencer* and *New Haven Register*. Cohen said, "I was the first to ever write a significant injury report that told people what the injury was, how long it takes to come back, and whether the player was practicing."

"Back then you didn't get the information off the internet," he said. "You picked up the phone. You had to call people—people had to take your calls, you had to network, you had to know who to call, when to call, when was practice over..."

Their faxed newsletter transitioned to the internet, allowing reports to be e-mailed. They created a website, footballinjuries.com. Although their focus was always on fantasy and predicting how well players would do—and not picking winners of games—they appealed to both fantasy players and sports bettors. Cohen said 50% of the NFL teams were subscribers. They peaked at about 10,000 subscribers.

It was a lot of work, as they put out reports Thursday, Friday, Saturday, and Sunday morning. Cohen's wife would have to wait for him to finish the Saturday report so they could go out to dinner. Cohen had to personally call all the press boxes on Sunday mornings to find out which players were inactive. Not just anyone could do this—Cohen had developed relationships with all teams PR guys from traveling with the Jets.

During his time at WFAN, from 1987-2004, Cohen also served as the executive producer for both the New York Jets Radio Network and New York Giants Radio Network. In 2004, Cohen was hired by Sirius satellite radio to help launch their NFL network (Chapter 11). His duties at Sirius became so great that he no longer had time to also run his business and sold it to John Hansen in 2005.

Will Carroll

In 2002, Will Carroll, who worked for an insurance company, realized there were no journalists covering sports injuries with any depth. So, he put together his own injury report, only for baseball, and gave it to some friends. His report detailed players' injuries along with details about their rehab process, estimates for how much time they'd miss and how effective they'd be upon returning. Carroll had no medical training but had an ability to cut through the medical jargon spewed by team doctors and explain things in terms the average person could understand.

People subscribed to his e-mailed reports. Some just wanted baseball information, some were gamblers, but most played fantasy. It grew solely by word of mouth until one day Carroll was listening to the radio and heard ESPN baseball expert Peter Gammons reference his report. "I about drove into a telephone pole," Carroll said.

His subscriber base quickly grew from a couple hundred to a few thousand. He quit his job and joined Baseball Prospectus in 2003, where he wrote a column "under the knife." He also started adding football injury content.

After eight years with Baseball Prospectus, he went on to work for *Sports Illustrated*, Bleacher Report and others. He has written two books and been a regular guest on dozens of radio shows. He remains one of the top injury experts as of 2024.

Stephania Bell

Eddie Aparicio and Greg McCarthy were high school baseball team-mates in San Francisco. They hadn't seen each other since graduating in 1987 when they happened to be on the same cruise in the Mexican Riviera 14 years later. They introduced each other to their wives and the couples became friends. They went to dinners together, and among other things, played together in a fantasy football league, where Greg co-managed a team with his wife, Stephania.

Coincidentally, Aparicio was also starting a fantasy football related company with his brother-in-law, called Commish Kit which was making draft boards. Aparicio started attending FSTA conferences to promote his company.

Stephania was a physical therapist. She had majored in French literature at Princeton University and then earned a master's degree in physical therapy from the University of Miami in 1991. She noticed that league mates were coming to her with injury questions, such as, "How long will it take their player to recover from a sprained ankle?" She explained, "The injury reports issued by the NFL teams were so vague. People knew that I worked with athletes with these kinds of injuries, so they wanted to know, 'What can I expect?'"

Stephania realized this was valuable information and probably other fantasy players would also want this. She thought of writing a column. Aparicio suggested she shop the idea at FSTA conferences. In 2004, he began bringing her with him to conferences. He introduced her to members and when he was given time to pitch his company to the audience, he also added a plug for Stephania.

After doing this at a few conferences, she hadn't gotten any offers and was about ready to give up. But she tried once more, and this time William Del Pilar, of KFFL, told her, "I can't pay you very much, but I can use you. Come work for us, we have the traffic—you won't be with us for long because somebody is going to discover you."

Del Pilar only offered her $5 per column, and she wasn't even given her own column—just a small space inside someone else's column. But it was a chance for her work to be seen on an established site, so she accepted. "The first article she submitted had great information," Del Pilar said, "but someone had to be a doctor to understand it, so we had to teach her how to write in layman's terms."

Del Pilar was right—she wasn't with KFFL for long. After she wrote for that first NFL season, Peter Schoenke invited her to write for RotoWire. She would only be paid $25 per column, but would get her own weekly column, write about both football and baseball injuries, and get space in their pre-season magazines. She was teaching as well as working as a physical therapist, so she had to pull an all-nighter every Thursday to get her column ready for Friday. She became a frequent guest on RotoWire's radio show.

A few years later, Aparicio was at an FSTA conference and saw

Matthew Berry interviewing a woman. He told Berry if he was looking for female talent for ESPN, he should consider Stephania. Berry said, "Send me her resume and writing samples." In 2007, ESPN flew the 41-year-old to Connecticut for an audition. She had never been on television, but she was offered a six-month deal. It wasn't going to be enough to live on, so she negotiated to commute back and forth from San Francisco with ESPN paying her travel costs. She saw patients a few days a week and flew to Connecticut for three-and-a-half-day weekends. She taped segments for shows such as *Fantasy Football Now*.

ESPN extended her six-month deal for several more months, and then offered her a full-time job with enough money so that she could move to Connecticut near their studios in the fall of 2008. With exposure on ESPN, she became perhaps the most known injury analyst fantasy sports has had, focusing mostly on football and baseball injuries, but also doing a little for other sports. Her work appeals to non-fantasy players as well. For example, if Joe Burrow gets hurt, Cincinnati Bengals fans want to know just as badly as Burrow's fantasy owners how long he will be out.

Still there as of 2024, she appears regularly on *SportsCenter*, *The Fantasy Show* and *Fantasy Football Now*, in addition to co-hosting ESPN Audio's *Fantasy Focus Football* podcast. She has contributed to *NFL Live*, *Baseball Tonight*, ESPN Radio and ESPN.com. She was also elected to the FSWA Hall of Fame in 2017, becoming the organization's first female inductee.

20 Years Later

Stephania said, "When I started attending FSTA conferences there were almost no other women there. I'm encouraged to see how many more women are in fantasy sports now. And sometimes other women in fantasy tell me that seeing me encouraged them and made a difference. And it's because of men like William Del Pilar, Peter Schoenke and Matthew Berry who gave me a shot."

"The second I met her I knew she was going to be a superstar," recalled Peter Schoenke. "It's like when a scout finds a young player and just knows he's going to be great, and it's Barry Bonds or someone."

Dr. Chao

Dr. David Chao left the San Diego Chargers in 2013 after being their team doctor for 17 years. That fall, he sat at home, giving in-game injury analysis to his wife and newborn twins. His wife suggested he tell it to someone who cares. And she opened a Twitter account for him, @ProFootballDoc. By 2024, he had amassed more than 200,000 followers—he had a podcast, a website, and has been on SiriusXM radio and Fox Sports radio.

There are several other well-known experts including, Dr. Deepak Chona, Dr. Jesse Morse, and Ben Dinnery, who covers soccer in the United Kingdom.

CHAPTER 19

Innovative Entrepreneurs

As we've covered so far, the invention of fantasy sports led to stat services, news and advice services, books, magazines, radio shows, injury experts and more. Other entrepreneurs have come up with more innovative ideas.

Mock Draft Central

Jason Pliml would go to his fantasy baseball and football drafts knowing what he thought of the players, but he'd have to guess what his competitors thought. For example, would that tight end he liked be available in the sixth round or should he draft him earlier?

Pliml thought it would be great if he could get an opinion sample from others before his drafts, and this led to the idea of creating a website to hold "mock" drafts. These would be just like real drafts, except when it's over, that's it—you don't play out the season. But by doing these, you would learn what other people think of player worths. And they would allow him to create Average Draft Position (ADP) reports, showing the average time in a draft when each player was selected. So even if someone only did a couple of mock drafts themself, they could see the averages for everyone else who participated.

Although Pliml was a freelance software developer himself, he hired someone to build a website, because he could hire someone for less money than what he was getting paid by his clients. In 2002, the 28-year-old launched Mock Draft Central, from a small office in Grand Rapids, Michigan. It wasn't an immediate success because it was a new concept. For two years, Pliml wrote articles explaining mock drafting, ADP, as well as general draft strategy, and gave these for free to magazines. He was trying to educate the fantasy community about the concept. And he hosted industry drafts for free to get his company mentioned.

His paid subscription site gained traction and by 2006 was running at breakeven. His business became SEO-driven as more and more fantasy players started looking for mock drafting and ADP. He also got publicity with articles in *The Wall Street Journal*, *Forbes*, AOL Money, and CNN SI. Others, such as CBS and ESPN, started offering mock drafts and ADP as well.

Mock Draft Central became profitable, increasing to 130,000 paid subscribers. Football was the most popular, with five million page views one August. Baseball also did very well; basketball and hockey did okay; golf and NASCAR only had a small amount of business. Advertising accounted for 35% of his revenue. Pliml also did side projects, such as building the software for a fantasy contest for Dan Patrick and ESPN 1000 in Chicago.

In 2010, Pliml sold the company to RotoWire. He stayed on for a few months transition period and since then hasn't worked in the fantasy industry.

Fantasy Sports Insurance

Nothing can ruin a fantasy season more than having one (or more) of your star players get hurt and miss most of the year. Nothing can reimburse you for all the hours you spent preparing for your draft and the disappointment of not being able to compete for your league championship, but fantasy sports insurance companies can at least cover some of your lost league entry fees.

It's unclear who invented this idea, but the first may have been Jack

Shankman and his partner Justin Felber, direct marketing salesmen in their early 20s from New York, who launched Fantasy Player Protection (FPP) in August 2005. It immediately garnered national exposure when it was mentioned in an article on ESPN.com in September. More mentions followed in newspapers and sports radio.

The way it worked is people could buy a policy for one or more of their players, and if they missed a certain minimum number of games, they received a payout. That minimum number varied by sport, and the cost of each policy varied depending on a player's age, position played, and injury history.

Their first year didn't go well, as the NFL's most-protected player, Kansas City Chiefs running back Priest Holmes, suffered a season-ending back injury, resulting in their paying out many claims. Despite the setback, Shankman still envisioned a bright future as the popularity of fantasy football grew. After the first year, he said, "Obviously, we do better when fewer players get hurt, but the buzz has been too good to not keep it going. The goal isn't just to turn this into a full-time job. The goal is to earn enough money to buy yachts!"

FPP was out of business a couple of years later, so presumably they never bought those yachts.

A company with a similar name, Fantasy Player Protect, was run by a real insurance agency, MiniCo Insurance from Phoenix, Arizona, that offered insurance from 2013 to 2021.

Several other companies sprang up using a similar format, and while Fantasy Player Protect stopped in 2021, there are other companies still offering insurance as of 2024.

Fantasy Dispute Resolution

Another problem fantasy leagues sometimes encounter is when there are disagreements among participants—such as thinking a trade between league members is too lopsided and should be voided—or perhaps an unusual occurrence that isn't covered in the league rules, such as when the 2022 Bengals vs. Bills game was canceled due to Damar Hamlin's cardiac arrest. Sometimes disputes lead to people leaving a league or friendships being damaged.

This problem led to the creation of fantasy sports arbitration services. For a small fee per "incident," they offer an independent third-party opinion. One of the first of these companies was Fantasy Baseball Commish Services, which launched in 2000 and brought in a grand total of one customer. But they grew after that, changed the name to RotoUmpire, and were still in business as of 2024.

RotoUmpire was started by Robert Burghardt and Scott Pisani. Burghardt explained, "After playing in some leagues that were literally destroyed by unfair trades and arguments, we looked but didn't see any service that could reliably arbitrate fantasy baseball disputes and that's why we created RotoUmpire. There were a few services around that tried to have the computer automatically 'decide' if a trade was fair or not, but those were unreliable."

As the longest-running arbitration service, they typically serve 30-60 leagues during baseball season and arbitrate 300 to 400 incidents. They recently added football as well. By 2007, there were similar competitors, including Rotoruler, Sports Judge, and Fantasy Dispute. These were all gone as of 2024. Fantasy Dispute lasted from 2004 to 2017 and was started by attorney Bill Green, who had spent two decades defending accused killers and starting in 2004 was also arbitrating fantasy disputes for $10 each. He said his hourly fee as an attorney was obviously much greater, but this was more fun.

Marc Edelman, who started Sports Judge, knew he wouldn't make money by spending one or two hours per case for $10-$15, but said it was a labor of love. After starting this when he was an associate at two large New York law firms, Edelman went on to become a professor of sports law at Fordham Law School and has published extensively on fantasy sports law. He consults for many companies on fantasy sports legal issues and taught the first law school course in the country on fantasy sports law.

Fantasy Judgment was launched in 2009 by Michael Stein and was still going as of 2024. At $12-$20 per incident for all these companies, it's not a huge money maker but they love doing it.

Draft Boards

When fantasy leagues began, people would write down their draft picks on paper. The first company to start offering draft boards may have been DraftKit.com, launching in 1995. They sold a large draft board that could be displayed for all to see, with labels for every NFL player that would be attached to the board in each teams' column when they were drafted. The labels were color coded by position. Draft Kit also offers trophies, championship rings and T-shirts.

Similar companies followed, such as EZDraft.com around 1999 and then CommishKit.com in 2002. Eddie Frias and his brother-in-law Eddie Aparico founded Commish Kit. Their first year, they sold 178 draft boards, but after later landing a deal with ESPN, as of 2007 Frias said they started selling that many in a day. His relatives were convinced he was running an illegal bookmaking operation.

Draft Kit, EZ Draft, and Commish Kit were all still in business as of 2024. Hundreds of US military members stationed around the world have fantasy leagues. For many years, Draft Kit has sent free kits to many of these leagues.

RotoWear

While some others like Draft Kit have sold T-shirts and other items, RotoWear launched in 2017 with an extensive line of fantasy related T-shirts. As of 2024, founder Kenneth Tevelowitz still ran the company all by himself out of his house. He has more than 250 designs, including the popular "Lineups and Chill" and "Waiver Wire Warrior."

LeagueSafe

When people form leagues with friends, collecting entry fees from everyone can be a pain. And sometimes whoever is holding the money doesn't pay everyone's prizes when the season is over. This is even more true when people are joining leagues over the internet and trusting a stranger to hold the money.

Paul Charchian had the idea of forming a company that would collect league dues—including nagging people who were late paying, so the commissioner didn't need to—and then hold the money and pay prizes at the end of the year. Essentially, a fantasy sports escrow service. He launched LeagueSafe in 2008. Earning consumers' trust was a problem, as some thought he'd collect the money and then take off to the Cayman Islands. But some trusted him—after all, some had previously been burned by friends or strangers on the internet. And he had credibility as an FSTA board member, even becoming president of the FSTA in 2009.

As time went on, the business grew. As of 2023, there had been more than 600,000 LeagueSafe users since its inception. The original idea was to make the service free if people paid by check, charge a small fee to cover costs if paid by credit card, and then earn money on the float, as interest rates were around 5%. But interest rates crashed to zero and they had to create new methods of creating revenue, such as various optional convenience fees.

Several companies have tried to copy LeagueSafe, but most didn't last long.

Guillotine League

Another Charchian innovation, contestants in "Guillotine Leagues" start with 17 teams (changed to 18 when the NFL expanded their schedule) and each week the lowest scoring team is eliminated. All players from the eliminated team are put back into the free agent pool.

Charchian got the idea from one of his Twitter followers, Jeff Wood, who tweeted him in 2018 and said he was playing this way. Charchian loved the idea, tried it with some guys at his office, and they all loved it, so Charchian gave it the name "Guillotine" and started a company offering the game.

Charchian describes himself as the CEO—or Chief *Execution* Officer—of Guillotine Leagues.

Trophy Smack

Many fantasy leagues want to give a trophy to their winners and in some cases, dating as far back as Bill Winkenbach, they also want to give the last place team a loser's prize. While there have always been many companies that make trophies, Matt Walsh and Dax Holt were not happy with the standard, outdated and limited trophy options that were available—so they decided to start their own company.

They launched TrophySmack in 2018 by investing $250,000 of their own money. They also won the FSTA elevator pitch that year. They developed a collection of unique and customizable trophies, along with other items such as championship belts, rings, wall art and an innovative collection of items for league losers. They sold $850,000 of merchandise in their first year, netting a $200,000 profit that they used to buy more inventory. The next year, 2019, they sold $1.9 million with a net profit of $500,000. And in 2020, they appeared on NBC's *Shark Tank* and Mark Cuban agreed to invest $600,000 for a 17% share of the company.

As of 2024, they have expanded to offer awards for any occasion, not just fantasy sports. They have 20 employees who work at their 800,000 square foot California facility and have hit $10 million in lifetime sales.

Women Against Fantasy Sports

In 2008, Allison Lodish, who owned a retail store in California, launched Women Against Fantasy Sports with a website and Facebook page. It was a forum where wives and girlfriends could support each other and post their tales of frustration. Lodish said, "We can't beat fantasy sports, but we can torment it."

Lodish said, "My husband would be driving with one hand, checking scores with the other, and almost crashing into vehicles—and I'm telling him 'We're only five minutes from home, can't it wait?'" At parties, the husbands would gather and talk about their teams and all the women would roll their eyes, thinking "This again?"

The site was up for a few years, with thousands of visitors. Lodish sold items such as T-shirts reading "Fantasy Sports Widow" and "I Thought I Was Your Fantasy." The top-selling item was women's underwear with the slogan: "Closed for the fantasy season."

CHAPTER 20

Experts Leagues

According to Ron Shandler in his book *Fantasy Expert*, Jerry Heath, who ran an early stat service, suggested to John Hunt the idea of a fantasy league comprised of industry writers. And Heath offered to be the stat-keeper.

Hunt loved the idea, and the first "experts" league was created. There were two 12-team leagues, one using only American League players and the other using only National League players. Experts included Keith Olbermann, Bill James, Glenn Waggoner, Rod Beaton, Danny Sheridan, two women—Dottie Enrico from *New York Newsday* and Lisa Winston from *Baseball Weekly*—and several others. Olbermann suggested the name League of Alternative Baseball Reality and it was commonly called LABR for short.

The first draft was held on March 8, 1994, by conference call. After everyone called in, Hunt realized he only had 11 participants, and everyone waited while he scrambled around the *USA Today* office to find someone else to play. After the delay, Bernie Williams of the Yankees was the first player nominated. Olbermann thought it was a joke, as he thought this was going to be the National League auction. Hunt told him, "No joke, tonight is the AL."

Olbermann said, "AL? I thought this was the NL. I can't do this. I will embarrass myself!"

Hunt said, "We have NL tomorrow, do you want to do that?"

Olbermann responded, "Yes, I'll do tomorrow," and hung up.

Once again, they waited while Hunt found someone else. The auction lasted until 1:45 a.m.

The results of these auctions were published in *USA Today*'s March fantasy baseball guide, receiving lots of attention. After another conference call in 1995, LABR started in-person auctions, first in St. Petersburg, Florida, in 1996, and later many years in Phoenix.

Greg Ambrosius recalls going to the 1996 weekend. "I was a little nervous," he said, "having not met anyone before. But when I arrived at the hotel, the first thing I saw was guys hanging out by the pool drinking beer and smoking cigars. And I thought, "This is my kind of group!" Larry Labadini, from *Fantasy Baseball Scouting Report*, was handing out Cuban cigars. Ambrosius added, "The entire pool was smoke filled and I think we drove all the vacationers away, between the smoke and the thick Northeast accents, debating the Red Sox starting lineup."

In 1999, Hunt decided to invite one "regular" guy to join LABR and compete with the experts. The winner selected was Mike Brown, a Jewish American who was then working with the Gaza Community Mental Health Program. The trip from Gaza to the auction in Tampa took 40 hours. Brown had made a Palestinian friend, Malek Shubair, and he co-managed the team. They made their weekly moves from an internet café in the Gaza Strip and won the 1999 AL LABR championship. In 2000, Brown was invited back to defend his title, but Shubair was no longer allowed to participate. Brown won again and dedicated his title to Shubair. John Hunt said, "I loved having them in the league. The thing I've always loved most about fantasy is its ability to bring people together—even in Gaza."

LABR was a huge success. When Hunt left *Baseball Weekly* in 2006, Steve Gardner took over and, as of 2024, has been the commissioner ever since. The March special draft guide peaked at more than 300,000 sold in a year, and the LABR results became a must-read for auction league players. The early March draft dates gave readers time to see the results before their own drafts. LABR added a snake draft mixed league in 2012 and a mixed auction league in 2020.

In 2013, Hunt said, "The original goal was to put out a good fantasy guide that people could use. By doing that, I brought all these people together in a league. It's remarkable to think about how it started and see what it's grown into now."

LABR has offered great publicity for participants and their companies. And more than that, the auctions and weekends are fun, and many friendships have formed. Participants will get together for lunch, spring training games, and late-night drinks after auctions. For several years, Rick Wolf and Glen Colton booked a hotel suite and hosted after-auction parties that would go into the wee hours.

Tout Wars

There was, however, one problem with LABR. It started out as a win-win for both USA Today, who sold massive quantities of their special fantasy issue and the participants who got national exposure. The auction results were published with the name of the expert, their company name and contact info. This was huge back then, as people couldn't just "google" someone's name or company and find out how to contact them.

But the second year of LABR, the results were published without contact information of the participants. And the third year when they changed to a live auction in St Petersburg, it required everyone to pay for their own travel and hotel. And again, no contact information was published. So now they were asking everyone to take the time and expense of coming to Florida and weren't even having the decency to publish their contact information.

This angered several members. One was Shandler. He realized the idea of the experts league was valuable, and he also realized that USA Today didn't have exclusive rights to the idea. In January 1998, Shandler e-mailed several current and former LABR players to gauge interest in a new league, one where they could have control over the promotion. After getting a great response, Tout Wars was born.

The name was suggested by Alex Patton, in honor of the Star Wars movies. A Tout Wars website was established. Zwilling, with his connections in the sports and entertainment industries, offered to make the draft a media event and get sponsors to cover the costs.

Zwilling convinced the All-Star Café sports bar in Times Square to host and sponsor the event. But they were only willing to do one day, so the Tout Wars auction for the American League was held as a two-night conference call a few days before. On March 28, 1998, the NL auction was held at the All-Star café with about 15-20 spectators. A draft grid was shown on a large wall-mounted screen, and press releases had been sent to local media. Zwilling recruited former MLB player Billy Sample as the celebrity auctioneer.

Despite their complaints about LABR, Zwilling, Melnick and some others played in both Tout Wars and LABR that year. And Shandler returned to LABR in 1999 because it was being held in conjunction with the first FSPA conference. But Tout Wars was very successful, due primarily to the participants promoting the leagues in their columns and websites, and linking to the Tout Wars website.

As with LABR, there has always been great camaraderie with participants, many who would see each other both at LABR and then a few weeks later at Tout Wars. Friday night pre-auction get-togethers at Foley's NYC bar became a tradition for many years until Foley's didn't survive Covid and closed. After Covid, the Friday parties have continued at other locations. As of 2024, Tout Wars had eight different leagues (some draft online) and about 100 participating experts.

Sam Walker, a sports columnist for *The Wall Street Journal*, asked to join the league for a year to see how he could fare against the experts and chronicle it for a book. He was granted a spot in the AL league in 2004 and finished in eighth place (of 12). But his book that followed, *Fantasyland*, was a bestseller and was later followed by a documentary film. Walker continued in the league and won the next year, and again in 2008. After the 2009 season, he retired from Tout Wars.

FanEx

Greg Kellogg wrote a column called *Kellogg's Komments* in the mid-'90s. He was perhaps the first to syndicate his work to multiple fantasy sites, with Komments appearing on more than two dozen sites. He later started his own site, Komments.com, where he provided a forum for new writers to be published. His business wasn't making much money and took about 50 hours a week in addition to the 50 hours a week he spent doing his day job. When FOXSports.com offered him a full-time fantasy job, he jumped at the chance.

Joe Bryant started writing about fantasy football in 1995. He and Kellogg knew each other, saw what *USA Today* was doing with LABR, and thought, "Let's start something like that for football."

They elevated themselves to be "experts" and, in 1996, started a fantasy football experts league, FanEx. Some of the original and early members included David Dodds, James Serra, Jim Lenz, Emil Kadlec, Ian Allen, John Hansen, and Bob Harris.

They started doing live drafts at fantasy football conventions, such as the 1998 Tropicana event and the 1999 expo at Mall of America, where Paul Charchian put together a program book for the event with the last 10 pages blank except for the numbers 1 through 10. He told the audience of about 500 that after each FanEX pick, they should hold up a number indicating whether they thought it was a good pick. While the next expert was on the clock for a pick, Charchian ran around with a microphone letting people express their opinions.

After the first two years, some members wanted to add a second draft, to give their readers an additional draft to analyze. Some members wanted to play out the league, but many wanted it to be just a mock draft, saying that managing two teams for the whole year was too time-consuming. Kadlec came up with the idea to do a draft, have no free agency, no need to set a weekly lineup, but each Tuesday after the games were played the league commissioner would determine your optimal lineup and record the points. These leagues became a very common and popular fantasy football format, eventually called "best ball," with commissioner software automatically calculating everyone's optimal lineup.

As of 2024, there were two main 12-team draft leagues, plus a 12-team auction league, that all play out the season, and a 12-team "best ball" league that drafts in June. FanEX has no website, but participants will write articles about their drafts and post updates as the season progresses.

Scott Fish Bowl

Scott Fish started in the fantasy industry as a content creator in 2005 and, as of 2024, he ran SafeLeagues commissioner services, specializing in Dynasty League formats.

In 2010, the 31-year-old Fish invited 96 people—a combination of both "experts" and random players—to compete in a fantasy football tournament called the Scott Fish Bowl. His intent was to connect the widespread fantasy community, "to bring us all closer to each other," he said. He was letting "some regular Joes play with the analysts they read and listened to."

Inspired by a 2014 Toys for Tots GoFundMe drive run by his Dynasty League Football co-worker at the time, Jeff Miller, Fish created a 501c3 charity called Fantasy Cares and requested participants in the 2015 Fish Bowl make a small donation. He raised $1,500, sent $750 to Miller, and they each went shopping at their local Toys "R" Us and donated to Toys for Tots.

Fish said, "Toys for Tots is one of my favorite charities. I see how excited my son gets when he gets a gift, and the thought of kids that don't normally get those and what it must be like for them, and to just brighten their holiday season...I just love that."

The competition, which is a mega-league composed of many smaller leagues, grew from the original 96 to 120 to 240 to 360 and then 900 players in 2018 when it raised $44,500.

It has grown to include many celebrity actors, musicians, former and current professional athletes and just about every analyst in the fantasy industry. Hundreds of entrants have come from all over the world—more than 50 countries—including ESPN Australia & New Zealand personality Laurie Horesh.

Fish has raised hundreds of thousands of dollars for charity, with the majority going to buy toys that are donated to Toys for Tots. Other donations have included hurricane relief after Hurricane Harvey, the National Coalition Against Domestic Violence, Best Christmas Ever, Coats for Kids, and Feeding America. The 2023 competition received more than 30,000 requests for the by-invitation-only tournament, which had only 3,324 coveted spots. More than $250,000 was raised.

Matthew Berry, who has been in the contest since 2019, said, "The event shows all the very best sides of fantasy football—the competition, the camaraderie, and the community."

Fish hopes to inspire individual fantasy football leagues to set aside one entry fee each year to put toward a charity—just on their own, without his Fantasy Cares involved. "There are hundreds of thousands of fantasy leagues," he said. "If every league set aside one of the entry fees for charity, we could do a lot of good."

Fish won the FSGA's 2019 Humanitarian of the Year award and 2021 Matthew Berry Game Changer Award. And he was named one of The Athletic's Persons of the Year in 2018, alongside people like Patrick Mahomes, Drew Brees and Larry Fitzgerald.

In 2023, looking back at what has transpired, Fish said, "It's surreal, and it's a realization of how good the people in this community are."

TGFBI

Lawr Michaels was posthumously inducted into the FSGA Hall of Fame in 2019. He had written about fantasy sports since the early 1990s, first with John Benson, and subsequently for many publications and websites. He was also a guest and host on dozens of radio shows. Nicknamed the "Zen Master," Michaels was beloved by the fantasy community.

After his passing in 2018, Tout Wars created an annual award to honor their longtime participant. Named the *Lawr Michaels Zen and Now Award*, it is to honor a Tout member who exhibits Michaels's qualities of positive energy and inspiring others in the Tout Wars community and across the fantasy baseball industry.

Justin Mason, an addiction counselor, entered the fantasy industry as a part-time writer and podcaster in 2016, starting his own website, Friends with Fantasy Benefits. In 2017, he also began writing for Fangraphs. When Mason was hired by Fangraphs, the members of his local friends league told him he was getting too good, and they kicked him out after almost 15 years in the league. He knew some people in the industry also lived near him in San Francisco, such as Ray Flowers and Lawr Michaels, so he reached out to see if there was interest in creating a league. Michaels loved the idea, and recruited Flowers, as well as Howard Bender. Collectively they got several other local analysts and a couple non-analysts and started BARF (Bay Area Roto Fantasy). Michaels became a very good friend and a mentor for Mason.

In 2017, Mason went to the Tout Wars weekend in Manhattan to observe the drafts. He told his friend Michaels if they needed any help setting up anything or whatever, he was available. Stephania Bell had the flu and Mason was asked the night before to step in and draft for her. On a brief phone call, she instructed him, "Just be sure to get Brandon Belt. Other than that, I'm too sick to think about anything." He drafted her team, including Belt, and then Bell ran it herself for the season.

Mason was envious of the people who played in Tout Wars and LABR, and figured as a new writer his chances of ever being invited to one of these leagues were slim. He decided to start his own competition, thinking, "Maybe I can show people that I'm pretty good at this." The next year, 2018, he created The Great Fantasy Baseball Invitational (TGFBI). The idea was to get industry writers and content creators to compete against each other in what would essentially be an "experts" league but have room for more participants and especially newer writers. The competition had 15-team leagues, with an overall champion as well. His goal was to get 45 teams, but with the help of Michaels he got 105, including some big names in the industry.

To his great surprise, shortly after setting up the first TGFBI drafts, Mason received his own invitation to join Tout Wars. His initial thought was, "I guess I didn't need to do this TGFBI." But then it dawned on him: "There has to be a lot of other people in the industry who felt like I did, so I should keep it going for them."

Fantrax sponsored the event and gave a $500 prize for the overall champion. Clay Link, from RotoWire, won and asked that his winnings be donated to a charity. That inspired Mason to turn the event into a charity event. He started requesting that participants donate—he would designate a charity to receive 50% of the donations, and each year's overall winner would decide which charity would be given the other 50%.

Big names in the industry continued to join, as well as new writers and everyone in between, and TGFBI caught fire. By the 2023 season there were 435 players, including several from outside North America. The vast majority are analysts, writers, podcasters, and other content creators, but Mason also allows some behind-the-scenes industry people such as programmers. It's all done online, with lots of mentions and conversations on social media.

Mason added about a dozen "satellite" leagues for non-industry participants who are willing to make charitable donations, and the winner of each league earns a spot in the following year's TGFBI. The season-long event has typically raised $4,000 to 6,000, but in 2020 he also did a pre-season 12-hour live stream event that raised $8,000 for charity. The next year, he made it a full weekend event, which also served as a kick-off for that year's TGFBI. In 2023, when industry radio and podcast host Dan Strafford lost his wife to cancer, Mason donated all the contributions that year to a GoFundMe to help Strafford raise his three girls.

Mason was given the 2022 Lawr Michaels Zen and Now Award. He was brought to tears when he learned he was being given the award honoring his good friend and mentor. When presenting the award, Ron Shandler said, "Given the explosion of writers, analysts, and podcasters contributing content these days, Justin's role in helping to grow this industry can't be underestimated."

Mason said, "I think TGFBI has been great for the industry because it gives everybody a sense of belonging. It gives new people the chance to compete against industry giants such as Tristan Cockcroft or Todd Zola or Jeff Erickson. And the new people get to show that they belong in this industry just like the giants."

Dan Strafford said, "Moments after sharing on social media that my wife passed away, the messages, tweets, DMs started to come in. The fantasy community showed me they cared. The community goes much deeper than relief pitcher debates."

When Winkenbach, Gamson, Okrent and others helped invent fantasy sports, they never could have imagined that, years later, there would be such a large close-knit community of industry content providers.

CHAPTER 21

Daily Fantasy Sports

One of the biggest reasons someone might stop playing fantasy sports—or never want to try it in the first place—is the time commitment of managing a team through a months-long season. After people got the idea of having contests as short as just one day or one week, Daily Fantasy Sports (DFS) was born. Prior to this, the term "season-long" fantasy sports didn't exist. It was just "fantasy sports"—no need to differentiate a length of time.

One of the keys in the creation of DFS was the 2006 passage of UIGEA, which exempted fantasy from being considered gambling. The legislation didn't require a fantasy contest to be a minimum length of time in order to be exempt, meaning a contest as short as even just one day was allowed.

Two of the earliest significant DFS sites both launched in 2007. One was called Fantasy Sports Live and the other Instant Fantasy Sports. But the real story of DFS begins one night in 2007, in Scotland, at a University of Edinburgh event for aspiring entrepreneurs. It was there that Nigel Eccles, a 32-year-old executive at a media company, met two men in their 20s, Tom Griffiths, and Rob Jones. Nigel wasn't happy with his career and wanted to start something of his own, while Tom and Rob—friends and former classmates—wanted to start the next Facebook.

They became friends and discussed their various ideas. Their best idea was Nigel's vision of a news prediction site with virtual cash to bet on real-life events. Tom and Rob had a contact who invested $1.2 million, and they started Hubdub. They added two other co-founders to their group, Nigel's wife Lesley—a former management consultant—and Chris Stafford, another former classmate of Tom's.

After 16 months of working seven days a week, they had big distributors such as the Huffington Post and Reuters, with a player base of about 250,000, but not nearly enough ad revenue coming in. Eccles knew they would soon run out of money. Nigel recalled, "We knew we had to go back to investors and say, 'This isn't working,' which is never good. We wanted to be able to say, 'This isn't working, but we've got this other thing.' So, we had to come up with what the other thing was."

They knew that most traffic on Hubdub was for sports predictions. And they knew that although they were based in Scotland they wanted to continue to go after the huge US market. They ended up investigating fantasy sports and saw an opportunity for daily games that few were already pursuing. They scrapped Hubdub and launched FanDuel on July 21, 2009, with Nigel as CEO.

Nigel said, "We seemed to know how to build games that people like to engage with, but we needed something that people were willing to pay for." They had also noticed that most fantasy games at that time weren't particularly mobile-friendly although the smartphone and app ecosystems were starting to snowball. From their very start, FanDuel was designed for mobile.

Nigel is unlike almost every other fantasy sports pioneer in that he never followed American sports and had only a vague concept of what fantasy sports were.

FanDuel's first game was a player pick 'em, where participants would predict who would get better stats in a head-to-head matchup, such as Tony Romo vs Peyton Manning. That didn't catch on, so they tried a format where entrants ranked players and filled out a roster via an auto-pick draft. Then Nigel received an e-mail from a player who had a suggestion. He said that the idea was cool, but the format was all wrong. Eccles said, "My first thought was, 'What does this guy know?' But I started talking to him and realized he knew a lot. He suggested a salary cap format. He was right."

That suggestion led to their salary cap game. The game is like other fantasy salary cap games, where participants must fill out a roster and include certain positions—every player is assigned a salary, and the total salary must stay under a certain limit. The difference is that for baseball, people pay the entry fee one day and the next day the game's over and they collect their winnings. (For football, it's a one-week contest.) There's no season-long commitment, and if, for example, it's May, a person doesn't have to wait until next year to draft a baseball team. They can enter a daily game at any time during the season.

Eccles said their research showed that the average fantasy players were in their mid-40s, and when sports fans in their 20s were asked why they didn't play fantasy the most common reason was that it took too long—baseball being six months and football 17 weeks. Eccles said their daily game would attract this younger market as well as appeal to some who played season-long. And with DFS, they also make every day "draft" day—people always say draft day is their favorite day of the year.

Users can play lower cost, head-to-head games where, for example, they each put up $10 and the winner gets back $18. Or they can join larger leagues and compete with more players for bigger payouts. FanDuel takes 10% from each pool and distributes the rest of the money among the top finishers.

FanDuel landed partnerships to white-label its game with several large US newspapers including the *New York Post* and *Philadelphia Daily News*, as well as radio stations. They quickly became the largest DFS company, paying out $1.5 million in prizes in 2010 and then $10 million in 2011. By 2012, they had raised $6 million more in venture capital and opened a corporate headquarters in New York. They had 18 employees, including 10 engineers, to ensure everything ran smoothly.

DraftStreet

Mark Nerenberg was an options trader, who had an idea to essentially combine online poker—which was very popular at the time—with fantasy sports. When he met Brian Schwartz in 2009, he told him about the idea, and Schwartz loved it. They discussed it with two others, and the four met one weekend to create a formal business plan, which would be followed by soliciting investors.

What they didn't know as they were dreaming of the fortunes they would make, was that the idea they had was DFS, and already existed. The weekend they got together, Mark was on his computer and stumbled upon a site called DraftZone that said, "Win daily cash games playing daily fantasy." He felt like a fool for not having checked earlier to see if anyone was doing this. And he was crushed, thinking this meant it was too late for them. But Brian had a different reaction. For him, it validated that it was a good idea.

Upon further searching, they discovered more DFS sites, including the new FanDuel. None of the sites, including FanDuel, seemed to be doing much marketing or business—at least, as far as they could tell—so they launched their own DFS site, DraftStreet. They thought if they could raise $100,000 for marketing, they could do well.

And they did do well. For a while they battled FanDuel as the most played DFS site. In 2012, FanDuel acquired more venture capital and new customers at a rapid pace, emerging as #1. But then a new competitor entered the arena...

DraftKings

Jason Robins, Paul Liberman and Matt Kalish all worked in middle management at the online printing company Vistaprint. Robins was a Duke graduate, Liberman a Worcester Polytechnic Institute grad, and Kalish had a BA from Columbia and an MBA from Boston College. They all loved fantasy sports and had an entrepreneurial spirit. Robins and Kalish had been talking about starting a company as early as 2008. Those conversations went nowhere, but they got the bug again in 2010. Along with Liberman, the three spent several months going out for drinks and dinner, batting around ideas. One day, Kalish thought of an idea for a DFS company, which excited them. They decided this was what they would pursue.

They spent many nights and weekends at Liberman's house in Watertown, Massachusetts, working out of a spare bedroom. "We'd get there around 7 p.m. and work till about 1 or 2 in the morning," Robins said. "Weekends, we'd wake up around 5:30 or 6 and do the same thing, work all day."

When they had enough of a plan and a prototype, it was time to put money into the venture. They collectively invested $25,000. They hired a lawyer to form a corporation, but he also encouraged them to raise venture capital. The three co-founders were aware there were other companies pursuing this same idea, so they realized raising venture capital was probably a good idea. They were told "No" more than 50 times, until finally a few said, "Yes." They were given a $1.4 million seed round. "At the time," Robins said, "that seemed like a ton of money."

The three of them quit their jobs at Vistaprint. DraftKings launched their first daily fantasy game on MLB's opening day, 2012. Nobody could have envisioned what would happen over the next several years.

The War Is On

Robins and his co-founders wanted to offer bigger prizes than his main competitors, FanDuel and DraftStreet, to attract customers. But they had trouble filling all their contests and lost money on many of them. And yet, they continued with that strategy, burning through their $1.4 million capital in less than a year. But their main venture capital firm was still confident enough to give them $7 million more in 2013.

In April 2013, Robins landed a meeting with Bob Bowman and Kenny Gersh, from MLB Advanced Media. Robins assumed he'd need to educate them on how DraftKings worked and why participants loved it. He rehearsed his pitch in his head many times. But right away Bowman and Gersh told him, "We know what you guys do. Would you like to do a deal with us?"

This was a seminal moment, as it was the first DFS marketing partnership with a professional sports league. MLB was given an equity stake in DraftKings, and at MLB's request the deal was kept confidential. Suddenly DraftKings signs were seen in MLB ballparks and on MLB. com sites. One of the incentives for MLB was that, as Nigel Eccles had predicted, DFS had attracted a younger audience—MLB desperately needed this, since their fans skewed much older.

That year, DraftKings paid out $50 million in prizes to thousands of players in their weekly fantasy football games, and daily games for baseball, basketball, and hockey. They had overtaken DraftStreet as the second-largest DFS company behind FanDuel. And in July 2014, they bought DraftStreet. One month later, they received $41 million more in investments from several prominent venture capital firms. For the 2014 NFL season, they offered a $1 million first prize each week.

DraftKings became the official DFS provider for the NHL in 2014 and for Major League Baseball in 2015. In July 2015, they announced funding and deals with ESPN and Fox Sports worth $550 million. They went from 200,000 registered users in 2014 to two million in 2015. Long gone from the spare bedroom in Liberman's house, their office took up almost an entire floor of a swank building in the heart of Boston's financial district. The break room featured two beer taps.

Robins described one key to their success: "For the customer, we want everything to be fun, easy to use, and engaging." He added, "The beauty of sports is that you already start with a great product. It's the world's greatest reality show. We don't have to create the content. It's already there. For us, it's more about how to add to an already interesting experience."

Meanwhile, FanDuel was also growing rapidly and kept their lead as the largest DFS site. In 2013, they started advertising on TV. In December 2013, they awarded their first million-dollar grand prize to Travis Spieth who won their football contest. In 2014, they secured $70 million in new financing. That summer, they struck a deal with the Orlando Magic, the first individual pro team to get involved with the industry. And in November, they entered a partnership with the

NBA that reportedly gave the league about a 2.5% ownership of Fan-Duel. Nigel Eccles said that quite soon so many teams were contacting them that he needed to hire a full-time consultant to negotiate all the deals. (The same week that the NBA deal was announced, DraftKings announced an exclusive deal with the NHL.)

In 2013, FanDuel had spent $10 million on advertising for the entire year, but, spurred on by the DraftKings competition, they spent $43 million advertising just for the 2014 NFL season. This included TV, radio, print, digital, and their partnerships with leagues and teams. FanDuel became the largest advertiser in the US. They were at war with DraftKings to acquire users. In 2014, FanDuel and DraftKings had, between the two of them, $1 billion in revenue.

In 2015, FanDuel raised another $275 million from investors including Google Capital and Time Warner. Not to be outdone, that same year DraftKings raised $300 million in new funding and spent enough on ads to close the gap in market share with FanDuel. In response, FanDuel increased their planned ad campaign from $50 million to $250 million during that summer. By mid-2015, both companies had several deals with pro sports teams and, for 2015, spent a combined $500 million for advertising, which included literally thousands of TV ads.

Both companies had more than one million registered users and yet, only about 8-10% of fantasy players had tried DFS. Both were valued at more than $1 billion. Their games had entry fees from 25 cents to $1,000, with prize pools that could pay as much as $2 million to the winner. Both companies awarded more than $1 billion in prizes in 2015.

Since their launch, FanDuel hosted some live event finals of their contests in Las Vegas and later the Playboy Mansion. DraftKings hosted live finals at locations including the Atlantis Resort in the Bahamas.

At the Jacksonville Jaguars stadium, and a couple of other NFL stadiums, FanDuel created a section called FanDuelVille, where fans had access to free daily fantasy football games and experiences, as well as multiple bars with signature cocktails, a live DJ, and opportunities to win premium hospitality experiences.

DraftKings investors included NFL team owners Jerry Jones and

Robert Kraft, as well as major media companies like NBC. Since their inception, DraftKings alone had awarded a million-dollar grand prize to 17 people: 14 from NFL contests, and one each from MLB, NBA, and the PGA.

"It's hard to overestimate the sweeping manner in which it changed our industry," said Paul Charchian, then president of the FSTA. "Those two raised more money than the history of our entire industry combined."

In the summer of 2014, both *USA Today* and *Sports Illustrated* started their own daily games. Yahoo entered the arena in 2015. But these barely made a dent in the FanDuel and DraftKings market share.

As DFS emerged, so did analysts and advice sites. RotoGrinders.com debuted July 2010 and was still quite popular as of 2024. It provides users with daily strategy articles for every sport, as well as research tools. There are numerous websites dedicated to DFS and other sites, such as RotoWire and RotoWorld, that were once only for season-long added DFS sections. The SiriusXM fantasy channel is full of DFS segments and discussions. The FSTA estimated that in 2012, DFS participants spent $3.4 billion on products, services, and entry fees.

Some DFS players have been so successful they have quit their jobs and turned DFS into a full-time profession. They spend hours every day studying lineups, matchups, and weather reports.

Legal Problems

As detailed in Chapter 17, a major scandal erupted in the fall of 2015, when there were accusations of DraftKings and FanDuel employees using inside information to win contests on their rivals' sites. The New York State Attorney General launched an investigation and questioned the legality of DFS. Some other states and the FBI launched their own investigations, and class-action lawsuits were filed against both FanDuel and DraftKings.

Lesley Eccles lost weight from the stress and was scared FanDuel could be shut down or even face criminal charges. Friends of her 7- and 9-year-old boys would ask, "Are your parents going to jail?"

Nigel worried about all the ways they could be shut down—besides the state and FBI investigations and class-action lawsuits, he worried that their payment processors could stop doing business with them, that they could be pulled from the Apple app store, and that the pro leagues might pull their support. In fact, ESPN did terminate a deal it had with DraftKings. And some financial companies, such as Citigroup, stopped allowing transactions with DraftKings.

As a result, the companies changed their policies and prohibited employees from playing games on each other's sites. Several months later, the New York state legislature passed a law legalizing DFS, and FanDuel and DraftKings weathered this storm. But it took its toll on the companies. During this period of uncertainty—which included a temporary ban on taking customers from New York State and some other states—FanDuel froze hiring and developing new games, scaled back expenses due to lost revenue and skyrocketing legal and lobbying costs. In the winter of 2016, they laid off 60 employees, and then another 50 two months later.

Facing similar problems, DraftKings agreed to merge with FanDuel in November 2016. The onetime rivals were going to join forces. But the FTC blocked what would have created a monopoly controlling 90% of the DFS market. The deal was dead by July 2017.

These events also took a toll on the rest of the DFS industry as some of the smaller DFS companies folded, a few without paying their customers. But both FanDuel and DraftKings recovered just fine from all of this and, as of 2024, remained the two DFS giants. They have expanded their games globally, beginning with DraftKings offering a daily soccer game in the United Kingdom in 2016.

In 2018, the US Supreme Court struck down the Professional and Amateur Sports Protection Act (PASPA) which, since 1992, had been a federal ban on sports betting outside of all states except Nevada. Suddenly, each state had the ability to legalize sports betting. FanDuel and DraftKings added sports betting to their offerings. In 2021, the

NFL announced FanDuel as their official sports betting partner. This came after years of the major pro sports wanting nothing to do with anything even resembling gambling, which included fantasy.

In 2019, DraftKings opened a 105,000-square-foot office in Boston, hosting 700 employees, with meeting rooms named after fantasy football legends such as "Brady," "Moss," and "Sanders." As of 2024, they had more than 4,000 employees with offices in London, Ireland, Israel, and Bulgaria.

FanDuel's headquarters is still in New York, and their more than 3,000 employees also work from five other US cities, from Toronto, and from Edinburgh and Glasgow, Scotland. Their Edinburgh office is the main location for the engineers, and includes a ping-pong table, mini basketball, a Space Invaders arcade machine, scooters, unlimited snacks, and a sports theme that permeates the space.

As of 2024, both companies had over 3 million users.

CHAPTER 22

Fantasy Sports Worldwide

Fantasy Sports has truly gone global, with people participating in more than 100 countries, either using locally owned fantasy companies or in some cases playing games offered by companies based in the United States or other countries. Many large companies such as ESPN, CBS and Yahoo have made efforts to attract foreign clients.

Other companies, such as RotoWire, have also gone global. They have freelance writers working from countries such as Pakistan and Australia. They translate soccer coverage into Portuguese and Spanish to reach players in South America. And they provide real-time updates to people playing fantasy cricket in India. RotoWire gets a lot of traffic from Europe as well as from South Korea, where American MLB and NBA is popular, and the Philippines, where the NBA is also popular.

Other global companies are business-to-business providers who run fantasy platforms for clients, such as Scout Gaming Group, which provides daily fantasy sports platforms. It has dozens of employees with headquarters in Sweden and other operations in Norway, Ukraine, and Malta.

This chapter will highlight some of the global expansion.

Europe

What is generally called "soccer" in the USA is usually called "football" in much of the world. In this section, "fantasy football" refers to the game played by the likes of Cristiano Ronaldo, not the game played by

Patrick Mahomes. And points aren't awarded for touchdowns or yards gained, but rather for goals, assists, goalkeepers saving shots, players lasting at least 60 minutes in a match, etc. Further, points can be lost for players receiving a yellow or red card, missing a penalty kick, scoring an own goal, being substituted for, etc.

Italian journalist Riccardo Albini is widely considered to be the inventor of fantasy football outside of America. In the late '80s, Albini was in Chicago and bought Cliff Charpentier's *Fantasy Football Digest* book and a baseball roto book. During his lunch breaks in Milan, he worked to develop a football version of the games. He launched Fantacalcio, which is Italian for fantasy football. His first contests were played during the 1988 European championships. He adopted the roto model of acquiring, by auction, players that would be on your team for an entire season. This limited the number of people who played.

A year later, he published the Italian Fantacalcio manual. By 1990, it was estimated that 15,000 people were playing. He proposed doing a game with Italy's most-read daily newspaper, which was dedicated to sports, *Gazzetta dello Sport*, but they said they didn't have the technology to manage a national game. But in 1994, they contacted him and were ready to do it. They created a salary-cap-style game, allowing for unlimited entries. It debuted for the 1994-95 championship with an estimated 70,000 players.

As with fantasy sports in the US and Canada, there were people playing versions earlier than the man credited with inventing it. One example is Bernie Donnelly, from England, who at age 13 in 1966 created a game and played with friends. By 1971, he had recruited seven friends to play for an eight-team league. Teams played head-to-head with only goals scoring fantasy points. It was a keeper league where managers would come and go, but the team rosters remained the same each year, except that teams could make trades with each other. The league was still going as of 2024—still with eight teams, and a long waiting list to join.

The man widely credited with introducing fantasy football to the United Kingdom is Andrew Wainstein. He was inspired after a family friend from the United States showed him a fantasy baseball game.

"The drive was enthusiasm for football," said Wainstein, who was a 25-year-old computer programmer living at home at the time. "I was a massive football fan—it's far and away the #1 sport in the UK and I just thought, 'People are so passionate about it—the stats are maybe a bit basic, but it could work.'"

Wainstein spent four months devising a scoring system and called his game, Fantasy League. He placed ads in football magazines. People would pay him for an information packet to start their league by holding an in-person auction. The first year, he signed up 80 leagues, with about 650 players, for the 1991-92 season.

Leagues would send their teams to Wainstein, who would produce league stats and standings. He worked out of his older sister's bedroom in London and was inundated with phone calls and faxes on Friday afternoons, the weekly transaction deadline. Wainstein said, "On a Friday afternoon the phone was nonstop, and then the fax as well—sometimes the fax would run out of paper, so I'd run over and change the fax paper while on one or two phone calls."

Wainstein wrote a software program that would start to print reports around 7 p.m., after the last games ended, and it took over 12 hours to print all the leagues. "Eventually my body clock was set to wake up every three hours, because that was how long it took for the printer to run out of paper," Wainstein recalled.

His business really started to take off when the game was regularly referred to on a BBC Radio show. And in 1994, he worked with the *Daily Telegraph* newspaper to create the first mass-marketed game. That same year, a British comedy show, *Fantasy Football League*, debuted, generating further interest in his game. Some 341,000 of the Telegraph's 900,000 readers played the paper's game. The grand prize winner was a 14-year-old boy who won a two-week holiday anywhere in the world to watch a football match of his choice. He chose a cup final in Brazil.

In 1996, Wainstein launched a website, FantasyLeague.com, that had grown into a huge company as of 2024. Over the years, he has run games for many sports in addition to football, and has provided games for BBC Sport, Sky Sports, *The Sun*, *The Times*, and many other companies. They report having had customers from 99 countries. Other newspapers started producing their own games. And the *Telegraph* game is still going strong as of 2024.

The Premier League, which is the highest level of the English football league system, started their own game for the 2002-03 season. They debuted with 76,000 players and, for 2023, grew to 11 million teams. It is unclear how many of those 11 million teams are the same people owning multiple teams, but clearly there are millions of individuals playing.

Fantasy football has also spread to Spain, Germany, France, Poland, Brazil, and many other countries. Its popularity has led to a sprawling international cottage industry of websites, forums, YouTube channels, and social media accounts.

India

Harsh Jain was born into a business family in Mumbai, India. From 2001-2003, he attended high school in England, where he became hooked on fantasy football, specifically the Fantasy Premier League. He told many of his friends back home and they started playing as well.

Jain went on to get a BS in Electrical Engineering from the University of Pennsylvania and then an MBA from Columbia University's Business School. When he returned home in 2007, he tried to find a fantasy cricket platform. Given how popular cricket was in India, he was surprised to see there weren't any. "I told my friends we have to solve this problem," Jain said. "There's a billion Indian cricket fans, and they don't have fantasy cricket."

He partnered with his childhood friend, Bhavit Sheth, and the 22-year-olds launched Dream11 in 2008. Jain borrowed "a couple of million dollars" from his father as starting capital and provided fantasy cricket, free to play, that relied on advertising revenue. But it didn't go well and after just two years, they found themselves strapped for cash. The 24-year-old entrepreneurs had lost millions of dollars. "It felt pretty terrible," Jain said. "Every founder, when you start something, you truly believe that this is going to explode, you're going to change the world—and ours crashed and burned."

Sheth, the company's COO, explained, "The ad revenue wasn't coming in because advertisers in India didn't understand fantasy sports. They needed to be educated. So, at that point we were wondering, what should we do now? We knew that fantasy sports as a model should work—there had to be some format in which it should work in India, we just didn't know what it was."

Jain was grateful he had a supportive family. "When I came home dejected," he said, "they stood by me and encouraged me to not give up on my dreams."

In 2012, Dream11 changed its platform from being reliant on ads to being "freemium." Users could choose to participate in a free or paid contest and the experience remained the same, except the paid games charged an entry fee and had prize pools. The average entry price was 40 rupees, or half a dollar, and the top player could win up to almost $250,000. The season-long contests also changed to a per-match format, which lowered players' commitment levels from many months to a single day. Dream11 kept a percentage of the entry fees. (If this sounds like DFS, yes, they essentially copied the DFS model.)

The changes worked, as they hit one million registered users in 2014, two million in 2016 and 45 million in 2018. Their growth has been aided by partnerships with some of the professional leagues and the use of cricket legends such as Harsha Bhogle and M. S. Dhoni as brand ambassadors. Jain said, "80% of users play the free contests to show off their knowledge in sports and for bragging rights among their friends."

But it also became a legal problem. Just as with the fantasy industry in the United States, they faced allegations of it being gambling. Dream11 spent a significant amount of time and money fighting to establish that their platform was a game of skill rather than a game of chance. It culminated with the Indian Supreme Court declaring Dream11 a legitimate platform.

As of 2024, the company had more than 800 employees. Dream Sports' investors have included Chinese tech giant Tencent as well as American hedge funds Tiger Global and D1 Capital. It took until 2020, but they finally became profitable. In 2021, they had revenues of $332 million, a net profit of more than $40 million, and the company was valued at $8 billion.

While cricket initially dominated their platform, other sports contests also became popular over time. As of 2024, 11 fantasy sports were offered, including cricket, basketball, soccer, baseball, kabaddi, badminton, futsal, rugby, volleyball, and handball. There are 200 million registered users. Jain said, "There are some contests with 10 million people playing against each other. We always try to make sure more than 50% of them at least win their money back, to keep it engaging."

Jain added, "It feels great to run a business that has come from solving a personal problem and that is contributing to the growth of India's sports ecosystem."

Australia

Peter Jankulovski and Kelly Barrett were in the United States in 2000 and saw how popular fantasy sports were. The pair, whose backgrounds were in online gaming, launched Vapormedia in 2001 with a fantasy game based on Australian rules football. Their first season drew 40,000 participants.

By 2012, it was estimated that one million people played fantasy in Australia. Vapormedia led with 700,000 players and offered 11 sports. Football was the leader, but other popular games included cricket, Australian basketball, rugby, and horse racing—where points are based on winnings of horses, jockeys, and trainers. They also offered games in New Zealand.

Japan

While attending Union College in Schenectady, New York, Ira Stevens did a term abroad in Japan. He later attended the Thunderbird School of Global Management in Phoenix, studying the Japanese language and business. After graduating in 1990, he lived and worked in Japan, and decided he'd like to start a business there.

Stevens had been playing roto since the early '80s and played the CDM game that started in the early '90s. He decided to bring fantasy baseball to Japan. In 1993, he cold called Brian Matthews, of CDM, and inquired about the possibility of bringing the CDM game to Japan. By 1994, he had met with Matthews in St. Louis and worked out a deal, and in 1995, Stevens launched Fantasy Sports Japan. This may have been the first time that fantasy sports reached Asia.

John Brison, one of the CDM partners and their lead tech guy, spent time in Japan to work on adapting the software. Stevens created a CDM-style game based on players in the Japanese Nippon Pro Baseball (NPB) league. The website was bilingual, with both Japanese and English. Due to their gambling laws, he offered product prizes rather than cash.

After starting with his game based on Japanese pro baseball, Stevens also offered all the CDM games based on American sports. Everything for those was identical to the CDM games, but presented bilingually.

Stevens marketed with ads in sports magazines, as well as passing out flyers in front of baseball stadiums. He passed out thousands of flyers over many years. Fantasy Sports Japan was still in business as of 2024, though it had yet to reach 1,000 registered teams for a season. Stevens says it's been a "labor of love" rather than a big money maker.

NeoSports is another company that has offered games in Japan. They also have offices in Australia, Vietnam, and Malaysia. But as of 2024, fantasy hadn't taken off in Japan like it had in several other countries.

There are fantasy games for sumo wrestling, although they are mostly played by people outside of Japan. Will Floyd is an American who grew to love sumo watching it on ESPN as a kid. In 2018, he started a fantasy league with a few friends and, the next year, offered

Fantasy Basho publicly. In 2023, he had a few hundred people, mostly Americans, playing. Another popular sumo game, called Kachi Clash, launched in 2020.

China

John Tang was born in China and raised in the United States. In 1999, the 19-year-old UCLA student had a summer job as a service rep at Cisco. He took up fantasy sports to keep himself entertained while working as late as possible. "You got paid for as long as you sat in your chair, so fantasy sports became a great time-killer for me," he said.

Tang brought fantasy sports to China in 2009 when he launched Fan Te Xi (pronounced "fantasy") Technology with the help of American company Hotbox Sports, which white-labeled a game for him. Prior to this, there were some small, unlicensed operators in China, and Chinese customers had the option of playing fantasy on western-based websites that weren't blocked. But FTX was China's first licensed fantasy website and leagues. And the first to have a fantasy website and platform in the Chinese language.

At the time, Tang reasoned, "If the US fantasy industry has 30 million users and makes $4 billion a year, what can it do in a country with four times the population and 290 million web users?"

He was counting on basketball to become popular, thanks in part to Yao Ming, who joined the Houston Rockets NBA team in 2002. Yi Jianlian, a former Chinese teammate of Ming, joined the Milwaukee Bucks in 2007. Tang said that when the Rockets and Bucks play each other, it's like the Chinese Super Bowl, with 200 million Chinese citizens watching on TV.

FTX quickly had 50,000 playing their NBA game, and later added soccer and other sports. But it appears the company shut down at some point during the 2010s.

Brazil

South America is no exception to the expansion of fantasy. In 2022, it was reported to have generated $1.4 billion in revenue, accounting for 6.6% of the global fantasy sports industry. Fantasy sports in its largest country, Brazil, is led by Cartola FC, which launched in 2005. Based on the Brazilian Soccer Championship, it has 38 rounds, from April to December, just like the real championship. Cartola FC is owned by Globo Group, the largest media conglomerate in Brazil. Its news, sports and entertainment programs reach 99.6% of the Brazilian population. As of 2021, the Cartola FC app had more than 17 million downloads and six million active teams.

Also popular in Brazil are fantasy basketball, baseball, football, mixed martial arts, ice hockey, boxing, golf, tennis, and motorsport. After Cartola FC, some of the most-played platforms are on ESPN, CBS, Yahoo, DraftKings, FanDuel and Reis da Bola.

EPILOGUE

When Andy Mousalimas thought it would be fun for customers and good for his business to offer fantasy football; when Peter Pezaris and his friends decided to start a business and initially tried an online restaurant guide; when Greg Ambrosius drove to Iola expecting to find a guy in a barn, none of them could ever have known that one day there would be a 24-hour radio station only for fantasy. Or fantasy games with million-dollar prizes. Or 200 million people playing fantasy cricket in India.

But they, and hundreds of other entrepreneurs, created a multi-billion-dollar worldwide industry. Some started at their kitchen tables while others began with millions of dollars in venture capital. What they all had in common was seeing a need that they could fill. Something that was needed but didn't exist, or something that existed but could be improved upon.

After finishing this manuscript, it occurred to me that I was doing the same thing. I saw a need for this book—nothing like this existed—so I created it.

The one key factor in the success of the fantasy industry is that fantasy sports are great. Emil Kadlec has explained, "Humans need a hobby—they need to get away from the stresses in their life—and fantasy football is a beautiful hobby."

Harsh Jain's take on fantasy: "I compare fantasy sports to popcorn for your movie. You have popcorn because it makes your movie better. Fantasy does that for sports. It deepens your engagement and makes that sports event 100 times more interesting."

People love fantasy sports. That's why there are games for everything from football to wakeboarding to Iditarod. That's why fathers and sons, mothers and daughters, co-workers, and people from all walks of life bond together. That's why Barack Obama played fantasy football while running for president. That's why 40% in an FSTA survey said they expect to keep playing until they die.

To where will the fantasy industry evolve in 10 years, or 20 years, or 50 years? I won't even hazard a guess, but I can't wait to find out.

BIBLIOGRAPHY

CHAPTER 1

APBAGames.com

BaseballGames.dreamhosters.com. "A Brief History of Tabletop Baseball." 2011 and 2019.

Drucker, Jim, interviewed by author, November 2022.

Furman, Eric. Spooky'sHobbyShop.com.

James, Bill. "Ballpark 'N Me." BillJamesOnline.com. December 5, 2021.

Kalb, Bess. "The Lost Founder of Baseball Video Games." Grantland.com. April 16, 2012.

Lemire, Joe. "Strat-O-Matic more than a game for its founder and devotees." *Sports Illustrated*, January 10, 2011.

Manly, Lorne, "Strat-O-Matic, the Throwback, Endures the Era of the X-Boxes." *New York Times*, January 13, 2006.

Nelshoppen, Thomas, interviewed by author, October 2022.

Rosen, Adam. "Celebrity Q+A with Jon Miller." Strat-O-Matic.com. May 27, 2014.

Spear, Tom, interviewed by author, January 2023.

Stark, Eric G., *The Ephrata Review*, April 24, 2019.

Strat-O-Matic.com. "Celebrity Q+A with Bob Costas." November 12, 2013.

Thorn, John. "First Baseball Table Game." MLBBlogs.com. June 2, 2014.

Witmer, Jason, interviewed by author, January 2023.

Zangari, Phil, interviewed by author, October 2022.

CHAPTER 2

Ain, Morty, "An Oral History of Rotisserie Baseball," *ESPN The Magazine*, March 8, 2010.

Berry, Matthew. "Untold Stories of 40 Years of Fantasy Baseball," ESPN.com. March 4, 2020.

Blandino, Joe, interviewed by author, December 2022.

Colston, Chris, Article in *USA Today*, 1999.

Connors, Mike, "Playing 35 Years of Fantasy Baseball," *The Virginian-Pilot*, April 6, 2014.

Ferretti, Fred, "For Major-League Addicts, A Way to Win a Pennant," *New York Times*, July 8, 1980.

Fleder, Nick, "A Conversation With the Founding Father of Fantasy, Dan Okrent," *The Hardball Times*, December 29, 2011.

Friedberg, Ardy, "Most Leagues Strike it Rich in Fun, Camaraderie, Not Loot," *South Florida Sun Sentinel*, September 27, 1990.

Goodwin, Tim, and Steve Wulf. "Steve Wulf and the Last Rotisserie Draft," ESPN.com, April 25, 2008.

Hassan, John, interviewed by author, November 2022.

Hilt, Ed, "Fantasy Baseball League Owners Still Bonding in Their 32nd Season," *Press of Atlantic City*, June 26, 2007.

Holdship, Deborah, "A League of His Own," *Michigan Today*, May 8, 2021.

Kelly, Jonathan, "Q+A: Fantasy Baseball Creator Daniel Okrent," *Vanity Fair*, March 21, 2008.

Okrent, Dan, interviewed by author, November 2022.

Okrent, Dan, "The Year George Foster Wasn't Worth $36." *Inside Sports*, March 31, 1981.

Sandomir, Richard, "Bill Gamson, Sociologist and Inventor of Games, Dies at 87," *New York Times*, April 6, 2021.

Strat-O-Matic.com. "Celebrity Q+A with Daniel Okrent," September 22, 2014.

Sweeney, R. Emmet, "Fantasy Baseball's Founding Fathers," BaseballProspectus.com, April 29, 2011.

Waggoner, Glen, and Robert Sklar. *Rotisserie League Baseball*. New York: Bantam Books, 1990.

Williams, Tom, "It's Now 40 Years for the Original Fantasy Baseball League," *The Gazette of Ocean City*, July 27, 2016.

Wulf, Steve, Article in *Sports Illustrated*, May 1984

CHAPTER 3

Ahlas, Harry, interviewed by author, February 2023.

Berry, Matthew. "Love, Hate and a Tribute to a True American Hero." ESPN.com, November 10, 2021.

Cooke, Ann, interviewed by author, February 2023.

"Death: John James Kumarelas," *Deseret News*, September 7, 1997.

Esser, Luke, "The Birth of Fantasy Football," *Fantasy Football Index*, 1994.

FantasyFootballIndex.com. "Andy Mousalimas: The Interview."

FantasyIndex.com. "In Memory: Andy Mousalimas (1924-2020)." May 2020.

FantasySportsBusiness.com. "Fantasy Sports History: The GOPPPL." August 5, 2010.

Franzese, Pasquale, interviewed by author, February 2023.

Green, Corinne, "Fantasy Football: We Owe It All to Wilfred 'Bill' Winkenbach," *Naples Daily News*, September 11, 2014.

Harris, Bob, and Emil Kadlec. "A Nod and a Wink to the Founders of Fantasy Football." FootballDiehards.com.

Hruby, Patrick. "The Founding Fathers of Fantasy." SportsOnEarth.com, December 2, 2013.

Keown, Tim. "50 Years of Fantasy Football." ESPN.com, November 11, 2012.

Podolski, Mark, "Fantasy Football League Originated in Northeast Ohio Entering 36th Season," *The News-Herald*, August 21, 2016.

Snapp, Martin, "Andy Mousalimas," *The Mercury News*, May 24, 2020.

St. Amant, Mark. *Committed: Confessions of a Fantasy Football Junkie*. New York: Scribner, 2004.

Whiting, Sam. "Huge Stat: 50 years of Fantasy Football," *San Francisco Chronicle*, November 21, 2012.

Whiting, Sam, "Andy Mousalimas, War Hero and Restauranteur Who Helped Launch Fantasy Football, Dies," *NewsTimes*, May 24, 2020.

Wilner, Jon, "Fantasy Football Was Born in Oakland, Original League Still Thriving," *The Mercury News*, September 13, 2015.

CHAPTER 4

Barton, Jeff, interviewed by author, August 2023.

BoxScoreBaseball.com.

Breznick, Alan. "Swinging for the Fences," *Washington Post*, January 4, 1999.

Carey, Bill, interviewed by author, February 2023.

Cotter, Larry, interviewed by author, February 2023.

Head2Head.com.

Hughes, Patrick, interviewed by author, June 2023.

Kadlec, Emil. "Patrick Hughes Fantasy Sports Pioneer," FantasyNation.com.

Kadlec, Emil. "Stacie Stern Fantasy Sports Pioneer," FantasyNation.com.

Lewis, Peter H. "Computerized Baseball Prodigy Baseball Manager a sure hit with rotisserie team leaders," *Baltimore Sun*, May 04, 1992.

Lombardo, John. "Dream Team," *Washington Business Journal*, July 21, 1997.

Mosher, Terry, "Rotisserie Baseball Enticing Players, Profits," *Kitsap Sun*, April 12, 1990.

Newman, Scott, "Fantasy Leagues Give Fans the Fun of Being an Owner," *The Pittsburgh Press*, May 30, 1990.

Polisano, Dan, interviewed by author, September 2023.

"Sandbox.com, Time Warner Link in $15M Deal," *Washington Business Journal*, April 24, 2000.

Sweet, David. "Visitors Find Sites' Games Are Right on the Money," *Wall Street Journal*, June 7, 2000.

Zaleski, John, interviewed by author, October 2023.

Zola, Todd. "A Chat With Jeff Barton From Scoresheet Baseball," RotoWire.com, August 25, 2022.

CHAPTER 5

Ford, Geoff, interviewed by author, July 2023.

Gibson, Bill, interviewed by author, July 2023.

Halbfinger, David. "Clock Runs Out on Fantasy League Firm," *Boston Globe*, October 13, 1995.

Johnson, Keith, interviewed by author, August 2023.

Kadlec, Emil. "Jeff Thomas Fantasy Sports Pioneer," FantasyNation.com.

Lev, Michael, "Real Money in Fantasy Baseball," *New York Times*, April 15, 1991.

Michaud, Anne, "Wakeman Files Under Chapter 11," *Los Angelese Times*, August 15, 1992.

Moser, Rob, interviewed by author, July 2023.

Thomas, Jeff, interviewed by author, May 2023.

CHAPTER 6

Ali, Rafat. "CBS Interactive Sues NFL on Fantasy Sports Stats." CBSNews.com, September 8, 2008.

Bailey, JJ. "Man in the Middle," *Entrepreneur Quarterly.*

Brown, Maury, "The Ledger Domain: The Impact of the Fantasy Stats Ruling," *Baseball Prospectus,* October 24, 2007.

"CBC v. MLBAM," *Harvard Law Review,* vol. 121:1439.

"CBS Faces Countersuit from NFL Players Over Statistics Usage," *Associated Press,* September 10, 2008.

DeMause, Neil, "Fantasy Firefight: When IP Meets WHIP." Baseball Prospectus.com, February 16, 2005.

"Fantasy Baseball Legal Win Could Change Game's Playing Field," *Associated Press,* August 9, 2006.

Fisher, Eric, "U.S. Supreme Court Denies Petition to Hear MLBAM/CDM Dispute," *Sports Business Journal,* June 2, 2008.

Florio, Mike, "Yahoo! Sues NFLPA," *NBC Sports,* June 4, 2009.

HarnessIP.com. "Litigation Victory for CBC and the $1.5 Billion Fantasy Sports Industry."

Isidore, Chris. "Fantasy 'Rights' and Wrong." Money.CNN.com, August 11, 2006.

Kadlec, Emil. "Charlie Wiegert Fantasy Sports Pioneer." FantasyNation.com.

King, Bill, "A Real Fight Over Fantasy," *Sports Business Journal,* November 14, 2005.

Kurtovic, Amir, "A League of Their Own," *St. Louis Business Journal,* May 4, 2012.

Loeb.com. "CBS Interactive Inc. v. National Football League Players Association, Inc." April 28, 2009.

Matthews, Brian and Carol, interviewed by author, February 2023.

PRWeb.com. "High Court Decision Marks Historic Day for Fantasy Sports Industry, Says Fantasy Sports Trade Association." June 3, 2008.

"Supreme Court Won't Rule on MLB Fantasy Lawsuit," *The Ledger,* June 3, 2008.

Telscher, Rudy, interviewed by author, January 2023.

Topaz, Bill, interviewed by author, March 2023.

Walker, Clay, interviewed by author, June 2023.

Wiegert, Charlie, interviewed by author, January 2023.

Yahoo.com. "The Reality of Fantasy." April 21, 2006.

"Yahoo Sues NFL Players Association," *Associated Press,* June 3, 2009.

CHAPTER 7

Allan, Ian, interviewed by author, April 2023.

Ambrosius, Greg, interviewed by author, April 2023.

Borelli, Stephen, "Appreciation: 30 Years and Counting: Baseball (Now Sports) Weekly Still Going Strong," *USA Today,* April 12, 2021.

Charchian, Paul, interviewed by author, October 2023.

Dan and Kelly Grogan, interviewed by author, April 2023.

Gardner, Steve, FSGA Hall of Fame induction introduction speech for John Hunt, 2013.

Gardner, Steve, "Leviathan to Crickets, Hunt Left His Mark on Fantasy Baseball," *USA Today*, June 18, 2013.

Gonos, David. "Reality Doesn't Bite: How Two Seattle College Students Created the First Fantasy Football Magazine." TheAthletic.com, Jul 25, 2019.

Kadlec, Emil. "Dan and Kelly Grogan Fantasy Sports Pioneers," FantasyNation.com.

Kadlec, Emil. "Ian Allan Fantasy Sports Pioneer." FantasyNation.com.

Kadlec, Emil, interviewed by author, July 2023.

Kadlec, Emil. "Jack Pullman Fantasy Sports Pioneers." FantasyNation.com, 2020.

Kadlec, Emil. "Paul Charchian Fantasy Sports Pioneer." FantasyNation.com.

Kopnick, Ben. "Fantasy Sports a Sweet Reality for EPHS Grad Paul Charchian," *Eden Prairie Local News*, September 6, 2022.

Landsbaum, Mark, "Fantasy Baseball: So How 'Bout Them Sludgers?", *Los Angeles Times*, October 21, 1987.

Shandler, Ron. *Fantasy Expert*. Chicago: Triumph Books, 2024.

Taylor, Bruce, interviewed by author, May 2023.

TheFSGA.org. "Fantasy Sports Hall of Fame: Ian Allan."

TheFSGA.org. "Fantasy Sports Hall of Fame: Paul Charchian."

TheFSGA.org. "Fantasy Sports Hall of Fame: Rob Pythian."

White, Paul, interviewed by author, June 2023.

CHAPTER 8

Bump, Lary, interviewed by author, September 2023.

Cavanaugh, Jack. "Who's on First? In Baseball's Rotisserie League, That Is," *New York Times*, April 5, 1998.

"Meet the Minnesotans Who Launched Fantasy Football." CBSNews.com, December 19, 2018.

Patton, Alex, interviewed by author, October 2023.

Shandler, Ron. *Fantasy Expert*. Chicago: Triumph Books, 2024.

TheFSGA.org. "Fantasy Sports Hall of Fame: Cliff Charpentier."

TheFSGA.org. "Fantasy Sports Hall of Fame: John Benson."

CHAPTER 9

Ambrosius, Greg. "Interview with Ron Shandler," You Tube High Stakes Fantasy Network Episode 32, March 2023.

DePasquale, Ron, "Football Fan Stumbles onto Gold," *The Boston Globe*, January 29, 2006.

Donahue, Ben. "The Life and Career of Virgil Carter." ProFootballHistory.com, October 2, 2023.

Finewax, Michael, interviewed by author, November 2023.

Gianella, Mike. "Fantasy Freestyle: How We Got Here," *Baseball Prospectus*, July 1, 2015.

Hoffman, Jascha, "Pigskin Pythagoras," *The Boston Globe*, February 1, 2004.

James, Bill. "Ballpark 'N Me." BillJamesOnline.com, December 5, 2021.

Kadlec, Emil. "Cynthia Frelund Fantasy Sports Pioneer." FantasyNation.com.

Kadlec, Emil. "Ron Shandler Fantasy Sports Pioneer." FantasyNation.com, 2020.

Okrent, Daniel, "He Does It by the Numbers," *Sports Illustrated*, May 25, 1981.

Okrent, Daniel, interviewed by author, November 2022.

Potts, Mark, "Baseball Sage Bill James Is Forever Asking Questions," *The Lawrence Times*, August 31, 2023.

Rodriguez, Ken, "Fantasy Football Gives Everyone a Shot as One of Joe Robbie's Headaches," *The Miami Herald*, October 20, 1989.

Schatz, Aaron, interviewed by author, November 2023.

Schucht, Eric, "Graphing the Game With David Appelman," *Washington Jewish Week*, April 27, 2021.

Shandler, Ron. *Fantasy Expert*. Chicago: Triumph Books, 2024.

Shandler, Ron, interviewed by author, November 2023.

Spezia, Mark, "Okemos Native Blazes Trail in NFL's Analytics Game," *Detroit Free Press*, February 4, 2018.

Springer, Steve, "Recreation Becomes a Vocation," *Los Angeles Times*, June 26, 1988.

Stambor, Zak. "Number Cruncher," *University of Chicago Magazine*, July/August 2008.

"The Ballad of Bill James." MLB.com, September 21, 2011.

TheFSGA.org. "Fantasy Sports Hall of Fame: Ron Shandler."

Wiedeman, Reeves, "The Sabermetrics of Football," *The New Yorker*, September 23, 2011.

Zavisca, Christian, "Pro Football Prospectus 2008 Review," *Knoxville News-Sentinel*, September 14, 2008.

CHAPTER 10

Adams, Russell, "Peter Pezaris," *Sports Business Journal*, November 10, 2003.

Arace, Michael. "The Fantasy Business Can't Manufacture Run," *Hartford Courant*, March 31, 1995.

Burger, Jim, interviewed by author, September 2023.

Burton, Rick, Kevin Hall, and Rodney Paul, "The Historical Development and Marketing of Fantasy Sports Leagues," *The Journal of Sport*, 2013.

Dewan, John, interviewed by author, January 2024.

Dewan, John, podcast appearance, Dewanfoundation.org.

El Kordi-Hubbard, Jonathan. "With Clients Like the NBA and Google, STATS is the Coolest Data Company You've Never Heard of." BuiltInChicago.org, February 25, 2014.

Forman, Sean. "John Dewan Biography," *Baseball Research Journal*, Spring 2016.

Furlow, Laurel, "Alumni Voice," *Carnegie Mellon Today*, January 1, 2009.

Lamm, Marcy, "Fantasy Game Developer Daedalus Sold to SportsLine," *Sports Business Journal*, January 3, 2000.

Oliveto, Mike, interviewed by author, August 2023.

Pezaris, Peter, interviewed by author, February 2023.

Phillips, Sam. "John Dewan's Perfect Game." SOA.org.

Pike, Rich, interviewed by author, August 2023.

"Sportsline.com Acquires Daedalus World Wide Corporation." CBSSports.com, December 22, 1999.

Wolf, Rick, interviewed by author, February 2023.

CHAPTER 11

Ambrosius, Greg. "High Stakes Fantasy Network Episode 33: Brady Tinker." March 15, 2023. Video on YouTube.com.

Berry, Matthew. *Fantasy Life*. New York: Riverhead Books by the Penguin Group, 2013.

Berry, Matthew, interviewed by author, January 2024.

Campbell, Morgan, "Fantasy Sports: Can New TV Network Find an Audience Among Poolies?", *Toronto Star*, March 11, 2013.

Charchian, Paul, interviewed by author, October 2023.

Cohen, Rachel, "Hansen Rode Popularity of Fantasy to a New Career," *Casper Star-Tribune*, December 7, 2014.

Cohen, Steve, interviewed by author, October 2023.

DiFino, Nando, interviewed by author, August 2023.

FantasyPoints.com. "John Hansen Biography."

Hansen, John, interviewed by author, December 2023.

Hitzges, Norm, interviewed by author, July 2023.

Kadlec, Emil. "Brady Tinker Fantasy Sports Pioneer." FantasyNation.com.

Kadlec, Emil. "John Hansen Fantasy Sports Pioneer." FantasyNation.com, 2020.

Kadlec, Emil. "Lenny Melnick Fantasy Sports Pioneer." FantasyNation.com, 2020.

King, Bill, "How Mr. Roto Came to Live a Life of Fantasy," *Sports Business Journal*, November 12, 2007.

Kleen, Brendon. "Matthew Berry: Best Former ESPN Talent to Get a Beer With?" AwfulAnnouncing.com, October 11, 2023.

Lebowitz, Larry, "Sportsline Puts Audio Programs on Internet," *South Florida Sun-Sentinel*, August 30, 1996.

Liguori, Ann, interviewed by author, July 2023.

Mayo, Jonathan, "Meet Roto's Dynamic Duo," *New York Post*, August 31, 1997.

Melnick, Lenny, interviewed by author, June 2023.

Midgley, Chad, interviewed by author, September 2023.

Mumm, Brad, interviewed by author, July 2023.

Schwartz, Cory, interviewed by author, October 2023.

Siano, Mike, interviewed by author, July 2023.

Silverman, Steve, interviewed by author, January 2024.

Simmons, Bill. "Matthew Berry." *The BS Report*. July 26, 2007. Podcast.

TheFSGA.org. "Fantasy Sports Hall of Fame: Matthew Berry."

Tinker, Brady, interviewed by author, June 2023.

Zwilling, Irwin, interviewed by author, July 2023.

CHAPTER 12

Bonini, Ryan, interviewed by author, January 2024.

Bray, Jim, "Turning on 'The Pitch,'" *National Post*, March 5, 1999.

Del Pilar, William, interviewed by author, November 2023.

Erickson, Jeff and Chris Liss. "History of RotoWire." Video on YouTube.com.

Erickson, Jeff, interviewed by author, December 2023.

FantasySportsBusiness.com. "Business Profile: RotoWire.com." November 27, 2010.

GrumblingsMedia.com. John Georgopoulos biography.

GrumblingsMedia.com. William Del Pilar biography.

Hardee, Howard. "At Madison-Based Company RotoWire, Fantasy Sports are Reality." TheBozho.com, August 22, 2019.

Kadlec, Emil. "Peter Schoenke Fantasy Sports Pioneer." FantasyNation.com.

Kadlec, Emil. "William Del Pilar Fantasy Sports Pioneer," FantasyNation.com.

LePore, Dennis, interviewed by author, August 2023.

Mulhern, Tom, "Fantasy Becomes Reality," *Wisconsin State Journal*, June 27, 2010.

Punzel, Dennis, "Flight of Fantasy," *The Capital Times*, May 29, 2008.

SandlotShrink.com.

Schoenke, Peter, interviewed by author, December 2023.

Shandler, Ron. *Fantasy Expert*. Chicago: Triumph Books, 2024.

Wolf, Rick, interviewed by author, February 2023.

CHAPTER 13

Bryant, Joe, interviewed by author, January 2024.

Dodds, David, interviewed by author, December 2023.

Dorey, David, interviewed by author, November 2023.

"Football Fans Turn Fantasy into Fiscal Reward." ABCNews.go.com, November 10, 2005.

Harris, Bob, interviewed by author, June 2023.

Kadlec, Emil. "Bob Harris Fantasy Sports Pioneer," FantasyNation.com.

Kadlec, Emil. "David Dodds Fantasy Sports Pioneer." FantasyNation.com, 2020.

Kadlec, Emil. "David Dorey Fantasy Sports Pioneer." FantasyNation.com, 2020.

Kadlec, Emil. "James Serra Fantasy Sports Pioneer." FantasyNation.com, 2020.

Kadlec, Emil. "Jim Lenz Fantasy Sports Pioneer." FantasyNation.com, 2020.

Serra, James, interviewed by author, October 2023.

St. Amant, Mark. *Committed: Confessions of a Fantasy Football Junkie*. New York: Scribner, 2004.

CHAPTER 14

Adams, Russell, "High-Stakes Fantasy Football Providers Drawing Scrutiny From Players, Inc.," *Sports Business Journal*, September 13, 2004.

Ambrosius, Greg. "High Stakes Fantasy Interview Series, Episode 25." January 24, 2023. Video on YouTube

Ambrosius, Greg. "High Stakes Fantasy Interview Series, Episode 26." June 2023.

Ambrosius, Greg, interviewed by author, April 2023.

Balkman, Eric, interviewed by author, August 2023.

CNBC TV interview with Emil Kadlec.

Dodds, David. "Interview with Lenny Pappano," FootballGuys.com, August 1, 2006.

FantasyNation.com. "Emil K."

Full Time Fantasy Football podcast with Emil Kadlec, FullTimeFantasy.com, 2020.

Gerczak, David, interviewed by author, July 2023.

Hayes, Stephen. "Beyond the Game: Ian Ritchie," TVSportsMag.com, December 24, 2020.

Kadlec, Emil, interviewed by author, July 2023.

Kaganovsky, Alex, interviewed by author, July 2023.

Leggett, Shellye. "Fantasy Football Connection." KOAT 7. June 4, 2020. Video on YouTube.

Muzio, Billy. "The FFPC: An Introduction to High Stakes Fantasy Football." FantasyData.com, March 18, 2021.

MyFFPC.com.

Pappano, Lenny, interviewed by author, July 2023.

Ritchie, Ian, interviewed by author, September 2023.

Schroeder, Chad, interviewed by author, July 2023.

Shandler, Ron. *Fantasy Expert*. Chicago: Triumph Books, 2024.

Simpson, Kalani. "Playing Fantasy Sports Like a Bat Out of Hell." StarBulletin.com, April 3, 2004.

St. Amant, Mark, "When Fantasy Players Go All In," *New York Times*, September 2, 2007.

TheFSGA.org. "Fantasy Sports Hall of Fame: Emil Kadlec."

Tucker, Ross and Joe Dolan. *Fantasy Feast*. 2021. Podcast.

CHAPTER 15

Behe, Regis. "Fantasy Sports Leagues Put Armchair Quarterbacks in the Game," TribLive.com, December 14, 2002.

Behrens, Andy, interviewed by author, January 2024.

Berry, Matthew, interviewed by author, January 2024.

Blaser, Vince, "Fantasy Football Is Booming," *Citizen's Voice* (Scripps Howard), August 24, 2003.

Blaser, Vince, "Fantasy Sports Games Now Multimillion-Dollar Business," Scripps Howard Foundation, 2003.

Colton, Glenn. Tout Wars Lawr Michaels award winner Rick Wolf nominating speech, ToutWars.com, 2021.

Fabiano, Michael, interviewed by author, March 2024.

Fischer, Sara. "ESPN's Big Bet on Fantasy." Axios.com, November 28, 2017.

Geller, David, interviewed by author, January 2024.

Harmon, Michael. *The Savvy Guide to Fantasy Sports*. Indy-Tech, 2005.

"Inside Sportsline: How Mike Levy Built a New Media Brand," Digital South, Fall 1997.

Johnson, Greg, "Fantasy Sports Draws Millions," *The Des Moines Register*, April 7, 2001.

Kadlec, Emil. "Rick Wolf Fantasy Sports Pioneer." FantasyNation.com.

Knuppel, Ryan. "Interview with Rick Wolf," *Knup Sports Show* #121. February 19, 2021.

Levy, Mike, interviewed by author, March 2023.

Marcin, Tim. "How Fantasy Football Exploded Online and Kept Yahoo Relevant." Mashable.com, October 17, 2020.

Mariani, Mark, interviewed by author, April 2023.

Melvin, Paul. "Starwave & ESPN: A Partnership That Built ESPN.com's Future." ESPN.com, March 30, 2015.

Ota, Kevin. "ESPN's Fantasy Success: It's All Real." ESPNpressroom.com, November 28, 2017.

Ota, Kevin. "New All-Time Record: 12 Million Fans Playing ESPN Fantasy Football in 2023," ESPNPressroom.com September 9, 2023.

Peyton, Dave. "Here's Where Baseball Enthusiasts Can Find News, Talk, Games and More," *Philadelphia Enquirer*, April 4, 1996.

Reiss, Geoff, interviewed by author, January 2024.

Robb, Sharon, "Cybersports," *South Florida Sun Sentinel*, August 17, 1997.

Robinson, Shawn, interviewed by author, January 2024.

Roefaro, Gano. "The Success Story of Mike Levy," Keys to Success interview. January 29, 2015. Video on YouTube.

Segars, Gary. "Interview with Rick Wolf, Fantasy Sports Pioneer." Winning Cures Everything. April 12, 2022. Video on YouTube.

St. Amant, Mark, *Committed: Confessions of a Fantasy Football Junkie*. New York: Scribner, 2004.

TheFSGA.org. "Fantasy Sports Hall of Fame: Rick Wolf."

Walker, Clay, interviewed by author, June 2023.

Ware, Scott, interviewed by author, January 2024.

Wilner, Richard, "How to be a GM – and Have Fun Doin' It," *New York Post*, February 13, 2000.

WinDailySports.com show #34 podcast.

Wolf, Rick, interviewed by author, February 2023.

CHAPTER 16

Ambrosius, Greg, interviewed by author, April 2023.

Clausing, Jeri, "Senator Unveils New Effort to Ban Internet Gambling," *New York Times*, March 23, 1999.

"Fantasy Leagues Motivate Many," *The Palm Beach Post*. May 16, 1999.

Fisher, Eric, "Fantasy Sports Trade Association Rebranding to Include Gambling," *Sports Business Journal*, January 22, 2019.

FSWA.org.

"How Many People Play Fantasy Sports? Interesting Facts and Figures," PlayToday.co, December 7, 2022.

IBISWorld.com.

Ruihley and Billings 2013.

Schoenke, Peter, interviewed by author, December 2023.

Seboldt, Allison, interviewed by author, January 2024.

Serra, James, interviewed by author, October 2023.

Statista.com.

TheFSGA.org. "Fantasy Sports and Gaming Association – Demographics Pahe."

Wasserman, Elizabeth. "Second Time a Charm for Net Gambling Bill." CNN.com, March 24, 1999.

Zaleski, John, interviewed by author, October 2023.

CHAPTER 17

Anderson, Curt, "Fantasy Leagues Threatened by Gambling Ruling," *The Monitor* (AP), February 3, 1991.

Chen, Albert. *Billion Dollar Fantasy*. Boston/New York: Houghton Mifflin Harcourt, 2019.

Conlon, Kendra. "Florida Lawmakers, Prosecutors Investigate Daily Fantasy Sports." WTSP.com, October 23, 2015.

Davidson, Tom, "Gambling Dismissal Settled Firefighter Wins Back Job With Department," *South Florida Sun-Sentinel*, November 10, 1991.

"DraftKings Employee Cleared in Daily Fantasy Sports Cheating Scandal." Casino.org, October 22, 2015.

Drape, Joe and Jacqueline Williams, "Scandal Erupts in Unregulated World of Fantasy Sports," *New York Times*, October 5, 2015.

Drape, Joe and Jesse McKinley, "New York State Lawmakers Vote to Legalize Fantasy Sports," *New York Times*, June 18, 2016.

Firestone, Jared. "FanDuel, DraftKings Face Class Action Lawsuit in Wake of Cheating Scandal," Expert Institute.

Friedberg, Ardy, "Most Leagues Strike It Rich in Fun, Camaraderie, Not Loot," *South Florida Sun Sentinel*, September 27, 1990.

Hyde, David, "Fantasy Baseball—Deliver Us From Evil!", *South Florida Sun Sentinel*, August 20, 1991.

Kadlec, Emil. "Geoffrey Stein Fantasy Sports Pioneer." FantasyNation.com.

Knotts, Bob, "Fantasy League Leader Loses Job," *South Florida Sun Sentinel*, November 28, 1990.

Matustik, David and Berta Delgado. "Bets Off in Austin After Raid," *Austin American-Statesman*, September 21, 1989.

"New York Investigates DraftKings and FanDuel Over Fantasy Sports Cheating," *The Guardian*, October 7, 2015.

Phillips, Jim, "Reduced Charges Recommended in Gambling Case," *Austin American-Standard*, May 30, 1991.

Phillips, Jim, "Travis Grand Jury Refuses to Indict for Fantasy Football," *Austin American-Statesman*, July 19, 1991.

Pierre-Pierre, Garry, "Ruling May Impact Firefighter's Case," *South Florida Sun Sentinel*, February 10, 1991.

Roberts, Daniel, "DraftKings, FanDuel Go to War with Eric Schneiderman," *Fortune*, November 11, 2015.

Rodenberg, Ryan. "The True Congressional Origin of Daily Fantasy Sports." ESPN.com, October 28, 2015.

Schoenke, Peter, interviewed by author, December 2023.

"Sports Shorts." Associated Press, August 21, 1991.

Vogel, Kenneth and Eric Lipton, "Cigars, Booze, Money: How a Lobbying Blitz Made Sports Betting Ubiquitous," *New York Times*, November 20, 2022.

Walker, Meg, "Fantasy League Leader Suspended," *South Florida Sun Sentinel*, September 28, 1990.

Wattles, Jackie. "FanDuel and DraftKings to Leave New York State." CNN.com, March 22, 2016.

Wegman, William. *Sports and the Law*. New York: Routledge, 1996.

CHAPTER 18

Aparicio, Eddie, interviewed by author, November 2023.

Bell, Stephania, interviewed by author, January 2024.

Carroll, Will, interviewed by author, November 2023.

Cohen, Steve, interviewed by author, October 2023.

Deutsch, Matt, interviewed by author, October 2023.

Kadlec, Emil. "Steve Cohen Fantasy Sports Pioneer." FantasyNation.com.

LoRe, Michael, "The Rise of Dr. David Chao AKA Pro Football Doc," *Forbes*, December 20, 2019.

Morse, Jesse, interviewed by author, October 2023.

Schoetle, Anthony, "Injury Expert Sports Huge Following," *Indianapolis Business Journal*, January 11, 2018.

Shandler, Ron, *Fantasy Expert*. Chicago: Triumph Books, 2024.

"Stephania Bell." ESPNPressroom.com.

TheFSGA.org. "Fantasy Sports Hall of Fame: Steve Cohen."

Tomlinson, Brett, "Stephania Bell '87," *Princeton Alumni Weekly*, November 4, 2009.

Wilton, Rick, interviewed by author, January 2024.

CHAPTER 19

Buckner, Candace, "Fantasy Football Making Financial Dreams a Reality," *Fort Worth Star-Telegram*, September 2, 2007.

Burghardt, Robert, interviewed by author, November 2023.

Charchian, Paul, interviewed by author, October 2023.

Edelman, Marc, interviewed by author, November 2023.

Greene, Jerry, "Fantasy Sports 'Widows' Unite," *Orlando Sentinel*, August 24, 2008.

Heitner, Darren, "Vault-Like Services Could Be Next Fantasy Sports Success Stories," *Forbes*, April 20, 2014.

Klayman, Ben. "Technology Spurs Growth of Fantasy Sports." Reuters.com, September 25, 2008.

Kuriloff, Aaron, "Disputes in Fantasy Sports Leagues Find People's Court," *Edmonton Journal*, March 15, 2007.

Lodish, Alison, interviewed by author, October 2023.

Pliml, Jason, interviewed by author, June 2023.

RotoUmpire.com.

SharkTankBlog.com. "Trophy Smack."

Shark Tank episode with TrophySmack, June 3, 2021.

Stein, Mike, interviewed by author, November 2023.

Taylor, Chris. "How to Keep Fantasy Football from Fouling Up Your Finances." Money.com, September 25, 2014.

TrophySmack.com.

CHAPTER 20

Di Fino, Nando. "Scott Fish: Turning Fantasy Football Obsession into Toys for Disadvantaged Kids," TheAthletic.com, December 10, 2018.

FanexFootball.com, 1996.

FantasySharks.com. "Fanex: Fantasy Analysis Draft." August 2, 2022.

FantasySportsBusiness.com. "Personal Profile: Greg Kellogg." October 1, 2010.

Fish, Scott, interviewed by author, December 2023.

Gardner, Steve, "LABR of Love: Experts Fantasy League Begins 20th Season," *USA Today Sports*, February 25, 2013.

Hunt, John, interviewed by author, November 2023.

Mason, Justin, interviewed by author, December 2023.

ScottFishBowl.com.

Shandler, Ron. *Fantasy Expert*. Chicago: Triumph Books, 2024.

Strafford, Dan, interviewed by author, December 2023.

TheFSGA.org. "Fantasy Sports Hall of Fame: Lawr Michaels."

"Variety of Strategies Can Yield Roto Success," *Daily Record*, March 21, 2001.

CHAPTER 21

Chen, Albert. *Billion Dollar Fantasy*. Boston/New York: Houghton Mifflin Harcourt, 2019.

Dyal, Tom. "The Super Bowl of Startups: Interview with DraftKings CEO Jason Robins." Redpoint.com, February 5, 2014.

Gardner, Steve. "Daily Fantasy Sports Site DraftKings Acquires DraftStreet," *USA Today Sports*, July 14, 2014.

Kartje, Ryan, "Daily Fantasy Sports: From Boom to Nearly Bust to Back in the Game," *Orange County Register*, July 13, 2016.

Kilgore, Adam, "Daily Fantasy Sports Web Sites Find Riches in Internet Gaming Law Loophole," *The Washington Post*, March 27, 2015.

King, Bill, "FanDuel Delivers Daily Dose of Fantasy Games," *Sports Business Journal*, February 6, 2012.

Mitchell, Tia, "Fantasy Sports Industry Spends Big on Lobbyists as It Tries to Change State Law," *The Florida Times-Union*, December 31, 2015.

Morris, Chris. "A Fantasy Sports Fan Bet About to Hit $1 Billion," CNBC.com, May 16, 2015.

Playma.com. "History of DraftKings."

Sawers, Paul. "Fresh From $275M Funding Round, Fantasy Sports Firm FanDuel Acquires App Development Firm Kotikan." VentureBeat.com, July 20, 2015.

Sawers, Paul. "How FanDuel Grew From Humble Scottish Startup into an American Fantasy Sports Giant." VentureBeat.com, May 22, 2016.

Sciple, Nick and Motley Fool Staff. "The DraftKings Origin Story: From Idea to Market Dominance in 8 Years." Fool.com, June 25, 2001.

CHAPTER 22

Cooper, Adam, "Fantasy Sports Enjoy Very Real Growth," *The Sydney Morning Herald*, March 27, 2012.

"Fantasy Sports Fever in Brazil Drives Segment Growth in Latin America," *Games Magazine Brasil*, May 3, 2023.

"Fantasy Sports Global Market Report 2023." ReportLinker.com, April 3, 2023.

Flannery, Russell, "Chinese Sports Fantasies," *Forbes*, July 12, 2010.

Floyd, William, interviewed by author, December 2023.

"Flutter Entertainment and Grupo Globo Announce DFS Initiative in Brazil." Flutter.com, November 23, 2021.

Hazell, Craig and Ash Kernsworth. *The A-Z of Fantasy Football*. Pitch Publishing.

"How Many People Play Fantasy Sports? Interesting Facts and Figures." PlayToday.co, December 7, 2022.

Jain, Harsh, interviewed by author, December 2023.

Kempton, Joshua, "The Rise and Rise of Fantasy Sports," *Western Independent*, June 6, 2023.

Kumar Jha, Aashish, "Meet Harsh Jain Who Co-Founded Dream11." Study.in, April 26, 2023.

Lopez-Menchero, Tomas Hill. "How Fantasy Football, and Fantasy Premier League, Went From Niche Hobby to Mainstream Boom." ESPN.com, December 24, 2022.

Mazzeo, Leonardo. "Why in Italy Fantasy Football Is Not Exploited Enough?", *NSS Sports*, June 18, 2020.

O'Malley Greenburg, Zack. "Global Couch Potatoes," *Forbes*, March 6, 2009.

"Riccardo Albini, interview with the inventor of Fantasy Football." Altervista.org, December 18, 2018.

Stevens, Ira, interviewed by author, December 2023.

Surya. "History of Fantasy Football and Origin of FPL." AllAboutFPL.com, May 1, 2020.

Tong, Goh Chiew. "A Sports Tech Startup Lost Millions—Then Made It Big." CNBC.com, December 22, 2022.

Wardale, David. "The Offline Era: The History of Fantasy Football (Part 1)." FPLTips.com, May 30, 2023.

ABOUT THE AUTHOR

Larry Schechter is the author of the 2014 Amazon bestseller *Winning Fantasy Baseball*. He has been called one of the best fantasy baseball players in the world. Larry was a two-time winner of the CDM Sports national salary cap contest, defeating 7,500 teams in 2002 and 6,000 teams in 2005. He has competed in the two most prestigious experts leagues, winning the USA Today-sponsored LABR league three times and the Tout Wars experts league six times. One of his keys to success in fantasy baseball is attention to detail. He used that ability in researching, conducting interviews, and writing *The History of Fantasy Sports*.

Larry is now retired and lives in Florida. You can follow him on X @LarrySchechter.

www.ingramcontent.com/pod-product-compliance
Lightning Source LLC
Chambersburg PA
CBHW030401130626
46549CB00004B/1585